The
E-Marketplace

The
E-Marketplace

Strategies for Success
in B2B Ecommerce

Warren D. Raisch

McGraw-Hill

New York   San Francisco   Washington, D.C.   Auckland   Bogotá
Caracas   Lisbon   London   Madrid   Mexico City   Milan
Montreal   New Delhi   San Juan   Singapore
Sidney   Tokyo   Toronto

McGraw-Hill

A Division of The McGraw·Hill Companies

1 2 3 4 5 6 7 8 9 0 DOC/DOC 0 9 8 7 6 5 4 3 2 1 0

ISBN 0-07-136123-5

This book was set in Times Roman by Binghamton Valley Composition.

Printed and bound by R. R. Donnelley & Sons Company.

McGraw-Hill books are available at special quantity discounts to use as premiums and sales promotions, or for use in corporate training programs. For more information, please write to the Director of Special Sales, Professional Publishing, McGraw-Hill, Two Penn Plaza, New York, NY 10121-2298. Or contact your local bookstore.

This book is printed on recycled, acid-free paper containing a minimum of 50% recycled, de-inked fiber.

This book is dedicated with love and appreciation to God and my family and friends who supported me through the writing of this book. To the people who see me in the morning before I've had a cup of coffee or shaved and showered and still manage to love me; to the people that really don't care what e-Marketplaces are all about and are more concerned about me making it to a soccer or football game to see them play; to the people that I have neglected entirely since starting to write this book; to the people that support me no matter what journey I am on, as long as I take them with me. This book is dedicated to my loving family—to Cara, my wife, who creates love and beauty in everything she touches; to my sons, Nicholas, who aspires to be a World Cup soccer player someday and already has a World Cup spirit and a heart to match, and Patrick, who also has a heart the size of Texas and aspires to save the world by going into law or police services; to my parents, William and Catherine. Without all of their love and support this book would not have been written. I thank God everyday for blessing me with such good fortune.

Contents

7 Global Knowledge Networks Take Flight   164

8 E-Marketplace Business Models   181

9 Value Trust Networks: The Future of Supply Chains   233

11 Developing Your E-Marketplace Organization, Culture, and Strategy   297

FOREWORD

What Is the Future Significance of the Content Component of B2B?

This book provides the reader with a vision of e-Marketplaces evolving into new forms of combined digital and physical value delivery platforms through the development of global *Value Trust Networks*. The B2B application space, which until now has been focused on goods exchanges and transaction systems, will evolve to embrace the exchange of knowledge. In fact, intra-enterprise knowledge exchange systems have been evolving for some time now (with mixed results, but inexorable forward progress overall). The time has come for interenterprise knowledge exchange. Knowledge exchange, as compared with information exchange, is the exchange of information in context, which is usable for decision making, as well as for learning. For example, "best practices" will be exchanged between willing enterprises, affecting the development of professional and management skills. Such knowledge must possess value.

The Value of Content in Context

Despite the broadly held prejudice that content on the Web wants to be free, content that has true value or that can be marketed so as to be perceived as having value will be priced in the future. Which pricing models will prove popular is still unclear. Michael Ruettgers, CEO of EMC, points out that the market value created during IBM's big-iron heyday was about $80 billion. Then the rise of PCs built up ten times as much market value, around $800 billion. Today networking companies are contributing to another ten-fold increase to $8 trillion. What's next? The content wave, creating $80 trillion in market value? The offset to "content wants to be free" perhaps is "value will out." Adam Dell, adjunct professor at Columbia Business School and managing partner of Impact Venture Partners, sees content service providers (CSPs) as being very interesting value propositions, especially to the extent that they can leverage a community of content contributors. Dell says that CSPs may ultimately dominate the provisioning of business data across the enterprise.

Lack of content in Web models to date generally results from the shared characteristic of haste, intensified by the pressure to be one of the first, if not the very first, mover. This leads to development schedules on "Internet time," and very early product launch. In the not-too-distant future, there likely will be a trend toward more highly engineered models, in which the processes are thought out in detail, and the functionality complement is well developed to offer higher levels of added value than before.

Organizations, commercial or within the enterprise, will emerge that will adopt the invention of intermediation techniques and recombinant function models as their core competency. And they will invest in processes to create relatively high-value models, which will likely lead to viable economic models in the general knowledge exchange business.

Whether sold commercially or distributed internally, knowledge will be under strong pressures to be priced. In fact, there is currently a noticeable rationalization of pricing levels in knowledge management (KM). Here is a brief possible basis for an evolving pricing theory of knowledge: The differentiation between information and knowledge is assumed to be a discontinuity in their respective values; knowledge is usually decision-relevant, and it therefore carries more identifiable value. So when a unit of information is certified as being in fact "knowledge," its average value may be estimated, usually through some informal negotiation or historical experience between supplier and consumer.

Just as in the hardware segment of our industry, there exists inherent "positive price-elasticity" of demand from period to period; in other words, when price per unit of knowledge goes down, then utilization of these lower-price units goes way up, resulting in some reasonable increase in total price. (This is remarkably analogous to the known IT trend that when price per unit of computer power goes down, utilization of this computer power goes up disproportionately.) Experience shows that as a result of this elasticity, both suppliers and consumers are happy.

Today, in practice, with virtually nobody exercising the discipline of measuring value, prices per unit of knowledge can and often have actually increased from period to period. This is not rational from the knowledge consumer's perspective and therefore needs to be rationalized. Because of the Internet and resultant new models that ensure that prices per unit *will* decrease over time, the improved value outlook is positive. This theory may lead to a revolution in the propensity of individuals and organizations to consume priced knowledge, which in turn will accelerate the development of B2B knowledge exchange service firms. (The emergence of *knowledge exchanges* and business models is further explored in Chapter 7.)

This book explores the changing business dynamics and the new business relationships which will be enhanced and supported through the development of Value Trust Networks that will interconnect individuals, organizations, and entire industries.

Gideon Gartner

INTRODUCTION

The Real Market Dynamics and Future B2B Business Models Beyond the Exchange

The media hype about e-Marketplaces is focused squarely on the projected transaction flow of over a trillion dollars in trade that will be passing through global digital markets. This is indeed a significant opportunity, and one that will impact your business and your entire industry value chain. This book will thoroughly cover these market dynamics and identify a clear road to profitability for these B2B business models. Equally important is the vision of the future that is provided in this book. The transactions are a necessary first step in the evolution of these new blended digital and physical business models.

But the transaction is only the beginning. Information flow and knowledge creation hold great promise to be the real value offered by digital marketplaces in the long run. This book outlines three key areas of evolution that will change your business dramatically: (1) e-Marketplaces as the transaction hubs for industries, (2) the evolution from transaction exchanges to knowledge exchanges and ultimately a global knowledge network, and (3) the evolution of industry value chains into Value Trust Networks that provide a secure global venue for real industry collaboration and integration.

Joining me with their perspectives are some of the visionary leaders of the Internet age, including Keith Krach, CEO of Ariba; Mark Hoffman, chairman and CEO of Commerce One; and Gideon Gartner, founder of the Gartner Group and Giga Group. These leaders have been rapidly forming the foundation for the new economy infrastructure, commerce flow, and knowledge exchanges. These visionaries provide their views and insights into the future B2B business models. Having this advanced view into the future will provide you with the power to define your business model today to leapfrog the competition and build lasting value propositions that will secure your company with a firm place in the leadership realm of the twenty-first century.

We are living in a time of incredible innovation, invention, and creativity. But with this innovation comes enormous change and confusion. This book was written as a tool to provide you with plain talk in a very complex time. My approach to writing this book was to provide the reader with an overview of the business dynamics behind the current and emerging digital marketplaces. The book also provides a clear vision of the future of B2B business models. Whether you choose to build your own or to participate in these global e-Marketplaces, or both, this book will prove to be an invaluable resource to you.

If you picked up this book, you are probably one of two types of people. Either you are a highly entrepreneurial spirit who is looking to understand as much as you can about this so-called new economy and the successful market makers that are driving the hyper-growth that we are experiencing. Or perhaps you are one of the lucky followers of these entrepreneurs who has been tasked to build the organization and technical platform to support your entry into this bold new world that mixes both virtual and physical realms into new business models and opportunities. Or maybe you're a bit of both. Either way, I am pleased that you have joined in on what I hope will be an informative journey of discovery into the inner workings of these new B2B business models.

Since a book can only offer a fairly one-sided discussion format, a companion Web site to this book has been developed where you will find updates on the latest e-Marketplace trends and opportunities. The online Web site will provide a venue for the readers to open a dialogue with myself or with other readers about key subject areas that the book covers. The Web site has been developed in collaboration with NetMarket-Makers.com and Jupiter Communications. The site is designed as a place of learning and sharing about these new business dynamics. Please join us there for updates, live Webcasts, and discussion groups about e-Marketplaces and B2B strategies for success. The URL is as follows:

www.netmarketmakers.com/b2bstrategies

or

www.nmm.com/b2bstrategies

Straight Talk

This book was developed at Internet speed in the hope to capture the latest trends and opportunities in a concise, easy-to-read format that will explain to you in straight talk what these new e-Marketplaces are all about. Also reviewed are the successful organizational models used to accelerate change, as well as the strategic business steps needed to guide your organization into the twenty-first century.

The vision of this book is to simplify the often confusing jargon and technospeak that permeates the ebusiness world these days. This is not meant to minimize the complexity of the situation. The world is, in fact, changing rapidly, and this requires knowledge tools for a knowledge society. So in that vein, this book is offered as a management resource to you. The aim is to empower you as an executive reader with enough timely and useful information about the emerging B2B e-Marketplaces and the overall ebusiness global network to allow you to move ahead with speed and foresight into the next generation of your business and your professional career.

This book will provide you with the key market data, terminology, and business model definitions you need to chart the significant opportunities that lie ahead. Leadership examples from today's forerunners in the B2B ebusiness marketplaces are reviewed, and insight into the various existing and emerging marketplaces is provided. Strategies are provided for where and how to play in the global ebusiness ecosystem that is forming the foundation of today's business society.

How This Book Is Organized

The book starts with an overview of the evolving e-Marketplaces, with coverage of the e-Marketplace evolution and a clear vision of what the next business models will be. Then, in Chapter 2, the e-Marketplace business dynamics are reviewed in detail, providing the reader with a firm understanding of the impact of these new business models, as well as the key terminology and principles. Chapters 3, 4, and 5 provide a detailed review of how to integrate content, communities, and commerce, respectively, into an e-Marketplace and a complete industry value chain. Chapter 6 reviews the opportunities and issues related to going global with your B2B strategies. Chapter 7 provides insight into the critical importance of knowledge and the emergence of knowledge exchanges and knowledge networks. Then, in Chapters 8, 9, and 10, we review the business models and infrastructure required to create a profitable and operationally sound B2B strategy. The final chapter closes with a review of the organizational models required to succeed in this fast-paced environment along with an 11-step business planning process to follow in order to develop your own e-Marketplace B2B strategy.

This is not a time to be on the sidelines; the leaders of the twenty-first century are forming right now as you are reading this book. Whether your dream is to become an innovative leader in your industry with new business models or simply to defend and grow your current base of business using the new e-Marketplace dynamics, you will find resources here to empower you.

Warren D. Raisch

Acknowledgments

A special thanks to Mr. Don Milley, an entrepreneur, who along with Bill Kane, an innovative leader here at marchFIRST, first contacted me about writing this book. Don is on to other pursuits racing in the fast lane with his own start-up. His entrepreneurial drive is exactly the spirit that I hope fills the pages of this book. For it is this spirit of innovation and discovery that is at the very foundation of these emerging e-Marketplaces. Writing this book has been a journey of discovery, and I hope it brings you both inspiration as well as some practical explanation of the phenomenon that is occurring in our business and personal lives due to the Internet.

The exceptional contributors to this book personify the sense of new innovation and creativity that is driving the rapid growth of the new economy. The people that gave freely of their time, energies, and expertise to the creation of this book are truly the new pioneers of our time. I am eternally grateful to each and every one who provided me with their insights, encouragement, and passion to create this book. Everything in the Internet world seems to be created in 90 days and this book was no exception.

My deepest thanks to the individuals and organizations that supported the publishing of this book. Following is a summary of the key contributors. For the detailed bios, please refer to the *Contributors List* at the back of this book.

Key Contributors:

Gideon Gartner, CEO of Giden.com, founder of Gartner Group and Giga Group

Mark Hoffman, CEO and Chairman, Commerce One, Inc.

Keith Krach, CEO and Chairman, Ariba Inc.

Anne Perlman, CEO, Moai and the Moai team including Ray Letulle, CTO & VP, Product Management and Mike Vargas, Product Marketing Manager

Robert LoCascio, CEO, LivePerson.com and the LivePerson team including Larry Wasserman, Tony Pante, Brian Gonzalez, and Julie Perkins

William B. Lipsin, CEO and President, Ironside Technologies and the Ironside team including Shelly Hofman, Derek Smyth, John Weiskirch, Rod Foster, and Bill Allan

Fred A. Snow, CEO and Chairman, WholeTree.com

William Raisch, COE, The American Group of Companies

Todd M. Stafne, CEO, Co-Venture Group

Keith Bennett, CEO, Symphony Systems

Michelle Reed, Editor, McGraw-Hill

Rich Sheldrick, Group Technology Partner, marchFIRST

Neal Goldman, Director, Internet Computing Strategies—The Yankee Group

Eric A. Crump, Associate Partner, CRM Solutions, marchFIRST

Scott Jordan, Director of Business Development, Polytec/Physik Instrumente

Tony Ward, Vice President, Supply Chain Solutions, marchFIRST

Lisa L. Morgan, Author and Executive Advisor

Mercedes Kronfeld Jordan, Author, Editor, and Educator

Curt Ippensen, Senior Vice President Strategic Marketing, Rhea & Kaiser Marketing and the entire Rhea & Kaiser team including Brad Back, Sr., Dave Grinnel, and Jeff Hammond

Carole Palmer, Executive Advisor

Charles Richardson, Technology Architect, marchFIRST

Special thanks to the following companies and organizations that supported the publishing of this book through insights, perspectives, and projections to support the principles discussed in the book.

Ariba, Inc.

Commerce One

CommerceNet

Forrester Research

Gideon.com

IBM—International Business Machines

IDC—International Data Corporation

Ironside Technologies, Inc.

Lehman Brothers

LivePerson.com

marchFIRST, Inc.

Microsoft, Inc.

Moai, Inc.

Morgan Stanley Dean Whitter

NetB2B.com/Crain Communications

NetMarketMakers.com/Jupiter Communications

Oracle, Inc.

Rhea & Kaiser Marketing

STC—Software Technology Corporation

Symphony Systems

The Gartner Group

The Giga Group

The Yankee Group

Tibco, Inc.

WholeTree.com

CHAPTER

B2B E-Marketplace Evolutions

The Internet. These two words have changed the face of how people all over the world view communication, entertainment, buying, and selling. The Internet has changed our workplaces and marketplaces forever.

E-Marketplaces are becoming the new business venue for buying, selling, and supporting customers, products, and services. Still in their early evolutionary stages, they are today primarily focused on the matchmaking of buyers and sellers. This chapter provides you with the planning assumptions and vision to see beyond the current state of e-Marketplaces and into the future of where e-Marketplaces are evolving.

The global development and acceptance of the Internet as the new standard for communication and commerce provides us with a powerful new global Internet-based ebusiness network that is projected to drive billions of dollars in revenues and dramatically reduce the costs of conducting transactions online. The promise of this global "network economy" has fueled billions of dollars in investment from the public and private capital markets. It has become a business imperative for companies who want to succeed to understand the new market dynamics and closely align their business objectives and processes with new business and organizational models as well as enabling technologies. This section reviews the power of this new global Internet business network and reveals how every business can learn to leverage its brand, its people, and its assets to capitalize on this new digital economy. This chapter also introduces you to the next phase of evolution of e-Marketplaces, the emergence of Value Trust Networks.

The Evolution of E-Marketplaces

E-Marketplaces will go through several key phases of evolution. As with everything else related to the Internet, these evolutionary phases will move at Internet speed and in some cases will be evolving in parallel to other phases as outlined in the following. Successful e-Marketplaces will be those that incorporate all of the functional elements of these evolutionary phases into new value-based business models.

E-Marketplaces will evolve from simple matchmaking services focused on transactions and ecommerce. The next phase of evolution will be centered around providing value-added services that support the transaction. This will spawn the transformation of the e-Marketplace from a central matchmaker into a value-added service provider. As the transactions and value-added services begin to take hold, the savvy e-Marketplaces will harness the information flow and convert it into decision support services for their members. A new line of e-Marketplace businesses will emerge as digital markets move into becoming knowledge providers. The next evolutionary stage for the e-Marketplace will be the integration of the transaction exchange, the value-added services, and the knowledge services into Value Trust Networks that add secure collaboration to the member communities.

The Evolution of E-Marketplaces into Value Trust Networks

In the early stages of e-Marketplace development, the introduction of fundamental matchmaking systems brings together buyers and sellers through a relatively passive exchange system. This type of rudimentary exchange works fine for well-branded, well-defined commodity products and services. As the global Internet continues its pervasive expansion into many aspects of our daily lives, this passive exchange model will need to become much more interactive and interconnected into the living flow of our business and personal lives. This is particularly true in the B2B (business-to-business) marketplace.

B2B markets are based on more than matchmaking of buyers and sellers and the pursuit of the best price. Many large organizations have procurement departments that have hammered the suppliers for years and have prenegotiated very competitive prices. They also have something equally important: relationships and trust in a set of suppliers that they

FOUR PHASES OF E-MARKETPLACES

Phase One: Commodity Exchanges and Marketplaces – These are e-Marketplaces that are focused on the buying, selling, and trading of commoditized products and services. The products and services that best fit this category include products/services that can achieve a standardized global pricing level and that have mature globalized product distribution and service delivery systems in place.

Phase Two: Value-Added E-Marketplaces – These marketplaces provide value-added services to support their customers with transaction support services, as well as enable the customer-driven creation of customized products and services. This is achieved through either the customized configuration of the delivered product or services and/or the hybrid integration of products and services into new value delivered to the customer in the form of combined products and service offerings into custom solutions. This type of new value creation through a combination of digital and physical value delivery systems is now more possible than in the pre-Internet economy. Value-added services also come in the form of services that facilitate the transaction such as financial settlement, in-transit insurance, escrow services, warehousing, and e-logistics.

Phase Three: Global Knowledge Exchanges/The Global Knowledge Network – The Internet is emerging as the central point for communication and collaboration of knowledge workers from around the world. The development and availability of knowledge tools for knowledge workers creates the building blocks for *global knowledge exchanges* and the *global knowledge network* to become a reality. The capture and use of information that flows through the value chain of any industry is a critical component to successfully solving industry pain points and creating new value propositions.

Phase Four: Global Value Trust Networks – E-Marketplaces will provide an integration point for business process, people, and technology, as well as products and services. These new Value Trust Networks (VTNs) come together to support industry value chains. The Phase Four marketplaces will provide a combination of interoperability and trusted relationships that will forge the foundation of new global innovation. The VTNs will weave enterprises, marketplaces, industries, and individuals together into empowered and productive digital workgroups. These Value Trust Networks will be the new business platform for the twenty-first century.

know will deliver both price and quality of service that they can count on.

The Three C's of Ebusiness

The evolution of e-Marketplaces follows closely with the evolution of ebusiness in general. While developing your e-Marketplace strategy, it is imperative that you take into consideration the three C's of ebusiness: content, community, and commerce.

Content Strategies. It all begins with the creation, updating, and publishing of content that represents your business value propositions, your products and services, your brands, as well as your company image and culture. The Internet is a content-rich environment that allows for the communication and presentation of multiple forms of content. Content can take the form of text, graphics, video, audio, or mixes of all of these mediums. *Rich media*, which is the mixture of multiple forms of media, is becoming a major factor in differentiation between companies in their content strategies. When you publish your content, it is important that it is tailored and customized to the audience that it is addressing. Content management and personalization is covered in detail in Chapter 3. As you publish your content on the Internet, keep in mind the following steps in the evolution of your content:

Community Strategies. Communities have formed for thousands of years. With the advent of the Internet Age, communities are forming on a global basis. Communities will naturally form around your content if the tools and resources are made readily available. Two general groupings of communities are as follows:

1. *Communities of interest*—Communities of people that gather around your content because they are truly interested in the subject matter (music, sports, education, news, specialty products, and so on) are referred to as *communities of interest*. These communities can be as small as two people discussing your content and as large as millions of people coming together around the world to discuss news issues on Yahoo.com.
2. *Communities of commerce*—Groups of people that gather around your company and its content and that are economically tied to your company because of a business relationship are referred to as *communities of commerce*. An example of this type of community would be a PC manufacturer communicating with three channels of global distribution. These people are tied directly to your company's content for their very

livelihood. Another example of a community of commerce would be General Motors Procurement Department communicating to their 18,000 suppliers of auto parts that are used to produce their automotive products.

These communities can represent a rich customer base for your products and services if they are provided with the right personalized information and communication tools. They also represent one of the most significant sources of information gathering that has ever been available in the history of business.

Commerce. Once content is published and communities form around the content, then the natural evolutionary next step is to provide commerce to these communities. In general, people work with whom they know and trust. If you have done a good job with your content publishing and community-building strategies, your commerce strategy should fit nicely into play with both your B2C (business-to-consumer) and B2B customers. Commerce enabling your e-Marketplace consists of providing the functional ability to negotiate, trade, auction, and so on.

Global Value Trust Networks

The Web enablement and improvement of business process is a critical next step and is followed by the seamless integration between multiple e-Marketplaces and enterprises. This will form the foundation of global partner networks and the Global Value Trust Networks of the future. For this to occur, relationships must be increasingly based on trust and negotiation skills will become paramount. There must be ample security, standards, and governance to ensure that companies are appropriately and securely exposing and integrating their enterprises into the new global digital network. A review of these areas helps to identify what is meant by each of these critical success factors.

Value-Based Services

The future of e-Marketplaces is dependent on the development and delivery of true value-added services that are offered in both digital and physical delivery systems through the evolution of e-Marketplaces into trusted intermediaries that form Value Trust Networks for their member communities. The value of the e-Marketplace should be greater than the traditional means of conducting the business process and should leverage the new and old economy business models. Time-to-value is a critical success factor for e-Marketplaces in today's highly competitive market.

The patience of the capital and investment markets has grown short. Expectations for true value delivery and profitability are far more demanding than they were during the Internet frenzy days.

Trusted Relationships

As the critical dependency on products or services increases, the need for trust and established relationships increases proportionately. For example, if a company is planning to purchase some standard maintenance, repair, and operations, or MRO, products, then it may be willing to try some suppliers that it has never heard of and never worked with before to try to save on price. However, if a company is chartered to arrange steady procurement of mission-critical parts that feeds the production of its own products or services, it would most likely rely more on trusted relationships with established suppliers.

Trust is a critical component to true partnering to create long-term solutions to industry pain points and to create new forms of value. It is imperative that a trust relationship be forged either through the e-Marketplaces or that established trust relationships be given a new safe harbor to expand through the Value Trust Networks. Through this established trust, truly open communication and collaboration can occur. The trend seems to be that independently owned and operated exchanges and e-Marketplaces are the venue for transacting commodity trades that require less trust and established relationships. Industry-backed consortia have the support of major companies to move beyond commodity buying and selling. These consortia, if managed properly, can build on the well established trusted relationships that exist within the industry value chain to address true supply chain solutions.

Keep in mind that *price is not the only driving factor*. Factors such as quality, reliability, established relationships, and consistency of timely delivery weigh heavily in the decision-making process. For B2B trading networks to work for the long term, there must be trust in the relationships.

Trust is becoming a core element of the Internet, as evidenced by the proliferation of standards such as public key infrastructure (PKI), digital certificates, and authentication. We must learn to accept trust models that do not include human intervention.

Global Network Effect

The Internet represents one of the largest most pervasive business networks on earth, second only to perhaps the telephone network (although the Internet is by some measure an extension of the telecommunications network). The strategy should capitalize on both the physical network characteristics of the Internet as well as the powerful network effects that can be leveraged from the Internet. The *network effect* defined by what is often called the *Metcalf Law*, which states that "the value of a network grows by the square of the size of the network." The network effect is often described by the introduction of the first fax machine. For the first person buying the first fax machine, the network effect was zero because there was no one else with a fax to communicate with. But as the second person bought a fax and hooked it up to the telephone network, the network effect for the first person doubled. This theory shows how the network effect goes up exponentially for every new person that joins the network and for those members of the network that already exist. With every new person added, the value increases. The Internet has the same network dynamics. For every person or company that joins in on the Internet and the emerging Value Trust Networks, the value of the network increases.

Negotiation

Another key factor to consider when developing an e-Marketplace or participating in one is the ability to negotiate. Digital business is still based on some basic human elements, and negotiation is one of the most human of them all. Many of the companies that are in the global procurement and sales area are seasoned negotiators and will not be satisfied with a passive exchange model. They need the thrill of the game and the sense of accomplishment that comes from the negotiation. They also want to know that they are dealing with another human being and somehow receive the digital equivalence of a handshake and a look in the eye. In the digital economy, money will not remain on the table unnecessarily. Increasingly, ecommerce solutions are providing the intelligence and means to negotiate the best terms on all types of products and services.

Negotiation is a feature that will need to be built into the next-generation e-Marketplaces and exchanges. Some companies, such as Moai, already have this feature available in their current offerings, while others have it under development. Those businesses that offer this feature will have a significant competitive advantage over e-Marketplaces that do not.

Security

As big a proponent as many individual experts and businesses are of the digital economy and the global ebusiness network, it is often quite scary to sit down with security specialists and study the impact of exposing enterprises via the Internet. That being said, we still must boldly go where no man or woman has gone before, right? Yet that is not entirely true. Fortunately for us, we have some industry players who have been at the security game for decades. For example, banks have been conducting electronic funds transfers for years. Also, the travel industry has been doing electronic business for many years and has tackled some of the toughest security issues. This is not to say that any business should take security lightly. Security should be one of your top agenda items every step of the way. This book devotes quite a bit of time to security, although this issue in general is better left in the hands of true security specialists, some of whom are listed in the appendix at the end of this book.

Standards

A number of official and nonofficial standards bodies are forming to tackle the issue of developing a common business language, taxonomy, business process, and methodology that can be used as a foundation for communication, collaboration, and commerce via the Internet. Many of these standards groups are industry-focused. Following are a few examples:

- *RosettaNet*—Standards organization for the computer and electronics industries
- *OBI*—Open Buying on the Internet for MRO-type products
- *OASIS*—Organization for the Advancement of Structured Information Standards
- *ANSI*—American National Standards Institute
- *UN/EDIFACT*—United National Directories for Electronic Data Interchange for Administration, Commerce, and Transport
- *WC3*—World Wide Web Consortium
- *UDDI*—Universal Description, Discovery, and Integration (UDDI) standard and registry for the description, discovery, and integration of any business over the Internet. Launched by Ariba, IBM, and Microsoft, with support from other technology firms like Compaq, Dell, and Sun Microsystems, UDDI allows any company to list an easily accessible description of its contact, product, and service information, as well as its preferred ecommerce operating processes. The standard will allow businesses to more easily find and conduct transactions with each other, regardless of the software and hardware they use.

A truism about standards is that *standards are driven by usage*. This has been proven time and again throughout history. Even bad standards follow this rule. Many of the world's roadways, tunnels, and transportation systems were built on the foundation that the transportation would be by way of horse or Roman carriage. The problem is the same with Internet standards efforts. Many try to mirror the physical way things get done in the old economy and map it to a digital version for the Internet in the new economy. However, in reality, even many of these old processes were never that strong to begin with. Also, most of the business processes in place around the world today are based on a fairly linear one-dimensional viewpoint of the world. They take into consideration issues like time and distance, price and quantity, or price and quality. In today's business environment and the Internet global network, businesses must think in multidimensional terms. While traditional businesses are used to thinking of a buyer and a seller, today there are one-to-one relationships, but also one-to-many and many-to-one relationships that change the business dynamics greatly. Businesses need to rethink their business process and standards with the new economy in mind. If the only thing accomplished through the standards-setting exercises is to mirror the physical world and map it to the digital world, then businesses will be missing the big picture of where they are in their evolution. Granted, it would be a major step forward just to get any body of people to agree on a standard. But let's take this time to do it right and not miss the opportunity to set our sights and our standards higher to meet the promise of this exciting new economy.

Governance

As with any form of orderly social system, the new digital economy will need to have tight governance to ensure that businesses do not abuse the systems and uphold their responsibilities and obligations. In many ways, the entire global monetary system and the economies they support are based on trust and governance. Without this, businesses are all just passing around pieces of paper and metal. The digital economy is no different. Businesses are seeing the emergence and standardization of digital signatures, digital certificates, cybercash, public key technologies, and so on. The governance of electronic business practices is a critical component to global trust in the digital nervous system.

A Case in Point. Wall Street and the headlines will tell you that Commerce One is a leading provider of global ecommerce solutions for business. Although Mark Hoffman, chairman and CEO of the company, appreciates the recognition, he has a much grander agenda. While Commerce One-powered e-Marketplaces are making headlines, Hoffman and his executive team are focusing on a much larger picture: the evolution of global ecommerce.

At a cursory look, one might assume that Commerce One's success depends on its ability to provide superior products and enable marquis e-Marketplace ventures—at least that's what the headlines imply. Hoffman has a different idea, however. He argues that in the long term, ecommerce requires the cooperative involvement of businesses and governments worldwide. To prove his point, he recently appointed an international trade expert to the position of chief operating officer and president to transform his vision into a reality, not only at the executive level but also throughout the organization.

At the highest level, Commerce One is partnering with world-class organizations in Asia, Europe, Latin America, the Middle East, and North America that will help engage the powers in international governments that oversee international trade policy. At the middle level, the company is attracting Net market makers focused on serving vertical, horizontal, and geographic markets. To enable the proliferation of e-Marketplaces and online services, the company provides a business framework, methodologies, and solutions that support trusted relationships and enable e-Marketplaces to operate dynamically. At the lowest level, the company is submitting work on enabling technologies, such as XML (eXtensible Markup Language), to standards bodies including the World Wide Web Consortium (W3C) and RosettaNet to ensure that global trading partners can seamlessly exchange business documents and complete financial transactions.

Hoffman is also demonstrating the importance of governance through the Global Trading Web Association (GTWA), an international alliance of mega exchanges that now comprises and cooperatively governs the world's largest online B2B trading community. The purpose of the GTWA is to ensure fair trading practices and interoperability among the hundreds of e-Marketplaces that compose it. On a grander scale, the GTWA foreshadows what must happen worldwide: governments and businesses must work together to create an online commerce structure that is in line with new economy business and economic models.

"It is a grave mistake to assume that entire cultures, economic powers, and global business practices can be simply reduced to a series of Web pages," said Hoffman. "We must address the needs of the new economy on its own terms, not by awkwardly adapting traditional business practices to the Web, but by combining conventional wisdom and innovation in a manner that is practically applicable for the era."

Humanizing the E-Marketplaces

The global Internet is fueled by the power of human connectivity. E-Marketplaces that recognize this human element and incorporate it into the marketplace experience will win in their market sectors and maintain strong customer loyalty and competitive advantage.

The humanization of the digital marketplaces can be achieved a number of ways:

Personalization.   There are a number of products and services that allow a business to customize the Web experience specifically to each individual visitor to an e-Marketplace. This is explored further in Chapter 3.

Great User Interface Design.   This is a mix between great creative design, technology, and knowing the customer. It is an art and a science and, fortunately, there are teams of people that are very good at working together to achieve this. When it is done well, the customer can see it, feel it, and experience the difference.

marchFIRST, the world's largest Internet professional services firm, worked to develop a Pottery Barn site, which recently was named "Forbes Favorite" in their Best of the Web issue. The site, www.potterybarn.com, is the online store for Pottery Barn (NYSE: WSM), a division of Williams-Sonoma, Inc. The site was honored as the best of the best in the "Luxe Shopping" category for home furnishings. "We consciously decided not to rush a Pottery Barn online presence, and this honor supports our strategy and reaffirms our efforts," said Shelley Nandkeolyar, vice president of the ecommerce division at Williams-Sonoma, Inc. "We wanted to give our customers the same high standards they enjoy when shopping in our stores and catalogs, as well as offer them unique online entertaining and educational experiences like the Home Tour and Design Studio."

This example of great design as well as consistent quality of experience between the online and offline worlds makes this site an excellent example of thinking through the human elements of the site. This site is also integrated into the back-office systems of Williams-Sonoma to provide real-time integration with the enterprise.

Interactive Communication.   Humans have a basic need for interaction. Even if it is not always the most efficient way to get things done, it is still a burning need that most people carry around with them in their DNA make-up in the physical world. This tends to carry over to the digital world, where businesses can (and where it is appropriate to) try to build an interactive communication between them and their customers, employees, partners, suppliers, and stakeholders.

An example of great user interaction design would be the integration of multiple customer support methods into a site. In Chapter 10, The Customer-Centric Power Shift, under the section called TeleWeb Integration, we review the integration of a company's call center team into the Web strategy. TeleWeb integration is powerful in that it offers a visitor to a site a clear path to value and support from the company. With a single click of the mouse, a visitor can get live, real-time help on the Web site. LivePerson.com is an example of this type of TeleWeb integration. For a very affordable solution, you can add LivePerson support to your B2B and B2C visitors. It leverages a company's call center investment and provides on average a 4-to-1 ratio of call center representatives to visitors versus a 1-to-1 ratio of people calling into the centers via telephone.

Moreover, the "I" generation expects it. Those who grew up with computers and video games are used to interacting with programs and other individuals through a digital medium. Traditional broadcast strategies that worked with the TV generation boomers simply won't work in the new economy.

Humanizing the Look and Feel. Sites and e-Marketplaces that have well-photographed pictures of real people have the psychological effect of making visitors feel that they are dealing with other human beings rather than machines. A friendly environment can go a long way to conveying your company's culture and style.

The insurance industry offers a few good examples of this type of humanization of the Web sites through use of people graphics. Allstate.com and Reliastar.com are good examples. Also, not surprisingly, the fashion industry offers many examples with sites like Levis.com, Guess.com, and others.

Remember also that there is a time and place for graphic use. In the B2B environment it is common to minimize the use of graphics and focus on personalization of the experience to the user providing the fastest, most efficient path to conducting business. So temper your desire to add graphics to match the usability of the site area you are creating.

Computerized E-Marketplaces

There will be a certain number of e-Marketplaces and portions of all e-Marketplaces that will lend themselves to integrating with a pure computer-to-computer interface. Through the use of XML and Java, documents that are passed via the Internet can contain attributes that identify the owners of the document, and they can carry certain access privileges and instructions for operations that they can perform. The first introduction of the World Wide Web was designed as a human-to-machine interface though a Web browser. Typically, a company was passively presenting their company information for human viewership through the browser. As the Internet becomes more interactive, there is a rising need for other interfaces to the Web. With the acceleration of Java and XML as standard protocols and programming languages, a business will see metadata attached to its standard communication with e-Marketplaces that will carry with it attributes about itself, the document, its access privileges, its account histories, its credit limits, and so on. This will lead to computer-to-computer types of interfaces where we will have document-centric computing taking place over the Web.

We live in a world where documents change hands every day in order to process business—for instance, checking inventory or order statuses. Imagine this scenario: An established distributor of PC equipment wants to check the status of orders with a key PC manufacturer with whom they have a long-standing relationship. Rather than telephoning or faxing the company and asking for a status report on all open orders, the distributor simply sends out an "intelligent" document request form to the company via email or electronic forms on the Internet. The form is recognized by the PC manufacturer as coming from the trading partner, it has the appropriate access rights to the company database, it negotiates the query of the company database in a secure manor, and it responds back to the distributor with the requested order status report. This is all automated and done in a computer-to-computer manner. This technology offers a hands-free approach to routine reporting between trading partners. XML can handle the underlying metadata or attributes to the form, and the Java can handle the presentation level so that the end result can be read by humans. This type of scenario will be commonplace in the twenty-first-century e-Marketplaces. The emergence of intelligent document-centric computing will be enabled through this exact type of application of the latest technologies.

Document-centric computing refers to an evolution of paper document to electronic document on to the next generation of intelligent documents that carry with them identity, attributes, security access, and intelligent agent-based technologies. These enable them to move about the Internet, conducting routine business on behalf of the senders and receivers of these documents. The future of document processing has changed forever. Add to this the multilingual and multicurrency capabilities of new technology platforms, and the possibilities for document-centric computing on a global basis are endless.

The reason this is introduced here is to highlight the importance of thinking in multiple dimensions when planning out your e-Marketplace strategy. By integrating both your physical strategies with your digital strategies, you now have additional dimensions of value delivery to explore.

Web automation is critical to the evolution of e-Marketplaces, and because of the sheer volume of business that will be conducted through multiple e-Marketplaces over the coming years, it is an integral consideration when you are developing your e-Marketplace strategy. If the current projections of trillions of dollars of transactions that are expected to be moving through these e-Marketplaces are correct, then the need for Web integration and automation needs to be a top business and technology priority for all companies hoping to win in this new networked economy. Companies like webMethods, TIBCO, and STC are addressing this cross-enterprise business process integration with new enterprise integration applications (EIAs).

This is an era in which success is measured by speed of action. The current business environment drives management toward taking immediate actions. Often, these actions are driven out of a sense of defensive protectionism of current business. Other actions are targeted toward an offensive attempt to win *first-mover advantage* in the current land grab for the new territories of the digital economy. Still others are attracted to the cost efficiencies and market expansion opportunities of participating in the buying and selling through e-Marketplaces available on the global ebusiness network.

All of the preceding motivations offer defensible foundations for the development of a new ebusiness strategy, but it is well worth the time to pause for a moment and define a clear business strategy prior to jumping into the deep end of the pool with both feet. For all of its wonder and opportunity, the Internet should still remain just one of the business strategies for success. It may be one of the most significant business strategies, but at the end of the day, this is a multidimensional world where both the physical and digital delivery of products, services, entertainment, and education will remain for quite some time.

Digital and Physical Worlds Coincide

Developing a solid digital strategy is critical for today's business environment. Customers, suppliers, and employees expect complete online access to a company and the resources needed to conduct business with it. It is becoming as fundamental as having a telephone or a fax. People will work with companies that are easy to work with. The most effective digital strategies are ones that leverage and complement the physical assets, people, and established relationships. The first step to integrating a digital strategy into the existing world is to Web-enable some of the core functions, including sales, marketing, order processing, and fulfillment. In parallel, it is critical to integrate the back-office systems into the digital network. Otherwise, your business will be a victim of its own success. Many of the early Internet adopters were surprised by the volume of business that was being conducted via the Internet and were caught off guard when the business came in with no systems or process in place to support it. This had dire consequence because, as the saying goes, a happy customer will tell five people about your company and an unhappy customer will tell ten.

Doing business in the networked economy means that you can offer new ways to deliver value to customers via the Internet. The Internet offers multiple ways to support business clients, from the early attraction and informing stages through to conducting commercial transactions and providing ongoing customer support to those clients. A business's digital strategy should be designed to support its clients through the entire customer life cycle. As with any business strategy, it is imperative to clearly define the current state, then look ahead toward the future state. Take this time to review your business strengths, weaknesses, and opportunities for success in the new economy. (See Figure 1-1.)

Jeff Hammond, director of interactive media for Rhea & Kaiser

Figure 1-1. *Individual-Centric Strategy Model*

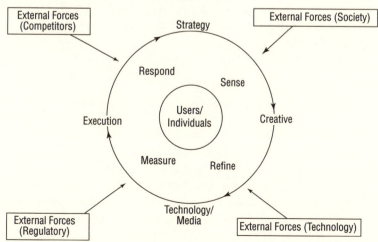

Marketing Communications, notes that "the customer's brand experience must be accounted for in any strategy . . . putting an 'e' in front of something doesn't change that. We've worked with both old-economy companies and new-economy companies who've found out the hard way that a successful strategy—online or off—must deliver against customer-defined needs while, at the same time, accounting for the forces that impact or influence how those needs are defined at any moment. Just because it's on the Web doesn't mean people are more willing to accept poor fulfillment, billing, and service."

Seen from this context, the integrity of the brand experience online must be assured through a strategic planning process that is centered on the individual, senses and responds to forces impacting the individual, and enables execution in an actionable, immeasurable, and time-bound manner.

10 Principles for the Success in the Twenty-First-Century Networked Society

1. Drive your success with a clear holistic strategy that incorporates an external viewpoint focused on your customers.
2. Define your customers and find new ways to serve them through a combination of physical and digital means.
3. Develop a customer-centric culture and organization.
4. Define what your core values and competencies are, master them, protect them, and outsource and partner every other element of your business.
5. Develop win/win-partnering strategies with your customers, employees, suppliers, and partners.
6. Develop a clear understanding of the dynamics of the digital economy.
7. Execute strategies to capitalize on the efficiencies of the global Internet ebusiness platform.
8. Humanize the front line and the last mile; automate the rest.
9. Never rest on yesterday's success, create an innovation culture and systems in your organization.
10. Know your competition better than they know themselves.

Those who master the art of customer satisfaction will win success in the age of customer empowerment. Drive your business's success with a clear holistic strategy that incorporates an external viewpoint of your customers. The winners in the new economy will be those that take a holistic approach to developing and executing their business strategies. Carefully review the entire enterprise. To win and maintain a leadership position in the networked society, companies should adopt an external viewpoint of their business.

Electronic Value Delivery Systems

The Internet represents an infrastructure for electronic value delivery that offers unprecedented efficiencies and customer-relationship building. Never before have organizations had a platform for delivering such clear value to customers that was as compelling as it is today with the Internet. The opportunity to develop multiple touch points with customers, support them on a 24/7 basis, and continue to add value through the entire customer life cycle is outstanding.

Understand the value chain from customer contact and support through delivery. *Add significant value in everything you do, or stop doing it.* Ask yourself every day, "Is what I am doing offering outstanding customer value?"

Define What Value Means to Your Business

Many businesses define customer value as low prices, high quality, excellent support, customized offerings, timely delivery, or ease of doing business. Once a business has defined what its value proposition is, then it should find ways to communicate and deliver on those values through a combination of both digital delivery and physical delivery of value. Be relentless about customer value delivery. Make sure that every employee in the company understands what the value proposition is to the customers. Reward and compensate the employees to deliver the value that customers expect. You cannot overcommunicate the value proposition to customers, employees, and partners. Define the value proposition in one short sentence or, if possible, one word. The more concise and focused the value statement is, the more success a business will have in communicating and delivering on the promise. It should become synonymous with the company name.

Brand Value Defined

A number of companies have accomplished this goal of defining their value through branding messaging and design. For years Apple Computer, Inc. personified the message of a new generation using personal computers through their slogan "The power to be your best." In the past few years, they have launched a new campaign with the slogan "Think Different." Apple has also won the hearts and pocketbooks of the consumer through great industrial design and fun use of colors with their iMac series. Apple embodies a company that truly understands value communication through branding, messaging, and great industrial design.

Learning to Leverage Brand Value in the Networked Society

The opportunity for people to encounter the brand on a daily basis has never been more possible than it is today in the networked environment. The winners in this new networked environment will be those businesses that master the digital and physical branding game and leverage their brand throughout their customer touch points. The brand is a critical component to continued success. It carries with it a brand promise that is communicated every day to every person that encounters it. To customers and potential customers, it is what attracts them to a company and keeps them coming. To employees and potential employees, it also holds a promise of the type of culture, environment, and products and services they want to be associated with. To external partners it carries with it a sense of whom they want to be associated with. The brand should also represent the company's strength and leadership in its industry.

According to Curt Ippensen, director of strategic resources at Rhea & Kaiser Marketing Communications, "Customers have a set of expectations about a brand whether experiencing it traditionally or interactively. MidAmerica Bank, a 77-year-old 'bricks-and-mortar' bank serving the Chicago area is a good example. MidAmerica's brand positioning is anchored by offering and promoting a higher degree of personal service than the competition. To maintain their position as the leading provider of home mortgages in the face of new e-competition, their initial e-strategy was to partner with several e-mortgage aggregators to serve those customers who preferred to do business by ecommerce versus traditional means. This entry strategy gave MidAmerica the time it needed to design and build its own full-service e-banking Web site. Even in the face of new e-competition, MidAmerica has maintained its leading market share and is having the best earnings year in its 77-year history."

As more individuals and organizations turn to e-Marketplaces to research and procure products and services, it is more important than ever to have a brand strategy that carries with the offerings the brand promise that has been developed. In the first wave of e-Marketplaces, there is a move toward driving out costs and inefficiencies from the supply chain that offers lower prices to customers.

Brands are one of a company's most valuable assets. They express the sum total of feelings and perceptions about a product or organization. Many B2B leaders have focused on the rational points-of-differentiation of their brand, but as traditional marketers have known for years, emotional benefits are as critical to success as one's ability to define functional benefits. Just think about how a customer feels *safe* in a Volvo, *excited* in a BMW, *important* at Nordstrom's, *warm* when buying a Hallmark card, and so on. These are all emotional benefits.

Learning to leverage brand strength and value in the networked society through digital branding strategies is critical to long-term success. The opportunity for people to encounter a brand on a daily basis has never been more possible than it is today in the networked environment that many of us live, work, and play in every day. The winners in this new networked environment will be those who master the digital and physical branding game and leverage their brand throughout your customer touch points. Your brand is a critical component to your continued success. Your brand carries with it a promise that is communicated every day to all who encounter it. To customers and potential customers, it is what attracts them to a particular company and keeps them coming back for more. To employees and potential employees, the brand also holds a promise of the type of culture, environment, products, and services they want to be associated with. To external partners, it carries with it a sense of whom they want to be associated with. A brand should also represent strength and leadership in its industry.

Just as there is a process to defining B2B strategies, there is a process to developing a successful brand strategy. Unfortunately, in their rush to market over the past 12 to 18 months, many dot-com players have failed to understand or address this, which may provide a correlation to those who are thriving today and those who are not. Rhea & Kaiser Marketing Communications, a branding leader based in Chicago, recognizes this and uses a proprietary process that works whether the brand is delivered through traditional bricks-and-mortar or online channels. Importantly, the Rhea & Kaiser Strategic Roadmap is a thorough, five-step process based on gaining competitive and customer insights, and ultimately developing strategic alternatives that are relevant and resonate with the intended audience. As stated in the company's literature, "Ecommerce consultants have stated that our branding process is the first among many that they've reviewed that is not only clear and understandable, but actionable, results-oriented, and easy to incorporate into other B2B strategies. Understanding what your brand does or should stand for will be more critical to any successful ebusiness plan as the industry moves forward."

In order to capitalize on the e-Marketplace opportunities it is important to move ahead with a clear action plan. The following section provides a perspective from Moai, a leading marketplace-enabling company, on developing a winning e-Marketplace strategy.

Moai Perspective on Ecommerce

Moai is a leading provider of dynamic commerce solutions for online exchanges, auctions, and procurement. Dynamic commerce involves the buying and selling of goods and services online through flexible transaction models that change over time based on multiple terms such as price, condition of goods, warranty, and shipping costs. Moai's solutions address the unique challenges faced by companies looking to initiate or expand their ecommerce initiatives in the technologically complex and rapidly changing Internet business climate. While Moai's primary focus is on customers in the business-to-business market, the company also has customers in the B2C and C2C (consumer-to-consumer) markets.

An Introduction to Dynamic Commerce and Negotiated Ecommerce

A Review and Analysis of Trends and Opportunities in Commerce on the Internet

With the advent of ecommerce, businesses have low-cost, global access to a highly focused and greatly expanded network of trading partners. Already, the ecommerce world has produced many undisputed successes, from entirely new Internet-focused companies, like Amazon.com and eBay, to existing companies that have extended their organizations to take advantage of the Internet, such as Dell Computer.

While the Internet represents a new channel for marketing and selling to customers, the future opportunities are far greater. Initial ecommerce applications targeted the implementation of online advertising, catalog, and order fulfillment systems, producing good bottom-line results for many companies. The online market has now embraced dynamic commerce, which is the buying and selling of goods and services through flexible pricing mechanisms that change with supply and demand. Moai is an innovator in this space and immediately recognizes the limitations of first-generation dynamic commerce applications.

These applications focus on basic price and quantity bidding. As the market has quickly evolved, Moai has introduced negotiated ecommerce that fully leverages the Internet's inherent potential to facilitate complex decision-making processes that require the ability to negotiate multiple factors. Presently, dynamic commerce manifests itself most commonly in exchanges and auctions. Companies employing these trading mechanisms are enjoying a number of significant benefits including:

- Higher yields on surplus, obsolete, or slow-moving inventory
- Access to new trading partners domestically and globally
- Additional sales channel for cross-selling
- Reduced overhead costs
- Streamlined negotiation processes
- Lower transaction and research costs
- Community building in vertical markets

Current estimates from Forrester Research on the future of this market illustrate the tremendous growth potential moving forward. Forrester predicts that by 2004, in the United States alone, total online trade will reach almost $2.7 trillion, with a little over half (roughly $1.4 trillion) coming from online marketplace transactions.

The Introduction of Ecommerce: Mapping Traditional Businesses to the Internet

When business first moved to the Internet and the term *ecommerce* was originally coined, companies simply replicated traditional business practices. Web-based models, relying on static pricing schemes, were popular methods for implementing ecommerce. While these models took advantage of the Internet's global reach and around-the-clock availability to deliver customer convenience, the actual business methods remained rooted in existing practice.

The migration of B2B activities to the Internet has been built upon existing pricing models and traditional distribution channels, and has used the Web's reach and responsiveness to improve the speed and lower the cost of doing business. Suppliers have found more efficient access to their customers, and buyers have expanded their ability to research available vendor options. However, the traditional purchasing paradigm has remained largely the same—buyers research the range of posted prices, compare their relative value, select the best option, and either purchase at the stated price or negotiate a final price offline.

Although these initial ecommerce implementations have given many companies immediate and uninterrupted access to an expanding population of online customers, these solutions have barely tapped the full potential for interactivity and market responsiveness inherent to the Internet.

From Static Prices to Dynamics Commerce

Static pricing models that grew out of the Industrial Age as mass production and extended distribution chains encouraged large economies of scale. Static prices became necessary to manage the increase in both volume and variety of products over far larger geographic regions. Despite these benefits, static pricing still had a number of shortcomings, made more apparent today with the fast pace of Internet commerce.

Static prices are slow to adjust to market conditions, thereby causing a gap between the price that is charged for a good and its actual market value. Providing just a glimpse of the overall market demand, static prices convey only whether or not there was a buyer at a given price. Consequently, businesses spend a substantial amount of money on market research to help them understand and forecast demand.

Enabled by the Internet, dynamic commerce solves the dilemma of "sticky" prices by providing virtually instantaneous knowledge about market demand, such as how many bidders exist, who they are, how motivated they are, and the prices and quantities they desire. Essentially, dynamic commerce breaks free of the relatively static pricing methods used in traditional business models, and uses the Internet's intrinsic capacity for continuous interactivity to create new types of fluid, market-driven environments. These markets inject unprecedented immediacy into the buying process and optimize value-driven pricing for sellers. Static pricing models grew out of the Industrial Age as mass production and extended distribution chains encouraged large economies of scale. Static prices became necessary to manage the increase in both volume and variety of products over far larger geographic regions. Despite these benefits, static pricing still had a number of shortcomings, made more apparent today with the fast pace of Internet commerce.

Static prices are slow to adjust to market conditions, thereby causing a gap between the price that is charged for a good and its actual market value. Providing just a glimpse of the overall market demand, static prices convey only whether or not there was a buyer at a given price. Consequently, businesses spend a substantial amount of money on market research to help them understand and forecast demand.

Dynamic commerce is the ability to buy and sell goods and services over the Internet where price and quantity change with supply and demand.

At the same time, dynamic commerce markets eliminate the need for layers of intermediaries and reduce the overall cost of sales. For buyers, these markets provide access to excess inventory, a wider variety of suppliers, and better, more widely available information—all of which reduce costs and increase customer satisfaction. For sellers, participation in these markets translates into higher revenues and quicker inventory turnover. By creating better parity between buyers and sellers, dynamic commerce facilitates a more efficient allocation of supply and demand.

Dynamic commerce involves the buying and selling of goods and services online through flexible transaction models that change over time based on multiple terms such as price, condition of goods, warranty, and shipping costs. Moai's solutions address the unique challenges faced by companies looking to initiate or expand their ecommerce initiatives in the technologically complex and rapidly changing Internet business climate. While Moai's primary focus is on customers in the business-to-business market, the company also has customers in the business-to-consumer and consumer-to-consumer markets.

Embraced by the marketplace, dynamic commerce has evolved as markets have grown and changed. The first generation of dynamic commerce applications focuses on the common negotiable: pricing. Depending on the business, quantity and time can also be negotiated.

Negotiated ecommerce is the ability to map complex negotiation structures in business transactions to the Internet. These structures can include multiple stages of negotiations with more than one bidding parameter.

The next generation of dynamic commerce applications facilitates complex negotiation processes. This new generation is called *negotiated ecommerce*, which is the mapping of complex negotiation structures in business transactions to the Internet. Augmenting dynamic commerce, negotiated ecommerce allows buyers and sellers to include multiple factors in the decision-making process. These multiple factors can include, among others, price, delivery time, condition of goods, or payment terms.

Initially, companies that wanted to employ simple dynamic commerce capabilities built the applications themselves. However as the benefits of dynamic commerce were recognized, solutions providers emerged with both the technical and business expertise to provide a full spectrum of dynamic commerce platforms. Companies, like Moai, have become specialists in this field and are able to provide businesses with the latest technology, expert business services, and rapid deployment capabilities. Today, ecommerce companies that want to augment their online strategies with dynamic commerce capabilities do not have to build it—they can turn to these experts.

Key Aspects of Dynamic Commerce and Negotiated Ecommerce

The emergence of interconnected exchange networks and the increasing acceptance of ecommerce tools and capabilities are only two of the many factors driving the dramatic growth in commerce on the Internet. While companies continue to discover innovative ways to apply new dynamic technology, it remains the most beneficial mechanism to sell excess or scarce inventory and is quickly becoming the predominant mechanism for procuring goods and services.

In essence, dynamic commerce solutions leverage the power of market-driven pricing and dynamically responsive, personalized transactions, while negotiated ecommerce uses the Internet to facilitate advanced negotiations and bidding functions. There are several characteristics of dynamic commerce and negotiated ecommerce that enhance a business's online practices.

Flexible Market-Driven Pricing Models

At the core of dynamic commerce is the ability to drive the final price point of every transaction to yield optimal value for both buyer and seller. Unlike initial ecommerce applications in which a fixed price is preestablished for each item, dynamic commerce solutions incorporate fluid bidding and pricing mechanisms, such as those used in traditional auctions and trading exchanges. These formats serve various purposes when they are employed. For example, a company that wants to move inventories quickly, but are not as concerned about price, may employ an open Dutch auction. A company that wants to increase competition among its suppliers for the best price for goods may choose to host a reverse auction. (See Chapter 5 for more information on types of auctions.) Within these new applications, individual buyers and sellers can track and update the current status of bids via easy-to-use, online interfaces. Current information is always available on bids, bid history, available inventory, time remaining for bidding, and so on. This information, in turn, facilitates increased activity between buyers and sellers.

Multiple Parameter Bidding

In addition to price, time, and quantity, negotiated ecommerce allows buyers and sellers to negotiate other factors synchronously or asynchronously. These other factors include warranty, shipping terms, or condition of goods that can be weighted and negotiated in a dynamic environment. The decision to purchase a new home, for example, requires consideration of a wide range of variables in which price is one factor among many. Other negotiable variables might include condition of the property, move-in dates, mortgage terms and conditions, or inspections. Complicating the process is the fact that many of these variables are negotiable and vary depending on how they are packaged in the final offer. By providing a centralized mechanism to negotiate each of these variables, negotiated ecommerce improves the ease and efficiency of the entire transaction.

Market Aggregation and Community Cohesiveness

Dynamic commerce environments foster a greater level of buyer loyalty and community cohesiveness by combining the global reach of the Internet with the flexibility to adapt to the changing nature of specific market needs. Because the interactivity of dynamic commerce gives buyers and sellers a greater sense of immediacy and influence over the pricing of transactions, participants become more involved and, consequently, develop an ongoing attachment to both the process and the hosting site. Additionally, relationships may develop, both competitive and cooperative, between market participants that foster a sense of community. The Internet's additional dimension of eliminating geographic constraints allows previously excluded buyers and sellers to participate from anywhere around the world.

Competitive Advantages Through Improved Operational Efficiency

The flexible responsiveness of dynamic commerce enables pricing to track changes in market conditions as they occur. This not only spurs buying activity but also improves the efficiency of distribution and inventory management. In B2B markets, this elimination of latency in supply chains will help raise the efficiency of all participants, whether vendors or customers. In addition, the immediate feedback mechanisms that are intrinsic in this environment enable companies to adjust their overall product strategies quickly to meet actual market demands.

Multiple-Stage Negotiations for Complex Transactions

The evolution of dynamic commerce to negotiated ecommerce has given rise to new, powerful solutions that enable corporations and independent market makers to create multistage, online negotiations in which complex terms can be settled upon at different points in the negotiation process.

A direct benefit of negotiated ecommerce is the simplification of the process to screen and select vendors. For example, a computer manufacturer needs to purchase 5,000 power supplies for delivery within two days. A quick search identifies 25 potential suppliers. Since the company does not have time to call each supplier individually to obtain quotes and does not want to award the contract to the lowest bidder automatically, an online, multistage, and multiparameter negotiation format is used for the selection process.

The 25 suppliers are notified of the request by email and directed to the company's ecommerce Web site where the negotiation is being conducted. The first stage of the negotiation involves delivery time, and the second stage of the negotiation is price and delivery package. In an environment similar to an online threaded discussion, the buyer determines that only five suppliers can provide the power supplies in the requested time frame.

In the next stage, the five suppliers are asked to provide their price and, as expected, there is wide variation. As a result, the buyer has the option to begin negotiating with each supplier individually on a price-delivery package. The buyer will determine, through negotiations, which provides the greatest value. These negotiations are dynamically communicated online simultaneously, and typically, the suppliers are unaware of the details of the other suppliers' negotiations.

These negotiations can also support third and fourth stages of negotiation depending on a buyer or seller's business needs. At any point, the purchaser or seller can accept, reject, or counter an offer. In the end, the multistage negotiation process allows companies to transfer more sophisticated business transactions to the Internet.

Initial Ecommerce

- Online catalogs
- Order processing
- 24-hour access to customers

Dynamic Commerce

- First Generation Applications
- Fluctuating pricing mechanisms
- Better access to information

Negotiated Ecommerce

- Multiple bidding parameters
- Multiple stages of negotiations
- Threaded discussions

Dynamic Commerce and Emerging Negotiated Ecommerce Implementation Models

The underlying mechanisms of dynamic commerce are beginning to appear in a wide range of specific implementations. All of these implementation models can include elements of negotiated ecommerce as described in the previous section, but here they are discussed primarily in terms of dynamic commerce. The four prevalent types of market implementation models emerging include

- Enterprise-driven markets
- Procurement-focused applications
- Marketplace-focused exchange environments
- Ecommerce portal and service provider marketplaces

Enterprise-Driven Markets

Businesses have learned a difficult and, in some cases, expensive lesson about the cost of carrying excess inventory. Aggressive international competition and faster product life cycles have forced companies to rethink manufacturing processes, inventory management, and supply chain activities in an effort to adopt continuously leaner practices. Despite their successes, it still remains impossible, if not economically impractical, to reduce surplus inventory levels to zero. The significance of this issue is easily underestimated. On average, businesses in the United States carry approximately $18 billion in surplus inventory annually, an amount equivalent to about one-tenth of all finished goods.

The current process for selling surplus inventory is inefficient. Many companies still trade orders by phone and fax, a slow and labor-intensive process. In addition, when companies yield control of inventory to third-party intermediaries, they lose their influence over where and at what price the merchandise is sold. Although some businesses need inventory to protect against variability in demand effectively, a more efficient way to manage excess inventory exists.

Dynamic commerce offers a more effective solution to this problem. Rather than selling off surplus inventory to third-party intermediaries, companies are now using the Internet to auction surplus goods to vendors. By leveraging the flexibility of the Internet to target a select group of highly motivated buyers or extend the reach of businesses across a maximum number of participants, dynamic commerce has a distinct advantage in generating competition and market liquidity. In addition to realizing improved returns and more efficient processes, companies are retaining greater control over their brand, extending a valuable service to their customers, gaining more valuable market insight, and reducing costs.

Procurement-Focused Applications

Another significant application of dynamic commerce lies in the field of sourcing and procurement, and applies to both long-term supplier contracts and unpredictable "spot buys." Several businesses have used dynamic commerce in common procurement activities such as supplier consolidation, annual negotiations, and corporatewide projects to gain savings through purchasing activities. These solutions can be applied to either strategic or direct goods and services related to a buyer's manufacturing operations, as well as to indirect purchases (commonly called maintenance repair and operating resources, or MRO). Although there are clear difference concerning financial details and procurement methods, the fundamental value proposition is identical for all of these purchasing methods.

Many companies already use simple forms of competitive pricing for sourcing or supplying goods. Typically, the process requires sealed bids from prospective suppliers, which are evaluated by the buyer. The buyer then selects one or more suppliers and negotiates detailed terms for specific contracts. This process can be labor-intensive for both parties and may result in contract terms that vary from supplier to supplier based on the market position of the supplier and the negotiating skills of both the trading partners.

By using negotiated ecommerce mechanisms, a buyer can automate the RFQ tender and bid processes. The Internet gives buyers the ability to eliminate geographic and cost barriers to potential suppliers, and to include additional suppliers into the bidding process at very low cost. A reverse auction greatly increases competition in the marketplace by giving suppliers instant feedback on where they stand along with the opportunity to submit new bids and win the contract.

Marketplace-Focused Exchange Environments

Dynamic commerce implementations are also gaining rapid acceptance as forums for creating industry-specific or marketplace-focused exchanges. These exchanges are "many-to-many" markets with multiple buyers and sellers. Using structured bid mechanisms, online exchanges can provide stable environments for fostering highly vibrant trading activity in commodities or other industry-specific products. By bringing together multiple sellers and a highly aggregated group of buyers around well-defined sets of products or service offerings, online exchanges leverage dynamic bidding on the Internet into an unprecedented opportunity for all parties to achieve maximum value.

Exchanges solve fundamental and pervasive inefficiencies that hinder trade, such as the fragmentation of buyers and sellers, high search and transaction costs, and limited market information or highly variable demand. Traditional exchanges (e.g., stock or commodity exchanges) also provide liquidity and a standardized process for trading commodity-type goods where long-term, highly integrated relationships are not necessary.

An exchange environment can also offer discrete auctions that may or may not incorporate online, threaded negotiations. These online exchange marketplaces, often hosted by vertical market makers, bring together buyers and sellers. Rather than selling their own products, these companies are focused on developing a marketplace and community by providing and distributing a range of information, products, and services. These businesses are often new venture-funded entities, or in some cases they develop as part of the Internet arm of an existing company. For companies entering or establishing new marketplaces, time-to-market is crucial. They need to get up and running quickly to compete in the marketplace. According to the Gartner Group's projections, there will be more than 10,000 market makers creating specialized markets by 2001.

Ecommerce Portals and Application Service Providers

The fourth major trend of dynamic commerce is the evolution of broad-based portals and service providers supporting a full range of turnkey ecommerce capabilities, including dynamic commerce solutions. These companies provide dynamic commerce capabilities to small and medium enterprises (SME), as well as offer larger companies a chance to "test the waters" before making a full or ongoing commitment. Companies provide access to a wide range of products or markets and often are the hosting provider for smaller organizations that do not have internal resources to support their own dynamic commerce infrastructure.

These portals and service providers provide a mix of the enterprise-driven and marketplace-focused exchanges as they aggregate these multiple sites into a single mall or catalog. Within this structure, individual businesses can operate their own dynamic commerce sites. The aggregation of multiple markets means that handling a high volume of traffic is a crucial factor for success.

> e-Market makers will capture $2.7 trillion in business-to-business ecommerce transactions in 2004.
>
> *Gartner Group*

Initial ecommerce applications provided an opportunity for many companies to move some of their business practices to the Internet. Companies experienced good results, and whole new entities focused solely on the Internet grew out of such successes. However, these successes have been limited by the dependence on existing business practices and static pricing models.

The current phase of ecommerce, driven by dynamic commerce and evolving to include negotiated ecommerce, breaks out of this mold and utilizes interactive, market-driven pricing. Large, small, and yet-to-be created businesses that utilize these interactive markets effectively have unprecedented opportunities to increase revenues and reduce costs. According to industry analysts, dynamic commerce will be a significant percentage of total ecommerce activity in the future.

The future of ecommerce could bring a rise in the number of digital marketplaces in conjunction with new technologies that could further leverage dynamic commerce. Electronic agents may first scour the Web for buyers and suppliers, searching for goods on sale or purchasing demand. Eventually, more sophisticated agents may compete in dynamic commerce markets on behalf of companies or individuals. Nevertheless, as prices approach their "true" market value, trade partners could increasingly compete on factors such as reliability, quality, and value-added services, not only price.

Once the decision is made to take advantage of these opportunities, the next step is deciding how to implement a solution. The very nature of dynamic commerce requires thinking "beyond the bounds" of traditional business practice and necessitates more than just buying a new software package and installing it. The effective creation of dynamic commerce to meet the demands of ecommerce will require a strong combination of robust software, hosting options, in-depth services, and expertise to support rapid and optimal deployments and innovative business processes.

Enterprises and market makers will require dynamic commerce partners that can provide a full range of professional services, domain expertise, and hosting alternatives along with their software offerings. In addition, the implementers of negotiated ecommerce sites will need highly adaptable software architectures that can provide the flexibility to tailor their applications to market specific requirements.

Chapter Summary

In today's business environment, taking into consideration several key factors when setting the companies overall e-Marketplace strategy is crucial. First, it is imperative that the company be highly customer-centric from all angles of the business, including market facing, employee facing, and partner facing. Second, you must organize for success, keeping the company structure lean, with easy access to decision makers with an open communication flow throughout the entire company value chain. Third, you must think, plan, and execute your strategy on multidimensions. All strategies should include multiple physical and digital value delivery methods to address the needs of all stakeholders. The following chapter will cover the e-Marketplace dynamics, providing an overall perspective on the evolution and operation of e-Marketplaces with a visionary perspective from one of the industries leaders and pioneers Keith Krach, CEO of Ariba, Inc.

CHAPTER

Twenty-First Century E-Marketplace Dynamics

The visionary electronic networks that we have been discussing for years are here, and many are taking the form of digital marketplaces. E-Marketplaces are becoming the digital trading zones of the world markets. These digital marketplaces will quickly evolve to offer higher levels of value and also become the digital workspaces for the knowledge workers who are designing, producing, selling, and delivering products and services that support these digital markets. The catalyst for B2B ecommerce growth is e-Market maker activity. The Gartner Group predicts that e-Market makers are projected to facilitate $2.71 trillion in ecommerce sales transactions in 2004, representing 37 percent of the overall B2B market and 2.6 percent of forecasted worldwide sales transactions. This chapter explores the dynamics of e-Marketplaces, including the recent trends, the future evolutionary projections, business models, and case studies that demonstrate the opportunities and risks associated with developing and participating in the e-Marketplace industry. The chapter also explores the current and future trends of e-Marketplaces and includes a perspective from Keith Krach, CEO and chairman of the Board of Ariba, Inc., on e-Marketplace dynamics in the new economy from the point of view of a technology enabling pioneer.

Key E-Marketplace Trends

The evolution of transaction-based business models is upon us. The business models of many e-Marketplaces in their early stages have typically been based on transaction fees. Many e-Marketplaces have even called out transaction revenues as a core element of their business plans. But the transaction-only model has fallen under the scrutiny of Wall Street as of late. Transactions and e-Marketplaces will no longer be synonymous in the near future, particularly as transaction fees come under severe competitive pressure. The transaction business represents the most simple of business models, but it does not provide a long-term sustainable advantage. For the buyer's convenience, wide selection and best price hold appeal. For suppliers, the extended global market reach and direct access to customers and consortiums of customers is powerful. The real long-term revenue opportunities lie in the value-added services and in the information and knowledge gathered around the supply and demand flow.

E-Marketplaces will evolve into digital work environments in which real industry collaboration can occur. The role of the e-Marketplace will evolve from simple matchmaker of buyers and sellers to trusted intermediaries and advisors and ultimately into *Value Trust Networks*. These Value Trust Networks will serve specific industry supply chains and/or provide horizontal trust-based value-added services to the members of the network.

E-Marketplace Evolution

As we first discussed in Chapter 1 and as shown in Figure 2-1, e-Marketplaces will evolve from simple matchmaking services focused on transactions and ecommerce. The next phase of evolution will be centered on providing value-added services that support the transaction. This will spawn the transformation of the e-Marketplace from a central matchmaker into a value-added service provider. As the transactions and value-added services begin to take hold, the savvy e-Marketplaces will harness the information flow and convert it into decision support services for their members. A new line of e-Marketplace businesses will emerge as digital markets move into becoming knowledge providers. The next evolutionary stage for the e-Marketplace will be the integration of the transaction exchange, the value-added services, and the knowledge services into Value Trust Networks that add secure collaboration to the member communities.

Figure 2-1. *E-Marketplace Value Evolution*

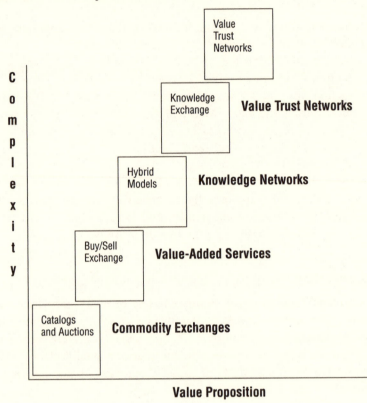

Transactions Drive Value-Added Services Revenues

Transactions, even with small commissions, remain crucial for current e-Marketplaces. This is because the first wave of value-added services that are being offered are centered around the transaction. The transaction itself becomes a loss leader as e-Marketplaces charge for services that facilitate transactions—financial services, escrows, in-transit insurance services, logistics, updating catalogs, project management, and the like—are driving the first wave of value-added service revenues.

E-Marketplaces Provide Transparency

E-Marketplaces provide multiple levels of transparency to the buyers and suppliers. When people discuss the transparency that the Internet provides, they usually center on the buyer transparency benefits, and there are many. But the transparency that the Internet offers is a two-way mirror that allows transparency for not only the buyers but for the suppliers as well. Following is a short review of buyer and supplier transparencies.

Buyer Transparency Benefits. Buyers receive many benefits from the transparencies offered by the Internet and e-Marketplaces. These benefits include *price transparency,* which provides the ability to compare prices across multiple suppliers. This can also cause commoditization of a supplier's products if price is the only consideration point. Transparency of quality, after-sale service, and reputation should also be factored into the buying decision in order to provide a more qualitative process. *Availability transparency* provides visibility into the location and inventory of products. Other forms of transparency are also made available, such as *supplier transparency*, which provides visibility into which suppliers offer specific products or services. Additionally, *product transparency* is offered to provide multiple selections of products. Further, buyers gain better control over their own procurement processes.

Supplier Transparency Benefits.   The suppliers also gain benefits from this transparency. Suppliers benefit from being included in a broadening number of markets that expand their distribution points and provide greater market transparency. Suppliers also can gain *buyer behavior transparency* and greater demand forecasting indicators, as well as competitive product and market analysis. Suppliers also gain a more predictable production planning process, a reduced inventory, the ability to target and customize promotions for buyers, and lower order-processing costs.

Current Trends and Keys to Success of the E-Marketplace

Following are several trends of the e-Marketplace, as well as integral elements necessary to thrive in the e-Marketplace.

Industry-Backed Consortia Are on the Rise

A highly significant recent trend in online B2B marketplaces is the entry of industry consortia in competition with independent vertical exchanges.[1] This represents new and powerful competition for start-ups and established B2B sites alike. The intent has correspondingly shifted from

---

[1] "Start-ups Leave Online Marketplaces in the Dust," *Upside Today*, August 2000, http://www.upside.com/Ebiz/3985df0f0.html

acquisition and aggregation of customers (which maximizes buying power) to corralling and leveraging existing buyer-seller relationships (thereby cutting costs and paperwork, and not incidentally slowing price erosion).

The first wave of consortia is forming between large incumbent players in highly competitive industries such as automotive manufacturers, utilities, airlines, high-tech manufacturers, and chemicals and petrochemicals manufacturers. Their goals are to combine their purchasing power, as well as to streamline supply chains and squeeze out inefficiencies from the process. These industry-backed consortia are forming their own e-Marketplaces, and they have established relationships, leading to real buying, selling, marketing, and financial power. It is unlikely that all of these industry-backed consortia will survive in the e-Marketplace industry. In fact, it is predicted that there will be a massive introduction of many consortia and then a consolidation of e-Marketplaces which will leave a few key e-Marketplaces standing in each industry once the dust settles. But these consortia should be taken very seriously by companies wishing to participate in multiple e-Marketplaces and by those companies building their own e-Marketplace. Alliance strategies or clear market differentiation strategies need to be put into action quickly to either capitalize on the opportunity or to defend against the consortia. The consortia players have the power to impact their industries, they have long-term trust relationships in place, and they have the financial power to execute a long-term strategy.

Combined with contraction of early-stage financing and a new-to-the-Internet emphasis on profitability, this is having a winnowing effect in an environment not lacking for harrowing mechanisms. Recent casualties include AviationX.com, which crashed and burned after a brief dogfight with industry-sponsored adversaries. Ventures built on the previously fashionable strategy of market-building and niche-defense find themselves not only competing with perhaps a dozen or more other entrants in the same space but potentially with well-financed, well-connected, sophisticated industry-sponsored consortium sites with immense capabilities and solid, established foundations in their market space. This has not yet been taken to the level of virtual trust building, but that notion promises to be fertile hunting ground for regulators, attorneys, and limping plaintiffs alike when the invisible line is finally crossed.

At the same time, old-fashioned churn and survival-of-the-fittest continue to decimate the ranks of B2B aggregators. The recent drought of funds from angel round to IPO killed more than a few young companies, even relatively successful ones. Diminishing CPMs (Costs per thousand impressions) are driving across-the-board contractions of all forms of revenue mechanisms; meanwhile, it is not getting any cheaper to market a site. These facts are propelling into fashion the old-fashioned virtue of differentiation by something other than promotional burn rate. Ultimately, B2B sites built on vertical aggregation of customers—the brute-force market-making of yesterday—are increasingly exploring supply-side opportunities, thereby facilitating collaboration between industry players.

Equity as a Tool for Locking in Communities of Commerce

E-Marketplaces will begin to offer equity sharing with customers in order to lock in their buying power and to combat the industry consortia that are forming in all major industries. But even equity participation does not guaranty loyalty. Market makers must move to value-added services as quickly as possible to survive and thrive.

Recognition that Industry Expertise Provides Real Value

Participants in e-Marketplaces will be looking for more than simply the transaction. Industry expertise applied to industry pain points will become a valuable differentiator to e-Marketplaces. With the rapid proliferation of e-Marketplaces, it will become a survival tactic for market makers to add deep value beyond the exchange services.

Current Focus Is on a Win/Win Value Model

It is imperative for the long-term sustainability of these Net markets that a balance of value is offered for both the buyer community as well as the supplier community. Focus on values that are long-lasting and high-margin for the market maker. The commodity exchange services will soon be minimized to low- or no-margin business. Focus on winning strategies that are deeply integrated into the buyers and suppliers, offering the market maker a long-term, profitable place in the overall value chain.

Vertical E-Marketplaces Are on the Rise

Vertically focused e-Marketplaces are those that are developed to support a specific industry or segment of a market. These markets are typically established by members of that community and hold value in the fact that they have all of the efficiencies and benefits of the horizontally offered digital marketplaces with the added value of having deep industry expertise. These vertical marketplaces are projected to proliferate over the next few years. Expect a massive consolidation of these by 2004.

The specialized markets that add real value beyond the exchange will survive.

Value Is Found in Collaboration

Collaboration is one of the key cornerstones from which to establish a foundation of value-added services for a Net market maker. Collaborative commerce will far surpass the revenue generated by exchange transaction services. E-Marketplaces that enable the formation of communities and that empower these communities with collaboration and knowledge tools will be at the forefront of their industries.

E-Marketplaces Will Substitute Information for Inventory

One of the most difficult problems facing companies today is having the right product at the right price at the right place. To compensate for this problem, the answer has been to have lots of product in lots of places where the demand is anticipated. This causes excesses in one place and shortages in others. The root of this problem is poor or unreliable information exchange. E-Marketplaces stand in an excellent position to move into the information exchange business. Ultimately, with the addition of collaboration and knowledge management tools, e-Marketplaces will be the preeminent knowledge providers to the industries they serve.

Independence and Neutrality Are Key Success Factors

E-Marketplaces must maintain independence from both their buyers and suppliers even if equity sharing is a part of the loyalty strategy. Independence in management and operations is critical to sustained survival. Partner-oriented hybrid models will prevail in reality-solving industry pain points. And offering true value-added services throughout an industry's value chain is no easy task. The winners in this new space will be those who are able to meaningfully partner with technology providers, information providers, market makers, and direct industry participation to come up with new hybrid business models that provide a win/win situation for all involved. Partnering is key to success in the twenty-first century.

The Blend of Digital Value Delivery and Physical Value Delivery

The winning business models in this new economy will be those that leverage the best of both the digital value delivery systems offered via Web-based e-Marketplaces and solutions as well as the physical value delivery systems. E-Marketplaces will never fully replace the value of human contacts and relationships.

Timing Is Everything

The time is now to develop your e-Marketplace strategy and execute. The early innovators and entrepreneurs have made the early tests. The boardrooms are supportive and the industry climate is right to take the lead.

"Cooperative Liquidity"—A Strategy for Survival and Success

Kevin Jones, cofounder of NetMarketMakers.com, argues that Net markets have a vested interest in their mutual survival and should share their buyers with noncompeting Net markets. He suggested online buying clubs for bandwidth, office supplies, or equipment leasing as ways markets can share buyers by bringing them to other Net markets. The idea has good merit and should be considered when setting your e-Marketplace strategy.

Cash Is Still King

Cash is getting harder to come by since the capital market justifications of mid-2000. Financially sound business models are critical. Public or private companies with deep pockets (mostly consortia-backed) have an advantage over start-ups with limited cash. Ventro CEO Dave Perry speaks of the $395 million his company has in the bank as a competitive advantage but admits that watching his stock fall from 240 to 25 was not one of his favorite moments. If you're a new IPO or heading for IPO, stock price volatility is a reality of the e-Marketplace business. This may be a good time to review and refocus the cash being spent on branding and target accelerated time to value delivery and profitability models.

It's Time for E-Marketplaces to Deliver

To date, most discussions of e-Marketplaces have focused on their potential, not real transactions or value delivered to users. The "land grab" mentality, justifying huge financial losses in the name of snaring market share, is out. Investors are demanding a path to profits someday. The brick-and-mortar coalitions will soon be asked to deliver too, creating opportunities for e-Marketplaces that can show results.

Mine That Transaction Data

Net markets possess a rich storehouse of information about buying trends in their industries, and packaging that data to sell to suppliers and buyers looks like a good revenue source, especially in a zero-commission environment. We explore the emerging knowledge exchange in Chapter 7.

Early e-Marketplace models are based centered on the transaction. The next wave of value delivery will be in the form of e-Marketplaces evolving into *knowledge providers.*

Tech Vendors Add New E-Marketplace Features to Their Software

Pressed by e-Marketplaces seeking turnkey solutions for complex businesses, tech vendors are opting to buy rather than build new features. Two billion-dollar acquisitions recently reinforced that trend: Publishing software maker Vignette snared cataloger OnDisplay. WebMethods bought Active Software. Look for more mergers and acquisitions of key technology companies that are seeking to provide full end-to-end solutions.

Integration with Legacy Systems Is Key

Linking systems of many buyers and many sellers through an e-Marketplace is much tougher than the direct B2B model of Dell Computer. But Net markets boost their chances of tapping into the supply chain by making easy connections to ERP software.

Universal Connectivity and Interoperability Are Key Long-Term Success Factors

To succeed long term, companies must think "external" to their four walls. In a networked economy, competitive advantage comes to those that appropriately and securely extend and open their enterprise to connect and interoperate with customers, partners, and e-Marketplaces.

Supply Chain Merging into Supply Webs

An illuminating case study is ForRetail.com. Originally an essentially undifferentiated exchange matchmaking retailers and manufacturers of consumer goods, it received $3 million from venture investors enthusiastic about B2B successes such as VerticalNet and undeterred by the glut of similar sites in the space.

However, bowing to financial and market realities less than six months after funding, ForRetail.com subsequently modified its business aim to focus instead on facilitating private ecommerce channels for manufacturers, their reps, and retailers. In their crosshairs: selling costs—the never-ending flurry of faxes, forms, paperwork, call slips, and general busywork—which in the wholesale retail industry can consume 25 percent of sales. Manufacturers and reps can compile their own e-catalogs and manage and track orders online using ForRetail.com's technology and services. The company projects cost savings as much as 10 to 20 percent of sales, which may be extrapolated to some $35 billion in putative cost savings to the industry.

In a way, this is a repudiation of the contention from not long ago that ecommerce would mark the demise of the middleman. Clearly, the trend is just the opposite, and a new type of middleman is being born.

The Digital Supply Chain

The trend deepens as it broadens. e-Chemicals, for example (one of an increasing number of B2B entrants choosing to eschew "dot-com" in their name, incidentally), places itself squarely in the middle of the supplier-customer chain. The company facilitates an "e-supply chain" bridging chemical manufacturers and their suppliers and leverages the Internet technologies to smooth logistical coordination across the channel. This is wholly in line with the trend away from price minimization via customer aggregation and toward cost optimization via improved efficiencies and tightened coordination between customers and vendors.

This is evolving rapidly to its logical conclusion: the linkage between the actual production machines that consume a commodity and the providers of the commodities being consumed. e-Chemicals is at the leading edge of implementing this sort of electronic supply chain. Eastman Kodak, an e-Chemicals partner, is aggressively pursuing direct linkages between itself and its established business partners. This represents an abrupt about-face for the chemical and photographics-product giant, which summarily withdrew from Envera, a vertical exchange.

Another example of this rapidly emerging paradigm is Campbell, California-based start-up Symphony Systems which, in its initial phase, is establishing a digital supply-chain infrastructure for the semiconductor manufacturing industry. This company is tackling both the software- and hardware-related issues involved in connecting the semiconductor industry's sophisticated and sensitive equipment to suppliers and customers using Internet technologies. For newly designed equipment, Symphony's secure bridge to the Internet can be implemented by integrating its server software into the tool's embedded computer. Legacy equipment can be Net-enabled by attaching a black-box hardware implementation of the Symphony server. Meanwhile, the company's centralized supply-chain portal activities allow equipment vendors, users, and suppliers to coordinate their efforts with closer coupling than ever before, making for a more efficient market than was previously feasible. This represents much more than the *reducto ad absurdum* of Japanese just-in-time philosophies popularized a decade ago. Noting the $100 billion that the semiconductor industry represents versus equipment utilization that hovers between 40 and 50 percent can summarize the stakes. Also, the industry has been characterized by dramatic boom-then-bust cycles as it has careened between being over- and under-capacity. Every percentage point gained in equipment utilization adds hundreds of millions of dollars to the industry's collective bottom line and potentially avoids pressures that might otherwise drive overexpansion.

Industry analysts view this trend as having legs. Cahners In-Stat Group, a leading research firm, estimates that virtual supply-chain networks will see $43.4 million of commerce flow through them in 2000, growing to more than $800 billion in four years. They estimate around 25,000 companies are testing the e-waters today, and that this number will balloon to more than 280,000 actively participating companies by 2004.

Clearly, a significant inflection point as to how business is done is thrashing itself out, both for large- and small-scale operations. The direction the ball will roll is anyone's to call. In fact, there is a likelihood that several seemingly polar-opposite eventualities will prevail. Independent virtual exchanges may well continue at the leading edge of each industry's churn as entrepreneurs strive to aggregate and leverage the combined buying power of a market. Then the scenario of the industry's largest players combining forces in the interest of efficiency will repeat, benefiting again the intrapreneurs and entrepreneurs capable of leveraging and facilitating the trend, perhaps from beachheads in the same vertical exchanges newly dominated by the consortia.

In the following section, Keith Krach discusses the structure and operations of e-Marketplaces and provides insights into e-Marketplace dynamics and trends.

Perspective: The Rise of the B2B Marketplace

Keith Krach, chairman and CEO, Ariba

The global ecommerce revolution is entering a new phase. While the vision and innovation of business-to-consumer Internet companies fueled the first stage, the leadership and market success of companies engaged in business-to-business ecommerce define the next phase. The early consumer-focused ecommerce winners created the Internet business model, but it will be their B2B successors that realize the full potential of the new electronic economy.

From the perspective of today's business leaders, this second Internet revolution consists of equal parts: threat and opportunity. The new B2B wave will split most industries' competitive field into two camps: the prepared and the unaware. Many organizations, reluctant or unable to initiate the deep change that the new business climate requires, have so far made only minor technical changes that barely touch their culture or business processes. These organizations have yet to make the investment in strategy, people, and money necessary to survive in the B2B ecommerce world. Those who fail to address the opportunity at hand risk becoming displaced by more forward-thinking and aggressive competitors.

For those who do respond to the new realities of B2B ecommerce, the worldwide B2B market offers opportunities on a grand scale. Still in its infancy, B2B ecommerce is already the fastest growth area in the superheated new Internet economy and carries potential almost beyond measure. A Boston Consulting Group report estimates that Internet-based electronic business relationships will account for $2.8 trillion in sales by 2003. The Gartner Group places this figure even higher—at $7.2 trillion. But although they are helpful in sizing the growth of B2B Internet sales, such projections of transaction volume may give a false impression of the future importance of the ecommerce market. More important than volume, from a business-to-business perspective, is *value*.

Today's volume projections only hint at the value that the Internet will provide in the years to come as an enabling technology for ebusiness. And the best mechanism to unlock that value are electronic marketplaces—private or public, aligning buyers and sellers in industry-focused Internet marketplaces for the exchange of goods and services.

Electronic marketplaces, also known as B2B marketplaces, are commerce sites on the public Internet that allow large communities of buyers and suppliers to "meet" and trade with each other. They present ideal structures for commercial exchange, consolidating and validating supply bases, creating new sales channels, and achieving new levels of market efficiency by tightening and automating the relationship between supplier and buyer. B2B marketplaces allow participants to access various mechanisms to buy and sell almost anything, from services to direct materials.

The extreme flexibility of these marketplaces, which may be customized to serve the full supply chain of virtually any industry or expanded to facilitate horizontal commerce chains, will establish them as the pillars of the new B2B ecommerce economy. Gartner Group predicts

7,500 to 10,000 B2B marketplaces to emerge by 2002, while Giga and IDC project that B2B marketplaces and exchanges will allow companies to save between $180 billion and $480 billion in transaction costs and related expenses by 2003.

Ultimately, all businesses will buy on a marketplace, sell on a marketplace, host a marketplace, or be marginalized by a marketplace. For organizations committed to participating in the coming wave of online business, B2B marketplaces offer a compelling entry point into the new economy at various IT comfort levels.

As ecommerce becomes more central to the operations of mainline companies, a diverse range of marketplaces is arising in every sector. So far, most of the early movers have been small, aggressive third-party dot-coms seeking first-mover advantage that they hope to leverage into market dominance. However, they will not have the playing field to themselves for long. Already, the established brick-and-mortar players are moving to leverage their existing trade relationships and access to buyer liquidity into established B2B marketplaces.

The options range from a neutral marketplace hosted by a third-party technology vendor, an in-house system designed for buy- or sell-side transactions, or an ASP (application service provider) type of model serving a particular commerce chain. The materials and services offered may either be industry-specific or horizontal across many applications. Additionally, the functionality varies between marketplaces depending upon the sophistication of the commerce chain and the end products. Functionality can include design chain collaboration, real-time dynamic chat between parties, ideal trading partner matching, various auction formats, OLAP (online analytical processing) tools for tracking commerce data, and market making capabilities.

B2B marketplaces are redefining how businesses interact with each other. Inevitably, all businesses will be affected by this revolution. The important question that all companies must answer is this: "How?"

The Value-Driven B2B Marketplace

Marketplaces and exchanges are emerging to serve each point of every industry's supply chain. Whether it's a spot market to clear excess raw materials in the metals industry or a new "virtual" distributor in the life science chemicals industry, these electronic markets bring buyers and suppliers together through new methods of dynamic collaboration and trade. They remove costly inefficiencies and deliver bottom-line savings to all participants.

Although still in their infancy, B2B marketplaces have the potential to drive the B2B ecommerce revolution. By virtue of their structure, which unites member companies in seamless trading communities of common business interest, B2B marketplaces maximize speed and efficiency. They offer buyers and sellers uniquely powerful forums to reduce transaction costs, enhance sales and distribution processes, deliver and consume value-added services, and streamline supply chain management.

Evolution of Ecommerce Mechanisms

To understand the shift forward that B2B marketplaces represent, it is useful to examine the progression of electronic business. The following is a brief overview of the rapid evolution of B2B ecommerce.

Electronic Data Interchange/Enterprise Resource Planning (EDI/ERP). Businesses with well-defined trading relationships use electronic data interchange (EDI) and enterprise resource planning (ERP) to create point-to-point interfaces with each other.

- *Advantages:* Useful for transactions involving replenishment orders for direct production goods tied to a previously negotiated contract.
- *Disadvantages:* Expensive to implement, outside the reach of all but the largest companies.

Sell-Side Storefront. The sell-side storefront, shown in Figure 2-2, is the primary model used in current business-to-consumer scenarios.

- *Advantage:* A single seller, typically a distributor, can construct a Web storefront that reaches many consumers (e.g., Amazon.com).
- *Disadvantages:* Expensive for buyer; does not meet the needs of corporate procurement organizations. Additionally, unless a single distrib-

Figure 2-2. *Sell-Side Storefront Model*

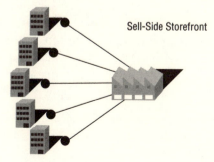

Sell-Side Storefront

Figure 2-3. *Buy-Side E-Procurement Model*

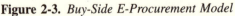

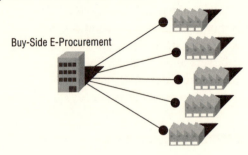

Buy-Side E-Procurement

utor can aggregate all the suppliers in a given industry, the buyer remains responsible for comparison-shopping between stores.

Buy-Side E-Procurement. Buy-side e-procurement, shown in Figure 2-3, involves buy-side applications generally consisting of a browser-based self-service front end to ERP and legacy purchasing systems. Corporate procurement aggregates many supplier catalogs into a single "universal" catalog and allows end-user requisitioning from the desktop, facilitating standard procurement for the organization and cutting down on "maverick" purchasing.

- *Advantages:* Purchases are made through this system are linked to the back-office ERP or accounting system, cutting time and expense from the transaction and avoiding potential bookkeeping errors.
- *Disadvantages:* This model yields reduced transaction costs but *not* lower purchase costs; no impact on size of supplier base, no enablement of dynamic trade; buying organizations must set up and maintain catalogs for each of their suppliers; too costly and technically demanding for most medium- and small-sized businesses; users from the build-to-order market need design collaboration capabilities and usually cannot order from catalogs.

B2B Marketplace. This latest evolution of B2B ecommerce, the B2B Marketplace, shown in Figure 2-4, enables a *many-to-many* relationship between buyers and suppliers. Buyers and suppliers leverage economies of scale in their trading relationships and access a more "liquid" marketplace. Users from the built-to-order market have the flexibility to interact and exchange product information in real time. Sellers find buyers for their goods; buyers find suppliers with goods to sell.

- *Advantage:* Many-to-many liquidity allows the use of dynamic pricing models such as auctions and exchanges, further improving the economic efficiency of the market.

Figure 2-4. *B2B Marketplace Model*

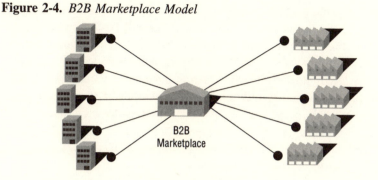

- *Disadvantage:* This model is far more complex to build and integrate with multiple buyers and suppliers.

Marketplace Requirements

As the new B2B trading hubs, marketplaces must enable certain processes and enterprise trading requirements. They should accommodate existing procurement processes and buyer-supplier interactions, as well as offer full interoperability with other markets. For example, marketplaces must be able to match ideal trading partners, not only by capability, but also by available capacity and predetermined vendor criteria such as minority ownership or annual sales. Additionally, marketplaces will develop into vanilla collaboration destinations. Enterprise Resource Planning (ERP), Computer-Aided Design (CAD), and Supply Chain Management (SCM) systems will become transparent to all users with emerging XML (eXtensible Markup Language) technology. This push for neutrality will only open the gates to allow more participation from the multiple tiers in the supply chain for the new global economy.

Procurement Processes. Procurement professionals configure a "virtual procurement system" within B2B marketplaces. This replicates the buyers' unique procurement process down to individual permissions, rules, and workflow, allowing the procurement organization to control the overall buying process while distributing the buying task to end users. Automation of the traditional procurement procedures allows companies to streamline the entire process. Additionally, integrations into ERP/MRP packages can streamline inventory, replenishment, planning, and production throughput operations for the plant.

Buyer-Supplier Relationships. Before moving to a marketplace, most buyers and suppliers will have existing relationships that must be reflected in the marketplace. Suppliers can configure the system to reflect prenegotiated discounts for certain buyers that will be automatically applied when those buyers access the marketplace. This many-to-many marketplace combines the advantages of both sell-side and buy-side models, but since it is hosted, it avoids setup and maintenance costs for the participants. Significantly, this can allow access by the smaller organizations that would not otherwise have the resources to trade online. Both buyers and suppliers gain the advantage of a much broader trading community, and both sides can decrease sourcing costs as well as easily collaborate with users around the globe.

There is much debate over the value of anonymous interaction between buyers and suppliers on marketplaces. We believe each model serves a particular purpose. For example, in an anonymous auction model, the suppliers are differentiated by their profile information. The contract is awarded to the best combination of vendor corporate statistics, core competencies, available capacity, and price. Buyers who utilize this model are often looking for validation for their supply base choices when phasing out an existing supplier or simply establishing a brand-new supply chain for a new assembly.

On the other hand, buying organizations dealing with highly specialized components and a known supply base will choose to deal in full disclosure on secure marketplaces. These types of transactions lend themselves to supply chain consolidation. Such contracts are determined by available capacity, since the supplier qualifications have already been determined.

Interoperable Marketplaces.   One of the key factors in building a successful B2B marketplace is to focus on meeting all the buying needs of the target user. These needs may go beyond the specialist capabilities of any single marketplace. To cater to broader buying requirements, marketplaces may link to each other and create a commerce chain, effectively extending the product range without giving up "control" of the buyer. Commerce chains, which include supply chains and value and service chains, represent the various classes of virtual links, relationships, or processes that can exist among trading partners. Commerce chain management focuses on applications that enable critical commerce processes, and the appropriate sequencing and implementation of new procurement systems. This process includes optimizing supplier and service partner management, financial services, and in-house or third parties logistics, as well as establishing efficient systems planning and effective commerce networks. The ability of marketplaces to interoperate extends the idea of liquidity and network effect by joining more buyers with more suppliers, but it does not sacrifice the ability of each marketplace to be highly specific to the supply-chain node or target buyer group it serves.

Benefits of B2B Marketplaces

Historically, buyers and sellers have suffered from a high degree of fragmentation and weak information flows. Necessary sourcing and sales efforts were time-intensive and costly. Buyers and suppliers went through a multistep process to fulfill a request for quote (RFQ). Many of these steps were unnecessary and dependent on each other, slowing fulfillment. Sellers, buyers, and market makers who take advantage of the opportunities offered by B2B each stand to gain vast benefits from the online marketplaces.

Seller Benefits

Sellers can lower sales channel and prospecting costs and access new customers through B2B ecommerce. Marketplaces extend that reach still further by creating and leveraging close collaboration between trading partners in a secure environment, tightening the relationship between supplier and buyer, promoting price discovery and spend aggregation and slashing supply chain costs. Supply bases can compete for new business based on their current capacities and throughput efficiencies.

Buyer Benefits

Buyers can use B2B marketplaces to reduce direct and indirect supply chain costs by leveraging their global scale and focusing their spend on preferred suppliers while utilizing advanced search engines to find qualified new suppliers. Additionally, buyers can take advantage of dynamic models such as auctions and bid-quote for efficient sourcing and spot buying. New tools for logistics, payment, and tax create opportunities to build transparency in the supply chain, decrease logistics costs, increase inventory turns, and improve the overall performance of the manufacturing and procurement processes, returning 15 to 27 percent back to the business in reduced costs (AMR estimate, 1999).

Market Maker Benefits

Market makers are the fulcrums of these new B2B ecommerce relationships, catalyzing the growth of the B2B economy by leveraging their domain expertise, customer relationships, and supply chain strength to fuel the growth of B2B marketplaces. In return for delivering incredible value, market makers stand poised to reap substantial rewards by sharing in the returns achieved by buyers and suppliers.

Marketplace Principles

Every market, whether online or not, represents a complex assembly of buyers and suppliers united by intricate lines of power and dependency. Although forces of supply and demand control the flow of business, each market carries a built-in measure of inefficiency. The B2B marketplace minimizes that inefficiency by tightening the relationship between supplier and buyer, promoting price discovery and spend aggregation, slashing supply chain costs, and increasing the reach of suppliers. If enough liquidity is built into the system, a B2B marketplace is the ultimate trading structure, the closest thing to a perfectly efficient trading system ever developed in the long history of commerce. If built properly, the marketplace will be able to highlight these new efficiencies to all constituents. Marketplaces must concentrate on developing tools for tracking not only dollar value savings, but also sales and planning savings. In this way, both the buyer and supplier will be able to incorporate these discoveries into their offline practices as well.

Buyer liquidity—the critical mass of transaction volume that is the lifeblood of every market—is essential to electronic exchanges. With so much speed and capacity, the B2B marketplace is the ideal technological platform for commercial exchange. Without enough buyers and suppliers on the network, or enough total purchase volume, the marketplace cannot capitalize on its potential for efficiency and will be bound by the same inefficiencies as an old-world exchange.

We have seen the powerful effects of marketplace liquidity even in the infancy of B2B ecommerce ventures. Even with the incredible amounts of money thrown into marketing programs, marketplaces without domain expertise, market-making capabilities, integration capabilities, and a flexible, intuitive GUI have collapsed from minimal transactions.

Marketplace Expansion Strategies

Electronic marketplaces create value for participants by playing three roles: connector, value-added service provider, and spend aggregator. The initial value proposition of every marketplace lies in the connector role, serving as the common platform over which trading companies route information and transactions. To become a value-added service provider,

B2B marketplaces must provide access to services ranging from baseline interoperability and directory services to specialty services such as online payment, logistics, and dynamic trade. Many marketplaces also take on the role of spend aggregator, negotiating lower prices for buyers by leveraging collective volume.

The early stage of marketplace development focuses on establishing enough basic capability and buyer liquidity to make the market competitive. In nearly all cases, markets start out with a narrow range of products and services and target either a product category or a buyer group. As they grow, they must expand from this sharp focus to support a broader base of buyers and suppliers.

B2B Marketplaces and Exchanges

A product-focused B2B marketplace may develop when a product or family of products is purchased across multiple industries (e.g., steel or PCs). Product-focused marketplaces typically serve industries in which extensive buy- and sell-side fragmentation makes it difficult for the players to achieve price and product discovery independently. That fragmentation, and the resulting natural friction in the market, makes these industries ideal candidates for B2B marketplaces. Online marketplaces allow product-focused marketplaces to drastically cut down on volatile and uneven pricing, improve information access, speed up transaction cycles, and slash transaction costs.

A buyer-focused vertical B2B marketplace emerges to serve the product needs of a particular group of buyers (e.g., ChemMatch, which focused on the needs of the chemical industry). Buyer-focused marketplaces deliver the same benefits and are structured along the same lines as product-focused markets, and they typically adapt over time to serve more categories of buyers.

The division between product- and buyer-focused marketplaces is sharpest for early entrants. As markets grow and mature, however, they must become more inclusive and functional to survive.

Procurement Portals

The newest example of the electronic B2B marketplace is the *procurement portal*, in which the market maker leverages relationships with small- and medium-size buyers to create an exchange. In this model, the market maker offers value to the exchange members—including lower pricing driven by its own spend consolidation as well as access to new customers and suppliers—while enjoying a range of special benefits. The procurement portal has the potential to become a powerful platform over which the host can extend brands, offer value-added services, and strengthen relationships with customers.

Companies with the strong competitive position and customer relationships to create and populate a procurement portal gain access to a unique range of opportunities. If leveraged intelligently, portals open the door to significant growth in the company's sales, service, and supply operations. Procurement portals can unite companies in a trading community of common interest driven by the market maker, who realizes substantial secondary business benefits from the endeavor, including branding advantage and increased exposure to potential customers.

Keys to Success

The success of every marketplace venture depends on a range of factors. Some of these describe existing market conditions; others involve elements of strategy and opportunity. Taken together, they are the keys to success that, if followed, can lead to the establishment of a successful marketplace, exchange, or portal.

Buyer Power

The single most important element in establishing market control is buyer power. Buyer power controls the flow of transaction volume that market makers can drive over their B2B marketplace. For single companies with enough present purchase volume to qualify as the dominant player in the market, or for a consortium of major buyers able to aggregate their spend, buyer power represents a potentially unbeatable weapon in the struggle to edge out rival market makers. Players with market-leading buyer power are able to bind a community of suppliers and smaller buyers firmly to their B2B marketplace.

Catering to Buyer Behavior

Understanding how today's market operates is critical to catering to buyer behavior. What preferences do buyers have around issues like business standards, supplier terms, and vendor assurances? What value-added services are in demand in the market, and which can be realistically supported over the exchange platform? Discovering the answer to these questions offers another leverage point in the struggle to establish B2B marketplace ownership.

Technology Enablement

The B2B marketplace model relies on light client-side technology—buyers and suppliers must be able to do business over the site through a standard browser. However, the B2B marketplace imposes special demands on the market maker, who must be able to manage the commerce process from requisition to order fulfillment and payment. This end-to-end support must take place over network application architecture capable of supporting thousands of users in a highly distributed, fully scalable Internet environment. The B2B marketplace platform should also enable complex business rules, workflow, potential design collaboration, question-and-answer sessions, and user relationships, and allow for integration with custom and third-party commerce modules.

To compete successfully in the B2B marketplace arena, market makers need a fully realized solution that accommodates the needs of their buyers and suppliers and allows them to extend advanced services to the trading community. The advantage will fall to those market makers who ally themselves with vendors with the technology solutions and expertise to launch and customize B2B marketplaces quickly.

Market leaders are emerging in the areas of interface, back end, scalability, database management, storage, load balancing, dynamic trade capabilities, design collaboration, sourcing, logistics, and payment. Just as in the offline world, the strategic alliances developed and aggressively nurtured by market makers will determine the success of the marketplace and, therefore, the success of the members.

First-Mover Advantage

Speed to market is another front on which small third-party players can potentially gain valuable ground over existing players. Slow-moving, complacent large buyers can be outdone by small, nimble competitors able to establish and quickly populate a B2B marketplace. If not anticipated by the larger market maker, this early-strike strategy can leave the market with no true consolidation of buyer power, allowing the third-party platform to grow into industry-standard status. Once established, the new marketplace may be able to resist any belated pressure from the larger rival.

Section Summary

The compelling benefits that B2B marketplaces offer for buyers, suppliers, and market makers are driving their rapid adoption of Internet practices. Marketplaces are the latest and most significant factor for reshaping B2B commerce relationships and will soon affect all businesses. Those who plan carefully and adopt a well-thought-out marketplace strategy will quickly become leaders in the new economy. Businesses that do not take advantage of the opportunities offered by online marketplaces or who grab at the chance to join the online community without planning ahead will soon be overwhelmed by the competition.

The primary beneficiaries of the coming B2B wave will be those who use the Web to extend, deepen, and create business relationships. Marketplaces offer companies the chance to develop and enhance their most important relationships—those with buyers and suppliers—while allowing market makers to open new revenue opportunities. Companies can use B2B marketplaces to strengthen their existing trade relationships, discover and develop new connections, and promote faster and more efficient trading.

The rapid adoption of B2B marketplaces will shape the future of global business. Marketplaces will multiply and leverage each other for specialist capabilities. In the years to come, marketplaces of all description and focus industries will proliferate on the worldwide stage, integrating into progressively deeper layers of the global business ecosystem. For companies seeking to establish a place of advantage in the economy, equipping for competition over B2B marketplaces is essential.

B2B Supplier Opportunities in the New Economy

To succeed in the new economy, sellers must commit fully to doing business on the Internet, understanding the digital infrastructure required to participate, and developing and executing a coherent plan of action. Web strategies should be appropriate to company size and scope and adapted to the competitive situation, industry focus, and available resources. Also critical to success is ensuring that the organization's ecommerce strategy works at a short-term and long-term level, ensuring rapid time-to-market while also incorporating defined plans for future initiatives.

Suppliers seeking to establish B2B Web business presences should concentrate on several objectives, including:

- Finding the right partnerships to create and exploit their Web businesses
- Seizing first-mover advantage in their industry
- Creating a scalable, digital infrastructure that integrates tightly with their physical infrastructure

- Establishing a single point of access to all markets of opportunity, allowing them to easily connect with all possible target customers.
- Achieving bottom-line business results, including increased revenue, lowered transaction costs, and lowered support costs, as well as developing a highly personalized, online presence that maximizes their electronic branding opportunity and creates competitive differentiation.

Sellers who act quickly and focus on their core objectives can soon begin participating in the B2B ecommerce explosion and secure their competitive future.

The New Economy

A new generation of aggressive companies has emerged to exploit the Internet's capabilities for information exchange and transaction processing, leveraging new technology and dynamic new business models to achieve success in their target markets. In industry after industry, these nimble, fast-moving players have challenged older and more established companies for market leadership. And while many of these early ecommerce winners focused on serving consumers, the next generation of leaders will be focused B2B players.

We stand on the brink of a major shift in the fabric of business, a mass movement toward new forms of technology-enabled commerce. The next stage of Internet business is now emerging in the B2B ecommerce market, which will set global business trends well into the twenty-first century and carry the Internet's impact throughout almost every industry. This paradigm shift will be so vast that it will launch a new and distinct worldwide market system: the digital economy. Currently in its formative development, the new economy offers opportunities on a scale difficult to quantify. Business-to-business is the fastest growth area in the superheated new Internet economy and is only beginning to realize its potential. Forrester Research estimates that Internet-based electronic business relationships will account for $1.3 trillion in sales by 2003 (Forrester Research, Inc., December 1998). A Boston Consulting Group report places this figure even higher—at $2.8 trillion (Boston Consulting Group, December 1999).

B2B is replacing B2C as the focus of the new economy.

Businesses have three choices in how they prepare for the coming B2B storm. They may ignore the trends and leave their organizations unchanged. They may take half-hearted steps to adapt for Internet busi-ness, superficially altering their organizations but leaving their core pro-cesses unchanged. Or they may recognize the tremendous opportunity offered by this paradigm shift, transform the way they serve their cus-tomers, and ensure their future in the digital age.

> *The Boston Consulting Group predicts that the B2B ecommerce market will grow to $2.8 trillion by 2003.*

The rise of Internet-based electronic commerce has changed the global business landscape forever. After a few years of explosive growth in the worldwide adoption of Web technology, business leaders have completely changed the way they perceive online technology. Once seen as an unfamiliar and threatening medium, the Internet has proven itself as a superb environment for commerce. In today's fast-paced, competi-tive atmosphere, no B2B supplier that lacks a strategy to conduct sales and operations over the Internet may be considered a leader.

> *Leadership among sellers depends on moving into B2B ecommerce.*

Organizations that move decisively and intelligently into Web busi-ness can register significant competitive gains. These include increased revenue, lowered costs, new customer relationships, innovative branding opportunities, and the creation of new lines of customer service. Sellers who fail to gear up for the coming B2B ecommerce explosion will not only pass up those opportunities, but in many industries will find their very survival threatened. As their customers and competitors outpace them, they will slide further into irrelevancy.

Requirements for the New Economy

Participation in the new economy means very different things to different selling organizations. Generally speaking, the most important require-ments for sellers seeking to push their business onto the Internet are a total commitment to success, recognition of the infrastructure challenges involved, and an intelligent plan of action.

Commitment

Whether an organization sells office supplies to multinational companies or provides specialized consulting services to a handful of clients, a strong commitment is needed to become equipped for Internet business. If the Web is to be central to the way any company operates, the ef-fort to gear up for ecommerce and an Internet-enabled value chain must be understood and accepted by key functional areas within the organization as well as by executive management. This is true for sellers large or small, highly centralized or distributed along several continents.

This commitment is necessary because each incremental advance down the path of Web-enabled commerce carries deep implications for business processes and organizational culture. Company leadership must be willing to commit the resources in people, money, and focus necessary to carry the ecommerce deployment through to fulfillment. Line managers and employees must embrace new tools for internal communication, sales processing, and customer fulfillment.

Web business deployment demands an organization-wide deployment.

No matter what stage of Internet business is pursued, the organization is being asked to transform itself and adapt to new ways of working and delivering customer value. The new processes and responsibilities required by world-class B2B ecommerce are demanding; management cannot easily force their creation and execution. Establishing leadership in the new economy requires a companywide commitment. The will to adapt and transform must be built into all levels of the organization.

Understanding the Digital Infrastructure

Suppliers seeking to make the Web a significant platform for sales and order fulfillment must gain an understanding of ecommerce infrastructure requirements. These infrastructure challenges are frequently misunderstood, and often exaggerated, by new deplorers of Internet business solutions.

Sellers are already familiar with the physical infrastructure that allows them to deliver their goods or services to their customers. Elements of this physical infrastructure include storefronts, processing centers, and transportation fleets. What is less familiar to new entrants to the electronic economy is the *digital* infrastructure of business—the combination of internal applications, network connectivity, online presence, and Web-based customer fulfillment that allows companies to track and satisfy a customer's total experience.

The organization's digital infrastructure should be integrated with its physical infrastructure. The Internet is creating a paradigm shift in B2B commerce, a transformation best thought of as enabling new business processes and improving existing ones.

The key to success online is to create a digital infrastructure that is tightly integrated with the company's physical infrastructure. Establishing the right flow of information links the organization's digital and physical infrastructures, providing target elements of the company with data about all aspects of the acquisition decision, including order fulfillment, payment, and customer support.

A Plan for Action

Whether driven by the profit motive or simply a desire to survive, businesses are rushing into ebusiness ventures like prospectors into a gold rush. Under pressure to perform in a new, unfamiliar arena, many companies sacrifice strategy to urgency. These initiatives fail because of a lack of forethought. By not taking the time to carefully assess the market, they fail to realize where the real areas of opportunity lie in this new economy.

Suppliers should develop an ecommerce plan for action appropriate for their

- Size
- Competitive situation
- Industry focus
- Available resources

Many sellers are already well down the path of transforming their business process and infrastructure for ecommerce operations. These companies may already have found their entry point into the new digital economy and are concentrating on expanding their operations or improving their business results. Other B2B players have not yet begun to address the challenge and face the need for a much more concerted and far-reaching deployment to integrate the Web into their customer communication and transaction processes. Regardless of their deployment stage, however, ecommerce ventures depend absolutely on the quality of their conception and execution.

Each supplier's specific strategy, objectives, and technical infrastructure for ecommerce will be shaped by variables that include its size, capabilities and scope, market pressures, industry focus, and available resources. Management must develop a coherent course of action that is both feasible and appropriate to the company's overall situation.

Also critical to success is ensuring that the organization's ecommerce strategy contains both a short-term and long-term perspective. For companies lacking a quality presence online, rapid time-to-market is essential; these organizations should seek the execution path that allows them quick access to business results. At the same time, the velocity of change online demands that companies also plan for the future, whether that is six months or three years down the road. The action plan for ecommerce deployment is never complete. It is best thought of as a living strategy, one that will evolve to fit the organization as its requirements and capabilities grow over time.

Success Strategies

Every enterprise's value chain may be enhanced through business-to-business ecommerce. While the details of a company's ecommerce action plan must be informed by its broader competitive situation, almost all companies will share several high-level objectives. How an organization goes about targeting these goals will determine the success or failure of its Internet initiative.

Increase Revenue and Lower Costs

The ultimate goal of every ecommerce expansion is to achieve bottom-line, measurable results—to increase revenue and reduce expenses. A well-executed Web strategy allows businesses to accomplish this on several levels. Aggressive Web-enabled businesses gain new revenue from multiple sources, including acquiring new customers and increasing business from existing customers. By expanding into the online medium, a supplier grows its pool of potential trading partners tremendously. And by developing a complete online business solution, the seller can gain increased revenue from existing technology-enabled customers that prefer to do business through ecommerce.

Suppliers lower their operating expenses by taking advantage of the Web's unique abilities for communication and transaction processing. By implementing new processes that automate functions long performed by salespeople or support staff—for instance, notifying customers of their order status—suppliers register important savings.

Find Partnerships of Opportunity

The right partnership strategy can allow a seller just entering the online space to accelerate toward a world-class business presence or help an established ecommerce player expand into new markets and services. It is neither necessary nor advisable for companies hoping to tap the flow of B2B ecommerce to go it alone. The alliance concept is alive and well on the Internet, where the special capabilities of the online medium can make such relationships especially advantageous. Simply by selecting the

right technology and marketplace partners—many of whom offer access
and services at low cost—suppliers can take a giant step toward true
ecommerce enablement.

> *Partnerships help sellers rapidly deploy ecommerce solutions and gain
> access to buyer liquidity.*

Sellers seeking to fast-track their Web plans should seek partnerships of opportunity—alliances with other companies that allow them to
quickly develop infrastructure, services, and access to new customers.
Pursuit of this strategy may mean joining a B2B marketplace, an electronic market on the public Internet that brings together buyers and sellers into a seamless trading community. These online marketplaces allow
sellers to gain broad access to buyers and develop new, highly efficient
lines of trade. Or it may mean selecting an application service provider
that will provide hosted access to the applications the organization requires to conduct its ecommerce solution. For suppliers of small size and
limited resources, Web communities exist that offer basic ecommerce
infrastructure, including hosting and transaction management.

> *The organization's digital infrastructure must support the full customer
> experience.*

Ensure a Quick Time-to-Market

Suppliers who move quickly to establish effective electronic business
presences put themselves in a position of strength. Those who adopt a
wait-and-see approach, hesitate too long over infrastructure decisions, or
are too tentative in execution run the risk of being passed by. Internet
business is characterized by its rapid pace and intense competition.

Once a competitor has fallen far behind, it can be too late to catch
up. Time-to-benefit is directly correlated with the speed in which a supplier establishes their B2B ecommerce presence. Rapid time-to-market
is an essential component to every ecommerce rollout.

Create the Right Digital Infrastructure

Even small or midsize B2B suppliers should not consider infrastructure
an obstacle to the development of an electronic market presence. In many
ways, it is easier than ever before for such organizations to gain early-
stage access to the benefits of ecommerce and an Internet-enabled supply
chain. The last few years have seen remarkable evolution in Web hosting,
dynamic electronic marketplaces, and applications that process and route
sales information. These are the essential building blocks of ecommerce

infrastructure, assuring the organization's ability to establish connectivity, put product or service information online, access a broad range of customers, process transactions, and fulfill orders.

Successful ecommerce demands the right alignment of human assets and technology elements, working together to support all phases of the customer experience: selection, purchase, delivery, and support.

- *Selection and customer review of key product and service information prior to the purchase decision.* This function is best served by a well-designed Web site that contains a complete range of information to guide the customer through the decision-making process.
- *Purchase sales transaction and processing.* This requires a tracking solution that routes information to all functional groups needed to complete customer order.
- *Delivery fulfillment of the customer order.* This should also include a customer response capability to keep end recipients apprised of order status.
- *Support customer service.* Often the forgotten element of ecommerce, support can be a make-or-break proposition in B2B, which is far more sensitive to service issues than B2C. From an infrastructure standpoint, this need is served through a Web presence that places technical information and access to company representatives within easy online reach of customers.

Create a Single Point of Access to All Markets of Opportunity

Sellers want to get their products and services in front of as many customers as possible while minimizing their online investment in time and resources. To achieve this goal, they should seek to join a system of interconnected B2B marketplaces. By using common data standards, these electronic marketplaces allow suppliers to maintain their product and service information at a single online location while participating in several markets.

> *B2B marketplaces let sellers access many customers, while maintaining one point of product and service information.*

Maintaining multiple points of online product information forces a seller to do expensive work in several places—updating prices and information, eliminating out-of-date content and managing customer data. This extra commitment leads to costly errors, drains money and time resources, and potentially makes the organization less responsive and less customer-focused.

Participation in a global network of integrated B2B marketplaces helps sellers gain tactical advantage and access to a virtually unlimited stream of buyer liquidity, maximizing the return on their investment in effort and money.

Exploit Branding and Customer Personalization

B2B ecommerce offers special opportunities for aggressive branding and customer personalization. Online business offers a special range of opportunities for branding and customer personalization. Both encourage customer loyalty—the all-important element of every ecommerce success story. The high cost of customer acquisition demands that organizations place a premium on holding onto existing customers through innovative branding and personalization initiatives.

Maintaining brand identity on the Web can be a challenge for B2B sellers. Buyers have easy access to so many competing suppliers that product and service offerings can be reduced to a commodity presence, if aggregated. Building a high-quality, distinctive Web site, particularly one that is enabled for integration via standards such as Commerce XML (cXML) to interact with network-based ecommerce purchasing solutions, can help suppliers stand out online by maintaining their brand identity and competitive differentiation.

Business-to-business trade puts a premium on personalization, the tailoring of offerings, prices, and services to specific customers. While personalization has its role in B2C, it is in B2B that is truly critical. Negotiated pricing, preferred customer relationships, and customized catalogs require a mechanism for focusing on specific customers. Personalization is important for sellers with a few customers or several thousand. While Dell Computer Corporation maintains over 35,000 Premier Pages on its Web site customized to the needs of individual customer organizations, a small supplier may see tremendous return from the creation of a handful of dedicated Web pages.

Section Summary

From the perspective of today's business managers, the new B2B ecommerce wave consists of equal parts threat and opportunity. It will split most industries' competitive field into two camps: the prepared and the unaware. Like every great paradigm shift, the global rise in electronic B2B trading relationships is also a potentially massive shift in power.

Small suppliers can establish access to an entirely new class of technology-enabled customer and rapidly develop into a major market player. Established giants can find themselves newly vulnerable, threatened by faster-moving and more technology-enabled competitors.

Suppliers who want to be among their industry leaders must seize the opportunity presented by the new economy. For those aggressive and focused enough to perform online, the upheaval and pace of today's electronic business world can yield tremendous benefit.

Chapter Summary

Keith Krach provided an excellent overview on the B2B phenomenon that is spreading across every major industry around the globe. New Web entrepreneurs and established brick-and-mortar business pros alike might wonder aloud what B2B is all about, what the best strategy is, what promises and pitfalls await them. Yet they'll likely not get any answer twice but this: B2B is here, and it already impacts all business, and you can delay your business's participation at great peril. Meanwhile, the opportunities belong to the fleetest and best executors. B2B might well be the Red Queen's land from Lewis Carroll's *Through the Looking Glass*:

> "... In our country," said Alice, panting a little, "you'd generally get somewhere else if you ran very fast for a long time, as we've been doing."
> "A slow sort of country!" said the Queen. "Now here, you see, it takes all the running you can do, to keep in the same place." The Red Queen continued, "If you want to get somewhere else you must run at least twice as fast as that!"

But at the same time, there is a certain timelessness emerging as B2B matures. Consider again what Keith Krach discussed: peppered throughout are eternal verities like *value, differentiation, efficiency, service, relationships*, and even that hoariest of old-economy chestnuts: *the bottom line*. And that's just it; all of a sudden, the Internet of the new century recalls business objectives and values familiar to all successful brick-and-mortar businesspeople—objectives and values that were, for a time, frankly out of fashion. These objectives and values now snap into focus as merely recast onto the new hyper-speed, boundaryless architecture of the Internet and propelled by hyper-competition. But they are no less familiar, and it is this new-but-old weave in the tapestry that differentiates the fresh, consortium-driven phase of B2B from the previous phase, in which the sudden, frictionless efficiency of the Web momentarily shot the pinions from under prices. Perhaps the efficiency of the Web overtook the efficiency of the market but if so, then only for a moment, like a race car flying over a slick spot on its way to victory. Viewed against that receding epoch, the emergence of market-making consortia presents a clearer validation of Adam Smith's notion of market efficiency than has ever before been witnessed.

In the following chapter we will explore the e-Marketplace dynamics in more detail, starting with the development of effective content strategies. Mark Hoffman, CEO of Commerce One, a global leader in e-Marketplace technologies, will provide his insights into the convergence of content and commerce. Whether your strategy includes building your own e-Marketplace or participating in multiple digital markets or both, content is still king and needs to be dynamic and real-time to win in the new economy.

3

CHAPTER

Dynamic Content Strategies

This chapter outlines the key areas of dynamic content creation, publishing, and management that will form the foundation of a winning *dynamic content* strategy for success. It provides an overview of the critical components of the *content value chain* that creates, distributes, hosts, delivers, and consumes content. Mark Hoffman, chairman and CEO of Commerce One, Inc., discusses the role of content management in the context of B2B e-Marketplaces. Research analysis on pervasive content on the edge of the network is provided in the second half of the chapter from The Yankee Group.

Much of what is outlined in data sheets and brochures about content management focuses on what content management is. The real challenge facing net market makers is the *why*. Look beyond the obvious first levels of content that are strongly needed to present information and conduct transactions, and one will find the real long-term value of content management is in the interactivity, the collaboration, and the personalization that leads ultimately to knowledge management.

Content Must Adapt in the New Economy

The long-term success of e-Marketplaces is predicated on their ability to provide not only transaction capabilities but dynamic, relevant content to trading partners. Content will drive the formation of communities and purchasing decisions. If the proper knowledge tools are provided to these communities of knowledge workers, then they will begin to collaborate, interoperate, and form *Value Trust Networks* (VTNs). These VTNs will be a platform for information exchange, knowledge creation, and collaborative global business practices. Flow of dynamic content via the Internet put into business process context will empower enterprises and individuals connected to global trading communities to conduct transactions, collaborate on projects, and create new forms of value for themselves and their customers.

Technology must support the realities and requirements of ebusiness discussed above. It should not be simply a point solution or, worse still, a closed solution for a single initiative. Because it's impossible to predict what initiative may be launched next, enterprises should select a technology architecture that can support all ebusiness initiatives. The right choice for ebusiness is

- *Open*—To reduce operational costs and to leverage outside innovation
- *Scalable*—To reduce time-to-market and to extend market reach
- *Controllable*—To manage risk and allow for constant innovation and reinvention
- *Rapidly deployable*—To reduce time-to-market and accelerate returns
- *Easy to use*—To ensure wide adoption and reduce operational costs

Every business has subject matter experts, which drive the success of its business entities. If a business is to be successful on the Web, companies have to get them involved in their online initiatives. But these employees are not necessarily technical experts, so they must be easy to use.

Accelerate with Outside Agencies

Companies are increasingly outsourcing services to ASPs (application service providers), systems integrators, ad agencies, and business partners, including content management. In today's dynamic business environment, companies must increasingly focus on their core competencies and outsource the rest. ASPs enable companies to rent content management software instead of having to buy it. Some also offer content management services.

Internet consulting organizations like marchFIRST and "The Big Five" are also in the content management business. These companies recognize that content management is an integral part of the success of any ebusiness or e-Marketplace. These traditional consulting organizations, as well as the new breed of global internet consultants led by marchFIRST, have dedicated hundreds of consultants who are deploying both content management solutions as well as the new integrated content and commerce offerings from companies such as Commerce One solutions that include content management. They know that e-Marketplaces must provide value to buyers and sellers at several levels. Suppliers must be able to sell and extend their reach to new communities of buyers effectively. Buyers must be able to locate products or services quickly and easily, as well as get access to new strategic suppliers. Finally, ad agencies are helping companies with content strategies, albeit at a different level. As the masters of branding and increasingly Web content strategy, ad agencies are working more closely with customers to manage what the customer see, when, why, and how.

Commerce-Enabled Content

There is a trend toward combining content and commerce closely into single integrated software solutions. This integration will make it easier for users of Web content to move quickly into a business and transaction mode as they navigate through the company's content. The optimum Web content strategy will always keep customers just a click away from commerce. The integration of content and commerce enables a more fluid flow for the customers, employees, suppliers, and partners that are accessing company content and using it for daily decision support.

Empowering this trend is the underlying technology standards of Java and XML (eXtensible Markup Language). XML is a metalanguage that allows for attributes to be added to a document or a piece of content such as the identification of its owner, its authorization levels, and its business process purpose. It enables a new class of *live content.* and computer-to-computer interfaces that don't require human intervention. It is one of the most exciting standards to hit the Internet programming environment.

All major software providers have standardized on versions of XML and most are also using Java. Java is another programming language that is enabling anytime, anywhere ecommerce. It is an end-to-end solution being designed into ecommerce servers, as well as the computers, hand-held devices, and cell phones that are accessing ecommerce services. Ergo, the combination of XML and Java is completely redefining how end users interact with content and transactions.

In the next section, Mark Hoffman discusses how content management strategies can be applied to B2B e-Marketplaces in a way that is beneficial to buyers, sellers, and e-Marketplace operators.

Perspective

Mark Hoffman, chairman and CEO, Commerce One

Commerce One is the leader in global ecommerce solutions for business. As the founder of the Global Trading Web, the world's largest business-to-business trading community, Commerce One enables buyers and sellers around the world to trade in a barrier-free environment and creates new business opportunities for all trading partners. Commerce One offers solutions for companies who want to establish and sell their products and services through an e-Marketplace and for those looking for a comprehensive e-procurement solution and with a high return on investment.

The Role of Content in Internet Initiatives

Content has always been central to the Internet. In its early days, primarily the scientific community and academia used the medium as a communications and research tool. In 1993, the World Wide Web revolutionized Internet content and human interaction with it.

Prior to the advent of the Web, a person would have to know where a file was physically located in order to access it. With the Web, physical location is irrelevant. In the early days, Internet content was text-based. The Web's underlying technology, Hypertext Markup Language, or HTML, enabled content to be graphically displayed. The difference between pre-Web and post-Web content is even bigger than the difference between black-and-white and color TV.

The Web represented en entirely new communications medium for the world. Its earliest B2B application was that of a virtual brochure. During 1993 and 1994, companies by the hundreds, then hundreds of thousands began establishing their own Web sites and publishing their own content. The excitement over the new medium began to wane when businesses realized that online brochures were a corporate expense as opposed to a revenue generator.

Enter ecommerce. Visionaries such as Dan Lynch and Jay "Marty" Tenenbaum understood that the long-term viability of the Internet hinged on its ability to generate revenue. Dan Lynch, the man who switched the ARPANET (the predecessor to the Internet) to the TCP/IP protocol that enabled the Internet, founded a company called CyberCash that was destined to become part of the new economy financial infrastructure. CyberCash understood early on that successful ecommerce had to work within the established financial industry structure. So, the company forged relationships with banks, credit card companies, and other financial organizations that could make end-to-end transactions on the Internet—true ecommerce—a reality.

The ability to complete transactions online does not necessarily result in sales, however, and is certainly not a strong enough foundation on which to base an e-Marketplace. In a B2B e-Marketplace, electronic catalogs and value-added content are essential. Buyers needs sophisticated decision-making tools, and suppliers need a means of presenting their products or services in a compelling way that will translate to sales. Content is the key to success.

The following diagram illustrates how the Internet's value proposition has shifted in the past few years. Content is central to each of these development stages. In the marketing phase, the Internet provided visibility on a global basis. In the sales phase, it provided a rudimentary means of buying and selling products and services. Today, the Internet is an integral part of any ebusiness strategy where the flow of content between companies, their customers and suppliers must occur in real time.

Internet Value Proposition

Marketing	Sales	Business
1993 —→	1996 —→	1999 —→

Source: Commerce One

The original commerce sites that basically provided shopping cart capabilities are not robust enough solutions for the business sector in particular. The supply chain represents a complex set of business processes that must extend out past the enterprise. Therefore, commerce solutions can no longer reside solely behind a firewall in a single enterprise.

The earliest marketplaces automated the procurement process, enabling the buying process to be reduced from weeks to a couple days. Now we are witnessing the emergence of complex e-Marketplaces that must support existing business processes and systems. Internet time does not allow for anything less. As a result, content is becoming even more critical for e-Marketplaces. Hosting catalogs is not enough. Buyers must be able to search them quickly, and sellers must have a means of differentiating themselves. Moreover, content must evolve to support strategic business decisions. Today, we are seeing the emergence of such solutions that support many-to-one-to-many relationships.

Content Drives B2B E-Marketplaces

Accurate and complete content improves the quality and speed of purchasing decisions by giving buyers the ability to search across multiple vendors and find the right products to meet their precise needs. For sellers, content differentiates their products and enables them to participate in multiple online marketplaces. And, to be successful, Net market makers must deliver content with value-added information such as ratings, reviews, regulatory compliance, and service information to attract new users and fulfill the needs of their diverse buyer and supplier communities.

Much of the content that is available today is inherently weak—a victim of the e-Marketplaces race to open new channels and to be first to market. Creating high-quality content is made difficult because different catalogs use different descriptions, attributes, and parameters to describe the same item. Content management issues became even more nettlesome with the addition of value-added content such as editorial articles, service information, and third-party reviews.

Unfortunately, most online marketplaces are ill prepared to tackle this content management challenge. They rely on time-consuming and expensive manual processes to extract, update, and aggregate content residing in disparate databases.

Content Landscape

Rich product content is at the core of every successful ecommerce transaction or service. Sellers need to communicate what they have to sell; buyers need to know what's available. The product catalog is the conduit for that communication. It establishes a common understanding between both parties to the transaction. As a result, the accessibility, usability, accuracy, and richness of that content directly impacts the transaction. If the information is complete, unusable, or unavailable, the buyer can't make an informed decision. Similarly, suppliers and e-Marketplace operators can't differentiate their products. If the information is inaccurate, the buyer is basing his or her decision on the wrong data. In either case, the user's experience may be less than satisfactory, which reflects poorly on the supplier, the e-Marketplace, and perhaps the idea of online transactions and their promise of cost savings.

Every buyer and supplier has his or her own preferences for the naming, descriptions, and information associated with every product. Where these preferences diverge is where the greatest potential for incomplete or inaccurate data exists. Two suppliers may assume that the same product description means something else.

The differences may be minimal for easily understood commodities such as pork bellies and pasteurized milk. However, as the products move further down the production chain, names and descriptions start to differ significantly. For instance, the naming of a product as seemingly codified as a golf club can vary greatly between manufacturers. Titleist refers to its similar club as a "gap wedger." Taylor Made calls its 52-degree wedge an "attack wedge." Cleveland uses the "dual wedge" moniker. Adams calls its 52-degree club a "pitching wedge." All four clubs have essentially the same loft and characteristics, yet all four are named something entirely different by their respective manufacturers.

The lack of naming standards make it difficult for buyers to get information on all available products, opens up the possibility that a supplier will miss out on a sales opportunity, and forces e-Marketplace operators to resolve the discrepancies as they construct their custom catalogs.

Beyond naming conventions, every supplier and buyer has their preferred listing of specifications. Suppliers typically list specifications they believe best highlight their products, while they avoid those that may expose less than competitive product attributes. Some suppliers simply list specifications out of habit with little more reasoning than "that's the way it's always been done." For buyers, preferred specifications may be based on special needs or features they believe are critical to maintaining their competitive advantage.

Most golf club manufacturers list the loft of their wedges and the availability of the left- and right-handed models. Many describe the shaft material. Some designate the make and model of the shaft. Some manufacturers describe face inserts or groove patterns. Others indicate bounce angle, the heel-toe camber, or the leading edge. No two companies use the same list of specifications.

For buyers this lack of consistency makes it difficult to compare products. Suppliers may lose a sales opportunity because their product description lacks a key specification a buyer is looking for. E-Marketplace operators must fill the gaps to make their catalogs more effective decision-making tools for fulfilling the needs of their diverse trading communities.

These disparate product descriptions and names impede ecommerce transactions by making the buying experience considerably more difficult and less effective. The redundant product descriptions not only bloat the catalog without adding more meaningful information; they force the buyer to conduct multiple searches using multiple names to generate a complete list of the products available through the e-Marketplace. Then the nonstandard information makes it difficult to compare products listed in the various search results.

In this situation, no one wins. Buyers get frustrated. Suppliers can get shortchanged when they aren't included in product searches even though they may be offering similar products. And the Net market maker loses by not being able to provide the best-possible online user experience.

If a buyer from a sporting goods retailer requested information on gap wedges, the search engine would overlook attack, lob, and pitching wedges even though these three categories represent essentially the same type of product. If the golf club buyer specifies a bounce angle of six degrees, only clubs from suppliers that list bounce angle would be returned.

The sporting goods retailer ends up making a subpar decision based on incomplete information. The attack, lob, and pitching degree suppliers lost out on a potential sale. And the Net market maker squanders an opportunity to help the suppliers and buyers expand their market.

B2B Content Management Solutions

Given the negative impact of varied catalogs, industry experts stress the importance of bridging the gap between supplier naming and formatting conventions. To maintain the content status quo is to limit the true potential of B2B ecommerce. Forcing suppliers to adhere to a common set of names and descriptions is unrealistic. Buyers aren't interested, nor do they typically have the in-house capabilities, to normalize and categorize catalogs. While all parties play a role in the management of content, the bulk of the task rests on the shoulders of the business-to-business online marketplace operator.

Though each trading partner and e-Marketplace operator needs to address content management issues, each requires different functions from the system. Buyers look for a content management system to provide their users with a common purchasing experience with minimal effort and cost. The solution should present an organization-wide product listing, including all pertinent decision-making information, search capabilities, and complementary services based on a user's role within the organization.

Suppliers want a content management system that enables them to manage their brand, as well as control their product descriptions, pricing, and discount policy. They also want a solution that helps them leverage their domain expertise. Given the dynamic nature of B2B ecommerce, content management must also provide the means for quickly and easily incorporating changes in product listing, descriptions, and pricing.

Because e-Marketplace operators must address supplier and buyer concerns, their solution needs to represent an aggregation of both. To accommodate buyers, e-Marketplace operators must streamline the buying process, provide decision-making information, and present a common buying experience. For suppliers, e-Marketplace operators must support the branding needs of the supplier, as well as the e-Marketplace.

Elements of Content Management

E-Marketplace operators must also choose a solution that enables them to add value, such as editorial content, collaborative tools, or third-party buying recommendations. Several application vendors are attacking the problem with varying degrees of success. The critical elements are normalization, rationalization, parametric searches, categorization, support of unstructured data and publishing models, scalability, automation, end-to-end scope, and interoperability. All those elements must be present in a content management solution to benefit buyers, sellers, and e-Marketplace operators alike.

Normalization. To save space in large, multiproduct catalogs, product descriptions are often constructed of abbreviations and acronyms that may be specific to a supplier. *Normalization* is a process used to expand these abbreviations and acronyms to full, uniform, and correct terminology. For instance, one supplier may list lack ballpoint pens using the abbreviation "BP PEN, BLK." Another supplier may refer to the same pen as "Ballpoint, BK." Through normalization, both abbreviations are expanded to the uniform description "black ballpoint pen" so all marketplace participants have access to each supplier's product. The uniform nomenclature makes it easier for buyers to compare products and costs, and ensures suppliers are included in relevant product searches. The expanded acronyms and abbreviations also make the marketplace content richer, with less room for misinterpretations. In fact, the Internet eliminates the need for acronyms and abbreviations entirely because space and cost are not issues to consider, unlike print media.

Rationalization. At a bare minimum, an effective content management system must combine data from multiple vendors. However, to simply input the existing names, formats, and data does nothing to resolve the issue. During the transfer of information, the content management systems must rationalize the data to match a common standard. This common standard can be the lowest common denominator—in essence, incorporating only the data that every supplier provides. Similarly, the common standard can be expanded to include all content categories. The latter, called *rationalization*, requires more work because the content management system must be capable of back-filing missing data from all suppliers. Yet, because it delivers more information, it is also the most effective form for standardizing content.

For instance, using our previous golf club example, the content management solution could link attack, lob, and pitching wedges so any query for one would return "hits" for all variations. Additionally, the product descriptions would be rationalized so each wedge would contain the same specifications.

Parametric Search Support.   One of the benefits of normalization and rationalization is support for parametric searches. With all names, descriptions, and data formats, matching a higher common definition, a buyer can input search criteria and the search engine will be able to access all matching products—even from vendors that use different naming conventions or data formats. In addition, with more complete product information, the parametric search can also provide a list of substitute products that meet most search parameters, alternative products that offer similar specifications, and inventory sharing for large-lot purchases that must be filled through multiple suppliers.

Categorization.   Categorization is closely related to normalization. Just as different manufacturers describe products differently, suppliers, buyers, and e-Marketplace operators may also place products in different categories. Some suppliers may use broad categories that encompass multiple product lines. Other buyers may choose narrower product category descriptions that focus on a handful of highly related products. Because categories are one of the first lines from searches, the content management solutions must resolve these categorization differences and segment product content into a common category structure such as United Nations Standard Product and Service Classification (UNSPSC).

Unstructured Data.   An effective content management system must also be flexible enough to incorporate both structured and unstructured data. While the majority of product information is usually highly structured, third-party review, product analyses, and industry reports, which tend to provide great value to buyers, are not. Additionally, certain purchasing transactions such as spot buys and RFPs (Request for Proposals) may be less structured. For these transaction types, key product information can be contained in a series of notes attached to the initial product descriptions. A content management system must be able to accommodate these unstructured and ad hoc attachments.

Multiple Publishing Models. Catalog content can be published at one to three locations: at the supplier's Web site, at the buyer's Web site, or on the e-Marketplace. Each publishing target has its own benefits, depending on the type of transactions or market. The content management system must be able to accommodate all three targets, in any combination, to ensure that the publishing model is determined by what is most effective for the market—not what is possible through the system.

Scalability. Scalability is also a major issue for content management systems. All e-Marketplaces expect to grow; however not all content management systems may be able to scale to the degree the e-Marketplace operator wishes. Some vendors manually normalize and input catalog content. Not only is this approach very expensive and time-consuming it also doesn't scale well. Ideally, the content management system should automatically handle the normalization of naming conventions and data formats.

Automation. The need for automation becomes obvious when one considers the ongoing management of content. E-Marketplace content is never static, so the content management system must be able to automate the processing and delivery of products and product description changes throughout the entire system, whether it's an enterprise or an e-Marketplace. All catalogs, regardless of where they reside, must be updated to reflect the changes.

Content End-to-End. One of the greatest lures of B2B ecommerce is the promised ability to integrate every aspect of the transaction. Moving procurement to the Web is the first step but to be truly integrated; content management solutions must be able to integrate with the buyers' and suppliers' internal enterprise systems. Effective content management solutions must share this same level of integration. Changes in supplier availability and pricing, data that is easily capture in their enterprise system, should be automatically communicated to the content management system and reflected in the catalog. Similarly, pricing and availability changes to the catalog should be communicated with the buyer's procurement and forecasting systems.

Interoperability. Content does no good in a void. For it to have value, it must be shared between parties. The more parties, the greater the value. However, original content is typically proprietary, developed as a point-to-point solution to represent a single supplier. As a result, Advanced Marketing Research (AMR) estimates that only 10 to 15 percent of all manufacturers' content is in usable electronic format.

For content to be shared between multiple parties, it must move from this point-to-point approach to an open framework for common electronic standards, schemas, and protocols. The central tenet is that the content must be exposed and accessible to external search engines and buying applications, regardless of the participant. While buyers, suppliers, and Net market makers all approach content management differently, this common framework enables each to share the same content. Content interoperability expands the potential market for the content and ensures each party can access content without implementing proprietary architecture.

Content Management Planning

Content management solutions can be broken down into three distinct stages: aggregation, publishing, and management. Aggregation is the process by which multiple vendor catalogs and third-party information sources are virtually or physically normalized and combined into a single catalog that contains all the content. Publishing is the process of standardizing and communicating the content so that it can be easily accessed and shared by suppliers, buyers, and e-Marketplaces. Ongoing management processes keep the content current, complete, and accurate.

Aggregation. The basic premise of aggregating content is relatively simple: Combine content from multiple vendors into a common catalog. However, the variety of supplier types and content make the actual process exponentially more difficult.

Earlier, we briefly discussed how different naming conventions, specifications, and data formats complicate the process for a single product. As the number of products increases, the complexity rises geometrically. The content management solution must enable the online marketplace operator to aggregate multiple products in multiple categories from multiple vendors across an entire industry, not just one segment.

From this churning chaos of names and formats, the content management system must be able to create a common high-quality content standard that encompasses all specification and content types and normalizes diverging naming conventions and information. The common standard must be information-rich to ensure that buyers have access to all the relevant information they might require. Content aggregation must be performed dynamically so the solution can determine how to handle missing information, ambiguous descriptions, and unknown terms on the fly.

A key concern for suppliers joining online marketplaces is the fear of losing control of their brand. Brand is critically important in today's Internet economy. Brand is the single near-constant that transcends the industry's continual state of change. Suppliers want a content management system that addresses the seemingly incompatible goals of normalization and brand retention. As such, the challenge is to meet a common standard but to leave room within that standard for the branding elements that help distinguish one supplier from another. Brand also provides an element of comfort and confidence for buyers so, though not as strenuously championed as the supplier, buyers also benefit from this incorporation of brand and normalization.

Within each category of participant—buyer, supplier, and Net market maker—there are vast differences in the needs and preferences. The content management solution must enable each of these users to customize their window into the catalog. By definition, the content standard used to normalize the multiple content sources must be quite extensive. However, not every buyer or seller is interested in every one of those specifications. The content management solution should enable each user to customize their interfaces to access only the information they deem important. By streamlining the information each user sees, the online marketplace can speed the process and improve the transaction experience by making it more relevant to the user.

The content management solution must also reflect preexisting buyer-supplier relationships. Some buyers and suppliers move their transactions to the online marketplace not to uncover new supplier relationships but to streamline the ones they already have in place. These relationships have been built on years of interdependence and negotiating that both parties want incorporated into their online partnership. However, suppliers and buyers don't want to make their hard-fought agreements available to the world at large. Online marketplaces are not necessarily malls where everyone enjoys the same pricing. The content management solution must be able to track these existing relationships and incorporate the resulting data access business rules, pricing, availability, and terms into the buyers' and sellers' customized content views.

Even with the complicated task of aggregating content, the market isn't about to grant anyone extra time. Time-to-market is still critical.

The marketplace that sets up shop first captures a competitive edge that makes it difficult for new entrants to compete. Because time is of the essence, packaged content management solutions provide an immediate advantage by enabling the Net market maker to create rich content faster. These ready-made solutions don't require extra time to create and ramp up. Online marketplaces, with their industry-centric focus, simply do not have the internal resources and expertise or the time to create a system in house.

Publishing.   After catalog content is aggregated, it must be communicated to all the parties in the trading community. A content management solution does this by publishing the aggregated content to one of three locations: the supplier's Web site, the buyer's e-procurement system, or the online marketplace.

Publishing aggregated content to the online marketplace is probably the most straightforward of the options. Once the content is aggregated, the marketplace simply posts the complete catalog on its site. Based on established permissions, buyers and suppliers can access the content through their standard Web browser or e-procurement application. These portal-based publishing solutions are excellent for communicating spot buys on a wide range of easily defined commodities.

Aggregated content can be published to the buyer's enterprise system behind their firewall. As a result, buyers can conduct product searches without ever leaving their internal procurement system. This buyer-centric publishing model is best suited to two product categories: plant-level commodities that can be supplied through multiple vendors and capital goods with special requirements. The common denominator is the need for control. For plant-level commodities, the buyer needs to ensure a continuous stream of the products necessary to keep their production line running. For capital goods, the buyer wants to be sure that the large-ticket items meet their requirements exactly. Because the catalog resides behind the buyer's firewall, there also is a perceived increase in security.

Typically, the content that resides at the supplier's Web site is not the aggregated catalog. Nevertheless, this content is still "published" because it's made available to the rest of the trading community. Some content management solutions simply point the buyer to this published supplier content. However, the more effective content management systems enable buyers to interact with the supplier site from within their e-procurement application. There are two reasons why a supplier might opt for this model. First, by retaining the content on their site, the supplier maintains their branding. Second, the supplier can make the industry specific search and product configuration engines at its site available to a wider audience. Because these applications can help buyers select product, this supplier-centric model is best suited to customizable, high-volume commodities.

Recently, a fourth type of publishing model has been introduced—content syndication. Content syndication is the publishing of content created or collated and provided by a third-party source. Much as a newspaper syndicate shares news stories, content syndication enables an on-line marketplace to share content created elsewhere and publish it to its own portal or those of the buyer and seller.

Management.   Once aggregated and published, content does not go into a perpetual holding pattern. No catalog remains static for long. Descriptions change. Prices go up or down. Products are deleted. Other products are added. All these changes need to be continually incorporated in the catalog. Out-of-date or inaccurate information is the major stumbling block for most ecommerce sites. Every time a buyer encounters information that is wrong or incomplete, it sours them to the experience. If they encounter this experience enough, they'll shift their buying allegiances to a marketplace where they have more confidence in the data.

A single catalog from a single supplier is a challenge to update, a challenge poorly addressed by all but the most efficient suppliers. Given the multi-catalog scope of ecommerce, moving those changes to the Internet is even more difficult. Regardless of the challenge, the modifications must be made systematically and quickly.

Because of the sheer number of sites where aggregated content can reside, a manual system would be quickly overwhelmed by the task of continually updating content. Under a manual system, Net market makers and exchange operators would find it difficult to determine when source catalogs have changed. With the myriad customized interfaces possible, it would be next to impossible for a manual system to communicate pertinent changes to the appropriate targets. The data entry processes required to input changes into a manual system would also quickly become a prime source for errors, especially as marketplace and exchange growth outpaces the ability to hire and train qualified content specialists.

For these reasons, an effective content management solution must be capable of automatically updating content. This content management solution must be able to automatically discern when changes have been made to a supplier's catalog. It must be able to normalize those changes into the aggregated content. And it must be able to pinpoint which publishing targets need to receive the updated content.

Content Management B2B E-Marketplace-Style

There are a lot of content management solutions on the market today. Some companies are opting to integrate commerce systems and content management software themselves, while others are turning to solutions providers. Commerce One is an ecommerce solutions provider that has integrated content management and collaboration as services into its infrastructure. Its solution is portal-based and includes applications, outsourcing options, subscription services, methodologies, and technologies designed to enable users to create, aggregate, implement, and manage rich, value-added content at the e-Marketplace level.

The solution is designed to accommodate global e-Marketplaces, as well as market makers, buyers, and suppliers. Content can be published once and posted to one marketplace or many. Parametric searches enable buyers to perform sophisticated searches that may include substitute products, alternate selections, and consolidated inventories of separate suppliers.

The content management services are part of a larger business services framework that provides a baseline infrastructure for interoperability. As a result, third-party content sources and services can be easily integrated to leverage each trading partner's existing infrastructure. E-Marketplace operators can quickly get to market with content and other business services, while trading partners get access to a rich set of services.

The content management solution consists of a content engine and refinery, as well as sourcing, contents, and "RoundTrip" services. The Commerce One Content Engine is the core application for dynamically aggregating catalog content. It enables marketplace participants to create, cleanse, customize, and manage catalog content. The Content Refinery is an integrated set of applications and methodologies that enable e-Marketplace operators to design and deploy content production and management operations.

The Content Sourcing Service enables e-Marketplace operators and buyers to access and search content from other e-Marketplaces. The distributed search capabilities can tie into the Global Trading Web, which is the world largest online B2B trading community. For buyers, this translates to fast global sourcing.

Some market makers may not want to create and manage content directly yet may want to offer these services to their trading communities. The Managed Content Service is a hosted option that is available through a global e-Marketplace, such as CommerceOne.net.

RoundTrip is a subscription service that is available to buyers and suppliers. Buyers can link to a supplier's Web site without leaving their e-procurement application. From a single window, buyers can search for and configure products on the supplier's site and then bring the completed order into the e-Marketplace to complete the purchase transaction. Further, they can take advantage of business services like payment processing and logistics that may be variable on the e-Marketplace.

The quality of the content drives the quality of the ecommerce experience. Complete, up-to-date, and accurate content will provide the greatest value, the fastest transactions, and the best overall purchasing experience for the buyer. In the hyper-competitive world of ecommerce, the positive experience is the foundation for success for all e-Marketplace participants.

Content management is an integral part of the value that is being created through B2B ecommerce. The newest ebusiness models include content and content management in their revenue models. This creates additional revenue streams for e-Marketplace operators and results in compelling new value-added services for trading partners.

Content and Context

Business process is driven to a large extent by dynamic content, which when customized to a certain event, takes on a context. For example, purchasing has its own set of context, selling has its own, and so on. When setting a content strategy, keep in mind context groupings and business process flow.

The next section of this chapter provides a perspective on *pervasive content* from The Yankee Group.

Perspective

The Yankee Group

The Yankee Group is an internationally recognized leader in technology research and consulting services, whose broad-reaching analysis encompasses all the areas crucial to ebusiness success: the Internet, electronic commerce, communications, wireless/mobilecomputing, and enterprise applications.

A Framework to Manage Pervasive Content at the Edge of the Network—Executive Summary

Today's World Wide Web is a giant tangle of material, as companies struggle to manage their content effectively both inside and outside the firewall. Web pages proliferate and are subject to unexpected and even expected daily traffic spikes, challenges in scaling rapidly, the immaturity of the Internet, the difficulties and inefficiencies of worldwide content distribution, the lack of ubiquitous broadband access, and much more. With the rapid proliferation of increasingly complex content on the Web, content providers, service providers, and consumers are increasingly relying on content management and delivery systems. These systems exist in multiple forms but can encompass content distribution, content delivery and caching, load balancing, performance monitoring, and personalization. And they manage pervasive, increasingly dynamic, and rich content effectively and efficiently, wherever it resides. Content management systems at the edge of the network are formed from a value chain (as described in Figure 3-1) that encompasses each of these elements. In the past, several models have failed because they took into account only part of the value chain. But the newest business models and systems successfully harness the entire value chain so that all parties benefit,

Figure 3-1. *Pervasive Content Value Chain*

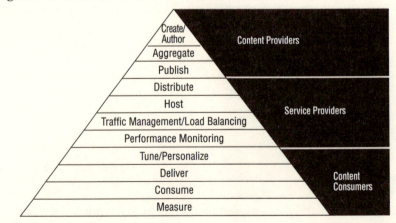

Source: The Yankee Group, 1999

which enables these new companies to collect revenues on the services they provide.

Part 1. Introduction

Content—the reusable information comprising text, graphics, audio/visual material, streaming media, and even applications that make up a Web page or Web site—is a critical element of all Web sites today and is the foundation for commerce. If a company can't tell people what it is selling on an ecommerce Web site, they won't buy. And if the company can't present content to knowledge workers, they will be unable to do their jobs. Content is the lifeblood of media like *The New York Times*, and of companies and firms that sell content themselves or that sell Web advertising based on their content. An inability to manage content effectively will cripple or severely impede the growth of these Web sites. Clearly, content is the center of everything that is Web-based. Without content, we would have blank Web pages.

This section provides an overview of the critical components of the content value chain that create, distribute, host, deliver, and consume content. We look at the impact of content management on content providers, service providers, and content consumers. *Content providers* are the companies that ultimately supply the content that is used by content consumers. Providers include media companies, portal sites, Web commerce companies, and any other company whose business is derived from some sort of content. *Service providers* include content delivery networks, collocation firms and Net sourcers (a term we will explain later in this section), ISPs, and ASPs. Finally, *content consumers* are the people who view the content: household or student users, business or government users, and users from within a company. We predict that the content delivery market will expand from $125 million in 2000 to nearly $1.5 billion in 2003 (see Figure 3-2).

The Foundation of the Value Chain.   In addition to the interdependency that is evident between its links, the value chain has been founded upon the need to push pervasive content to the edge of the network, the emergence of a platform for content delivery at the edge, and the need to deliver personalized content to content consumers.

Pushing Content to the Edge of the Network.   An important aspect of managing pervasive content is to push all types of content to the edge of the network. Bandwidth of all types is rapidly increasing in availability and decreasing in cost. But the size and complexity of the

Figure 3-2. *Content Delivery Solutions Forecast*

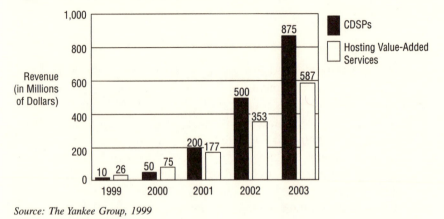

Source: The Yankee Group, 1999

different media are expanding as well. Thus, the need for ultra-distributed content management will continue to grow.

Even with increased bandwidth, distribution and delivery of rich media can be like sending an elephant through a garden hose. But by managing and controlling the flow, the content can move through the pipe evenly, and without shutting out other applications. For example, if a small ISP expects that a particular video will be viewed 1,000 times per day by its subscribers, it makes sense for the ISP to maintain that video on its servers to reduce the amount of time spent downloading that video from the content provider. By doing so, service to the ISP's customer will improve, while bandwidth consumption will decrease. The ISP can download content once and serve it up repeatedly. The downside of this approach, however, is that the cached content may not be current and that the content provider's Web site analysis software will incorrectly record the hit; the Web site only receives one hit, even though that hit represents 1,000 views per day from one ISP.

Today's newer and more sophisticated systems address this through advanced distribution technologies such as those by Inktomi/Web-Spective and F5 Networks that ensure current content, and through services such as Akamai's that redirect users to content at remote nodes only after recording their clicks. A systematic distributed content delivery approach such as that offered by Akamai and Sandpiper will meet the cost needs of ISPs, as well as the performance needs of content providers—all in a predictable, manageable, repeatable environment.

Finally, while static content has been sent to the edges of the network and into ISP caching servers, the next step will be to move more dynamic content and rich media to the edges of the network as well. This includes streaming media servers located at numerous remote sites, as well as increasingly distributed applications hosted at collocation sites around the world. This also includes "e-services," as envisioned by Hewlett-Packard: ultra-distributed, ultra-modular applications that can be called into action on the fly by anyone at any time. These might include online services to find a house, to book a plane reservation, to procure supplies, and so forth. Small, componentized applications and even some distributed databases will live on the fringes of the network, ever ready to quickly scale and deliver functionality on the fly.

A Platform to Manage Pervasive Content. Content management outside the firewall stems directly from traditional caching technologies used by ISPs, as well as internal content management systems, collocation hosting providers, and bandwidth providers. Although many solutions have been employed to improve Internet performance, until a few years ago, no company had developed a comprehensive system to address content or application performance issues. As a result, the door was open to new services developed by Akamai and Sandpiper, as well as new caching products offered by Inktomi, Novell, CacheFlow, Entera, InfoLibria, Network Appliance, and others.

Earlier attempts at performance improvement did not take a holistic approach, did not meet the needs of all of the parties, and, therefore, were not as widely deployed as they might have been. Because we are entering a new era in which the vendors and service providers take a more holistic approach, today's approaches are more likely to "stick" in the marketplace.

Pervasive Content. Similar to pervasive computing, pervasive content refers to reusable pieces of content—developed by anyone and delivered anywhere, anytime, on any device, and in any format, to anyone. Pervasive content relies on personalization and customization to the medium; it is not about broadcast. Pervasive content reuses content and includes text, graphics, photos, video, audio, dynamic, and static content, and is used throughout the extended enterprise. In the future, pervasive content will become increasingly dynamic—so much so that it will come to include applications and even e-services. Pervasive content flows throughout the content value chain. Most static content is composed of written text, graphics, and rich media (audio and video). Increasingly important, dynamic content is composed of data, such as stock quotes; personalized content transactions, such as in retail, banking, and brokerage; applications; and interactive content, such as brokerages and online

Figure 3-3. *Pervasive Content*

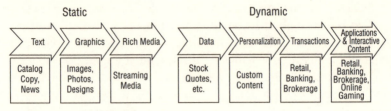

gaming. Today, dynamic content is a major and somewhat unaddressed challenge (see Figure 3-3).

The Content Delivery Platform. As increasing amounts of content move outside the firewall, more and more resources are required to manage them, and an ideal way to do this is through a platform. Just as content management within the firewall is built upon a platform, so too is content management outside the firewall. The content delivery platform comprises network routing and analysis, local routing and analysis, content distribution, and caching systems. A series of applications is built on top of that platform. These include tuning for specific media and for personalization, user profile management, content scheduling and subscription, file compression, traffic management, filtering, ad insertion, Web site performance monitoring, Web site analysis and reporting, and applications delivered at the edge of the network.

These content delivery platforms will become the foundation for content management outside the firewall. In short, these systems will enable ultra-distributed networks of static and dynamic content, applications, streaming media, and more—all available over a variety of devices.

In a manner similar to an operating system, these content delivery platforms enable a single unified view of content management, one that only a platform can provide. The platform provides a foundation for further expansion and the addition of new services that cannot be anticipated today. Figure 3-4 provides a view of the content management platform outside the firewall.

Content and service providers can take two approaches to these platforms. First, they can build the platforms themselves using off-the-shelf technology purchased from companies such as Inktomi, CacheFlow, Entera, InfoLibria, and Network Appliance. Or, they can essentially outsource the content delivery platform to content delivery service providers like Akamai or Sandpiper.

Figure 3-4. *Content Delivery Platform Outside the Firewall*

Tuning for • Media • Personalization	Content Scheduling and Subscription	File Compression	Filtering/Network Bandwidth Management	Web Site Performance Monitoring	E-Services and Custom Applications
User Profiles and Authentication	Streaming Media	Traffic Management Load Balancing	Ad Insertion	Web Site Analysis and Reporting	Transactions

API Layer

Content Delivery Platform

Caching Systems
Content Distribution Replication and Synchronization
Local Analysis and Routing
Network Analysis and Routing

Source: The Yankee Group, 1999

1. *Build/Buy.* The first set of vendors, especially Inktomi, enables service providers to develop their own content delivery platforms services in-house. Inktomi and others see themselves as "arms merchants" to all service providers. As such, they actually sell to both hosting firms and to content delivery service providers (CDSPs).

These packaged solutions enable hosting firms or Net sourcers to extend their offerings through new value-added services: content delivery and distribution, personalization at the edge of the network, advertising insertion, content tuning, and more. In most cases, these extensions will enable the hosting providers to garner additional revenue from existing clients. In addition, many of the hosting firms will find content providers interested because the hosting providers can control their own network quality in order to deliver on service-level agreements (SLAs).

Since the hosting provider owns the hosting facility, and possibly network bandwidth as well, it may be able to control its bandwidth costs, as well as its service levels, better than an outsourced solution. At the same time, the build/buy strategy requires service providers to build and manage their own content delivery networks with increased presence at the edge of the network—and this will present a major obstacle for many service providers. Most hosting companies have opted not to build these networks but rather offer caching solutions within their existing networks of data centers. This does not deliver the full value that is possible when content is pushed to the very edge of the network.

Proving just how complex these systems are, several specialized content delivery service providers have also implemented packaged content delivery platforms, indicating that even they did not have the expertise to build their own systems, and that their efforts were best spent running their network, not developing technology. This list includes most of the CDSPs—Adero, Mirror Image, and Sandpiper/Digital Island. Based on this, one might question how successful many Web-hosting companies would be in delivering content distribution services, since they will be competing against the specialized CDSPs.

2. *Rent/Outsource.* Alternatively, content providers and hosting companies may decide to outsource content delivery to CDSPs such as Akamai, Sandpiper, Adero, or Mirror Image. The CDSP approach has three advantages. First, CDSPs tend to be network-agnostic—particularly Akamai, and, to a lesser degree, Sandpiper. They have designed their systems to push content to the edge of the Internet, across several Internet backbones, and out to numerous ISP points of presence (POPs). Thus, these systems should be less prone to a single point of failure as would be the case for a hosting company deploying content only within its own network. Second, CDSPs actively monitor the Internet and their networks to route requests to the most appropriate cache. The CDSPs will typically factor in network conditions and the user's location to determine the most appropriate cache. CDSPs typically store network condition information in multiple tables that are updated at different frequencies; the frequency of these updates is one of the major differentiators between CDSPs. Finally, with a greater number of POPs than the hosted delivery solutions, CDSP networks should be able to deliver the fastest performance to the end user. By contrast, the hosting companies tend to focus more on distributing content within, rather than outside, their own networks.

Personalization.   Another major issue in content delivery is personalization. Personalization is the ability to deliver different content in various configurations based on a user's explicit or implicit profile, and on the content provider company's inference and delivery engines. The profile contains explicit information about the user—name, buying history, and so forth—and implicit information based on behavior on the Web site or elsewhere. The inference engine makes recommendations based on the profile, and the delivery engine translates recommendations into actions—perhaps a specific Web page with information on a recommended product.

Today, most of the content that flows through content delivery networks is static and is not personalized. Historically, the more static the frequently accessed content, the better suited it was to caching at the edge. So, when working with content delivery networks, many content providers generate dynamic Web pages at the origin server that point to static objects cached at the edge of the network. Pages are generated at the origin server instead of at the edge because much of the information required to drive personalization resides within the enterprise or near the origin server; it doesn't make sense for companies to distribute databases to the very edge of the network today.

But we expect that this will change in the future as personalization vendors come to see increased importance in content delivery. After all, the faster they can deliver content to the edge, the more effective their applications will be with fickle, time-crunched content consumers who are "quick to click" to another Web site. What's more, personalization places a heavy burden on origin servers; the more the burden can be offloaded, the better for the content provider. The only challenge will lie in ensuring reliable content delivery in a highly distributed environment. We are not suggesting that content providers will distribute thousands of copies of their profile databases—though those databases could certainly be shared among several companies. Rather, we believe that an increasing amount of the personalization work will be performed through caches and content delivery networks rather than on origin servers.

Challenges Addressed by the Content Value Chain

High Volumes. If companies could accurately anticipate traffic levels on the Web, they could effectively plan for that traffic. But traffic cannot be anticipated, which underlies many of the challenges that degrade Internet performance today. Also, Web traffic volumes exceed that of prior systems, and Web sites are prone to unexpected surges and flash (large, unexpected) crowds, which can degrade performance and crash Web sites. For example, the Victoria's Secret and Encyclopaedia Britannica Web sites collapsed on their openings because of unanticipated torrential Web traffic. Similarly, many Web sites experience slowdowns during peak hours because of heavy Web traffic—at their Web site or on the Internet in general. And with the potential for flash crowds and sudden increases in Web site traffic, content companies may not be able to add internal or hosted equipment and infrastructure capacity fast enough to anticipate traffic surges.

Network Immaturity. The Internet is still an immature delivery network prone to uneven response times, bottlenecks, network outages, and so forth. And although the Internet circles the globe, reliable systems do not. We expect that many specialized firms like Mirror Image and Adero will emerge to focus on the specific challenges of international content management. For content consumers, broadband *access* will not always equate to broadband *throughput,* because the bandwidth and reliability necessary to support that broadband connection may not be present throughout the network. And individuals employ many different types of Web browsers, ranging from basic 2.0 browsers to 5.0 browsers that support advanced features and Java.

Immature Content Distribution. Many content providers have not defined their strategies for content distribution. As a result, many are unable to effectively and expeditiously distribute their content to users. And even if they can distribute their content themselves, they may be unable to do so cost-effectively because of the large number of networks and content consumers. Companies need a way to methodically push and manage content at the edge of the network. At the same time, most content is not transportable to other formats because content has not been separated from layout.

Part 2. The Content Value Chain

Content management systems touch many people and companies, and they should meet the needs of numerous constituencies. These include content creators, editors, and publishers, as well as the company that provides the finished content—the *content provider*. At the same time, the content management system must meet the needs of the users who will view or consume the content. And, finally, the content management system must supply the service provider with a cost-effective means to distribute and deliver content to the end user. As companies develop new business models to service the content management market, we recommend that companies look at how well they service each of these constituencies, because, just like a link in a chain, each is a critical element of the content management life cycle.

Let's begin to look at the configuration of the content management value chain. First, we will look at the stakeholders who stand to benefit from improvements in content delivery. Next, we will look at their interaction within this value chain. Finally, we will look at the different components of the value chain in some detail.

We believe that this view of the value chain is a fundamental shift from past views. In the past, most stakeholders looked at their place as unique and separate from the others. The Yankee Group believes that a more holistic, comprehensive approach will ensure success for all participants in the content value chain.

Stakeholders. Solving the "worldwide wait" has been the holy grail of many Internet companies since the birth of the World Wide Web. *A variety of piecemeal approaches have been employed over time, but* *these have not been widely successful because they did not provide the end-to-end, platform-based capabilities we described earlier. Thus, the approaches were not able to meet the unique needs of different stakeholders.* These have ranged from client-side software that worked only with content served from a compatible server to ISP-based caching software that served content based on criteria established by the ISP, not the content provider. We believe that a platform approach that meets the needs of *all* stakeholders will be the most likely to succeed. With the advent of companies such as Akamai and Sandpiper (recently acquired by Digital Island), as well as new Net sourcers such as Intira and Digital Island, we believe that this time the holy grail will be found and that all stakeholders will benefit.

The Need for Speed: Consumers. Whether they are within the enterprise, outside the firewall, or in a living room surfing the Web, content consumers have sought an improved experience, usually directly associated with faster downloads. As a result, many of these consumers have selected broadband access. As performance varies from ISP to ISP, consumers will migrate to the ISPs that can provide the best throughput at a reasonable price.

Keep $ in My Pocket: ISPs. ISPs seek to reduce their costs through lower bandwidth consumption for the same user base. Many ISPs have deployed caching software from companies such as Cache-Flow in order to cache the most popular content locally instead of using bandwidth to pull it from the content provider each time. Second, ISP's would like to increase consumer satisfaction and offer value-added services, such as broadband or premium access, which can differentiate their offerings and bring in additional revenue—or at least prevent revenue erosion. ISPs aim to lower expenses and to protect their revenue base.

Growing Revenue: Hosting Providers. Other than building their base business, the primary goal for second-generation hosting companies is to provide value-added services that stretch beyond basic collocation— in other words, to offer a more complete suite of Net sourcing services. These services can bring in additional revenue from content providers and customers, as well as provide opportunities for differentiation.

We believe that the strongest and most competitive content distribution offerings will enable hosting companies to lock in their clients. This is particularly important as content providers become increasingly aware of the importance of content delivery.

Control: Content Providers. The primary concern for content providers is controlling the use of their content—mainly to ensure freshness and accurate hit rates. In the fast-moving Internet world, the fresher their content, the more they can maintain their competitive lead with current news, updated pricing, and so forth. Content providers simply want their content to be used as they intended.

At the same time, savvy content providers demand control over their hit rates, particularly those whose income is directly or indirectly dependent on these hits. Many ISP-deployed caches will not record hits each time content (for instance, a banner ad) is served directly from the ISP's cache server. These understated hit rates prevent the content provider from charging higher advertising rates for its Web site. Thus, more accurate reporting can directly improve revenue.

Content providers also desire timely, efficient, and cost-effective content delivery; and they want to ensure consumer satisfaction. A dissatisfied consumer may choose to go to another Web site without knowing that the slow download was caused by a company other than the content provider. That's why it's up to the content provider to make sure its content is effectively and efficiently delivered to the edge of the network. The content provider must balance consumer satisfaction and the need for fresh content with cost-effective systems to deliver on that goal.

Part 3. Adding Value at Each Link in the Value Chain

Refer again to Figure 3-1, which provides an overview of the content value chain. Each of the constituencies described in the preceding contributes to the value chain—content providers, service providers, and content consumers. Content providers manage the creation, authoring, aggregation, and publishing processes that ensure high-quality, useful content that meets business needs.

Service providers assist content providers and content consumers by distributing, hosting, tuning, personalizing, and delivering content. Sitting in the middle of the content value chain, these service providers are the linchpins of the content ecosystem. As service providers, their goal is to maximize revenue, profits, service value, and service quality.

The services closest to the content providers will be more focused on meeting the needs of content providers, while the services closest to the consumers will be primarily focused on meeting their needs or minimizing costs required to service them.

Content Providers

Creation, Authoring, Aggregation, and Syndication. Most creation, authoring, and aggregation processes are fed directly into the content management system outside of the firewall. These processes are covered in the December 1999 Yankee Group Report "A Framework to Manage Pervasive Content." These systems should integrate into the content management system outside the firewall wherever possible to provide a continuous system.

These systems should produce content that can be tuned to different media, even if the final media player is not known to the content creator. This can be accomplished by separating content from design and by using templates. For example, an author might create a generic news story using a standard template. Once published, that news story might then be viewed on a variety of devices including a desktop Web browser, a wireless PalmPilot, or a cell phone. Because the content has been separated from design, edge devices can easily tune this content for the appropriate medium, and authors need not know on which medium their content will be consumed.

Publish. The content provider sends content into the content management system through the publishing process. Several types of publishing models exist, each with its own advantages and disadvantages: static production, dynamic publication, and compiled publication. Static production is the traditional storage and publication of fixed Web pages. While this is acceptable for smaller or departmental Web sites, these systems restrict information reuse because design is inherently tied to content. Dynamic publication lies at the opposite extreme, generating Web pages on the fly each time material is requested. These systems are most useful for highly dynamic, rapidly changing, and personalized Web sites. However, completely dynamic Web sites place a heavy burden on databases and hardware. Finally, the compiled production model matches content to templates, publishing the completed material to the Web site. No one answer is always the right choice for a publishing model; we believe that companies should choose the model that best meets their business needs. The *use and consumption* of content should dictate the publishing model, not internal constraints. If consumption requires granular, personalized content, we recommend the dynamic model. If designers want to be able to change templates easily, we recommend a compiled model. The publishing model will have a tremendous impact on the capability of the Web site and should not be used to compensate for internal limitations.

Profiling and Personalization. The final element that is handled by the content provider is defining profiling and personalization that will be used later in the value chain. Profile variables will determine the types of personalization that can be utilized later.

Service Providers

Distribution. Distribution can be managed by content providers or by service providers. These systems and services replicate and distribute content to remote servers and caches, synchronize updates, and provide automatic error recovery and rollback.

The best systems will also maintain log files so companies can perform Web site analysis. We believe sophisticated content distribution will become more critical as content moves increasingly to the fringe of the network. Novell, F5 Networks, and Inktomi/WebSpective offer solutions in the distribution space; Akamai and Sandpiper offer services that cover this space, among others.

Hosting Services. Hosting services, whether of the first-generation collocation or second-generation Net sourcing model, enable content providers to maintain their Web pages and applications at a service provider with multiple locations. Several hosting firms offer content delivery services today including Exodus, Intira, Verio, and Concentric. GlobalCenter, Digex, and other firms resell content delivery services from Akamai.

Delivery/Caching. Delivery systems manage content on remote servers and move content from the remote servers to the content consumer or end user. While Inktomi is a major player in this space, several other vendors offer caching products, such as CacheFlow, Entera, InfoLibria, and Network Appliance.

The core concept of these systems is the ability to store content close to the user, at the edge of the network, often in a POP. In this way, each content request requires a shorter "hop" and is less expensive. Specialized caching software and appliances improve Web page response time and reduce latency caused by congested networks, congested servers, and packet loss.

Caches are available in several forms today. Multipurpose *proxy servers* offered by IBM, Microsoft, Netscape, Novell, and Sun all look like basic Web servers to browsers, and like Web browsers to origin servers. These servers are often used within the corporate firewall and provide security, IP address translation, and proxy caching. In many ways, proxy servers perform a variety of guardian and performance functions inside the firewall. By contrast, reverse proxies, server accelerators, or HTTP accelerators are designed to offload traffic from servers. These caches are deployed in front of servers or within POPs. When deployed near the origin server, these caches lessen the load on high-overhead origin servers that are caching the most frequently accessed content.

When deployed at the POP, these servers reduce bandwidth consumption, as content is stored at the cache close to users and does not need to be retrieved from the Internet each time it is requested by a user. In many cases, the same caching systems can be used as proxy servers and as server accelerators.

Caches may be deployed in either *nontransparent or transparent modes.* Browsers must be specially configured to point to nontransparent caches. But they do not need to be specifically configured for transparent caches, which intercept all traffic, generally making transparent caches more preferable. However, since all traffic in and out of the firewall will go through the transparent cache, these caches can be a single point of failure. Thus, transparent caches must be ultra-reliable and highly scalable.

Caches can be purchased as software installed on the server of choice or bundled with specific, sometimes proprietary, hardware. Inktomi's Traffic Server runs on several operating systems, and the Eolian, Cobalt Networks, Entera, and Novell (Internet Caching System) servers are flexible because they are not really tied to a specific hardware configuration or a proprietary operating system. The market leader, Inktomi, has built a strong business on this model.

By contrast, CacheFlow, InfoLibria, Network Appliance, and Cisco offer caches sold as appliances with integrated operating systems. Caching appliances are distinguished by hardware that has been minimized and optimized specifically for caching. These systems perform as stable and powerful servers because the hardware environment is completely known to the companies that develop the caching software. Further, these systems are stripped of superfluous hardware that would only slow them down. These vendors claim to offer a better price-performance ratio than the software-only firms—especially Inktomi (of course, we are not surprised that everyone tries to claim that they offer something better than the market leader, Inktomi).

As we have stated, caches are beginning to develop into operating-system-like platforms that support several caching-specific applications, such as streaming media, security, and more. Inktomi, Network Appliance, InfoLibria, and Entera envision the cache as a platform for additional applications that live at the edge of the network. While we believe that caches can indeed serve as platforms for content management at the edge of the network, these products must also walk a fine line between being general-purpose platforms and being powerful, limited-purpose appliances. Because the applications are still somewhat limited, we believe these players can reach that balance today—but this balance will become increasingly difficult as they support an increasing variety of applications.

Traffic Management/Load Balancing. Traffic management systems provide load balancing across multiple servers to ensure an even flow of traffic. The leader in this space is Cisco's Local Director, a hardware-based offering. Other offerings are available from Allaire, ArrowPoint (now part of Cisco), HP (QoS), HolonTech, IPivot, Platform, and Radware. In each case, these products bring in requests through a single IP address and distribute them out to the Web servers at the back end, depending on the amount of traffic on each server.

Streaming Media. Streaming media cuts across all of these, but it is a special case that deserves specific attention. Streaming systems deliver content to the end user through streaming media players such as RealNetworks' RealPlayer G2, Microsoft Windows Media Player, and Apple QuickTime player. Typical file formats are AVI, MPEG, MP3, WAV, and WMA (Windows). Streaming media are or will be supported by content delivery networks, such as Sandpiper (Digital Island) and Akamai; satellite distribution services, such as iBEAM and SkyCache; Net sourcers, such as Intira; and most caching vendors, including Inktomi, Entera, CacheFlow, InfoLibria, and Network Appliance. Most content distribution applications attempt to reduce latency. However, the optimal streaming media system will go a step beyond this to minimize *fluctuations* in latency as well, because these fluctuations cause uneven streams and create gaps. The more content that lives near the edge of the network, the lower the likelihood of fluctuations in latency.

Performance Monitoring. The only way to know that the system is up or down is to monitor its performance. This function is provided by performance-monitoring services, such as Keynote, Service Metrics (recently acquired by Exodus); application-level monitoring, offered by Freshwater Software; and others. This information is important because it provides an objective measure of the speed and quality of the end-user experience. This information can be used to monitor service-level agreements as well.

At the same time, a variety of network-centric products provide tools to measure packet loss at peering centers, hop counts, latency at network connections, and other variables to determine network conditions on the Internet. These tools enable the service provider or content delivery network provider to update the network map and routing to meet changing conditions on the Internet. This is of tremendous importance in a content delivery network that must constantly rely on the fastest possible communication between two points. In fact, this single element is one of the features that propelled Akamai into a leading position in the marketplace when it launched in April 1999.

Content Tuning. *Content tuning* is the process of preparing content for delivery to a specific consumption scenario. Scenarios are based on a combination of variables associated with the content medium, personalization to the content consumer, and business goals. We will cover each set of variables in sequence. We expect that many additional, as yet undefined, variables will become important as well.

Tuning to the Medium. *Media tuning* refers to content formatting and delivery specific to the characteristics of the device and the connections that feed it. This is a core enabler of pervasive content. The same content must be available in multiple formats tuned for each of the media variables listed below. In essence, content must be available in an *unlimited range* of permutations. Following are a few of the more common media variables, each with a large set of possible values.

- *Browser:* V 2.0, 3.0, 5.0; brand: Microsoft Internet Explorer or Netscape Navigator.
- *Level of standards support:* for standards such as Java, ActiveX, and XML.
- *The physical device:* PC, Palmtop PDA, handheld PDA (Windows CE device or 3Com PalmPilot), wireless phone, TV set-top device, hybrid device, or other devices of the future.
- *Physical output characteristics: Type* of output: display, print, audio, text-only, text to speech. *Size* of the display or printed page.
- *Connection or modem speed:* 28.8 Kbps, 56 Kbps, T1, T3, and so forth.

The power of the Internet is that it enables different browsers to view the same content. But each browser has qualities that cause the same content to appear differently in specific types of browsers. And an increasing variety of physical media will further challenge pervasive content management. We believe users will demand the ability to view and use the same content specially *tuned* to each situation and medium.

Looking to the Future. Today, most content is not media-tuned. But limited possible permutations will be replaced by an infinite variety in the near future. Thus, tuning will increasingly be handled by a sophisticated tuning system instead of by individual authors and contributors. In the near future, we will see a proliferation of new wireless devices, as well as broadband delivery over wireless, wire line, and cable networks. Content will become increasingly divorced from both format and receiver variables.

Tuning for Personalization.   Personalization is an increasingly important function that sits on top of the content management system. And as personalization increases in importance, so will the need for a robust content management infrastructure. As we have already stated, the major challenge of personalization is that most of it takes place at the origin server. We expect new methods to emerge that will move increasing amounts of processing to the edge of the network to speed up content delivery and reduce the amount of communication back to the origin server. Akamai's recently announced ICAP (Internet Content Adaptation Protocol) will have a significant impact on bringing personalization and other applications out to the edge of the network.

Content Consumers

Consume.   Content passes from the ISP to the last mile for delivery into the home, office, school, mobile, or other location from which it is viewed and consumed by a content consumer. Note that today's content consumers will change as new types of edge devices proliferate, including TV set-top boxes, Internet appliances, and mobile devices such as cell phones and PDAs.

Measure Behavior/Web Site Analysis.   The content delivery system is a core component of accurate Web site analysis and measurement. If the content delivery system does not provide statistics back to the content provider, the provider will have understated hit rates. For example, the Open Caching Interface (OCI) enables caching servers to report statistics to the Akamai network, which in turn feeds that information to content providers.

Part 4. Standard Protocols

A variety of protocols exist to integrate the various elements of the content delivery value chain into a cohesive whole. As is often the case, many of these standard protocols overlap or compete against each other. ICP is one of the most important and most common caching protocols; it enables coordination and load balancing between caches. More recently, CARP, HTCP, and Cache Digest have been developed to address some of the shortcomings of ICP, such as ICP's inability to work with the HTTP headers that provide data on access control and cache directives. WCCP enables load balancing of cache servers through a router. The recently announced Network Element Control Protocol (NECP) also enables load balancing. Also, Akamai and Cisco's OCI enable products from different cache vendors to cooperate and share information with the Akamai network, in part enabling more accurate Web site analysis for content providers. Finally, WPAD enables Web browsers to automatically discover the nearest cache to which they have access.

While the earliest protocols were based on cache sharing and coordination, the newer standards have continued to move upstream toward the content providers. The most recent protocol, Akamai's ICAP, promises to enable tighter integration between edge devices, such as caches, and applications themselves. As stated earlier, pervasive content will become increasingly dynamic and applicationlike. We expect that the ICAP protocol will be an important enabler of pervasive content in the future.

Part 5. Pulling It All Together: Delivery Methods

Different types of content have different transmission needs that will determine the most appropriate service model, as described in Figure 3-5. The key differentiators between the various types of content lie in the complexity of the operations being performed and the size of the files being transmitted. Large streaming media files with moderate complexity are well suited to satellite distribution, Net sourcing, and content delivery networks. Transaction-oriented content—with intensive database look-

Figure 3-5. *Where Should Content Live?*

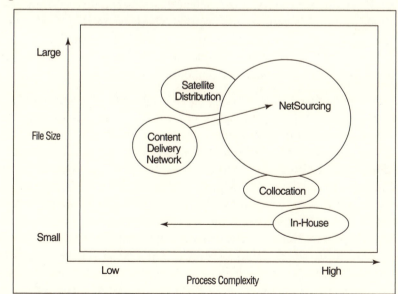

Source: The Yankee Group, 1999

ups, and personalization—is today well suited to in-house, hosting, or Net sourcing models. However, as content delivery matures, we expect that more and more of this content will live at the edge of the network.

In response to this, different service providers have devised strategies that are especially well suited to particular types of content. These providers bundle the services described above in different ways to meet those needs. Typical service bundles include distributed content/application hosting, content/application hosting and distribution, vendor-neutral content delivery networks, and satellite distribution networks. We will examine each in sequence, starting with hosting providers.

Hosting. Many content management services can be provided by hosting companies as value-added services—often at an additional cost. Many of these firms have successfully sold value-added content management services to augment and support their existing relationships with content providers. In many cases, however, the hosting firms are more concerned with operating the data center than with delivery at the *true* edge of the network—at the POP nearest the content consumer. We believe that hosting companies will continue to grow this market. But much of the growth will come from next-generation Net sourcers that offer a more complete and robust suite of services (than most of today's Web hosting providers), and from content delivery networks and satellite distribution firms as well. The "sweet spot" for first-generation hosting providers lies with relatively simple content that is best delivered from only a few locations. This content may include relatively simple HTML, some level of personalization, as well as some amount of transaction processing. As content becomes more complex and takes longer to transmit, the traditional collocation model will see diminishing returns.

Net Sourcing. *Net sourcing* is an outgrowth of collocation that adds multiple services. Net sourcing describes the combination of mission-critical, complex hosting; hardware/software provisioning; network connectivity; and infrastructure support and services. It provides a scalable, high-performance platform for hosted business, commerce, and multimedia applications. In addition, Net sourcers provide the critical infrastructure for next-generation, Web-based ecommerce and other business applications that span beyond the enterprise.

Examples of Net sourcers include Digital Island and Intira. These firms provide network services, content delivery, application services, and management. Content delivery is a natural extension of hosting services. We believe that content delivery services and the content delivery platform will be some of the key elements of Net sourcing strategy in the future.

Content Delivery Service Providers (CDSPs). CDSPs provide content distribution and delivery services. Two primary types exist today: satellite distribution networks and content delivery networks.

Satellite Distribution Networks. Satellite distribution networks move content through satellite networks to avoid the congestion and unevenness of the terrestrial Internet. Content is moved from the content provider to the satellite distribution network where it is broadcast directly to POPs with inexpensive receiver dishes. The POPs then redistribute content to their subscribers. These systems avoid the multiple hops and the sometimes-unreliable and variable connections required to move content through the terrestrial Internet.

Satellite delivery for Web content is a relatively recent phenomenon provided by iBEAM, SkyCache, and Edgix. Satellite distribution is ideal for real-time broadcasts to large audiences because the streams are not limited by capacity on the Internet and because they can provide even streams that avoid poor or choppy images. We expect that satellite distribution will be a key vehicle to provide the broadband content that feeds broadband connections at households.

Content Delivery Networks (CDNs). CDNs provide content without actually hosting the content. Satellite distribution could easily be a subset of this, though most CDNs today use terrestrial networks for distribution. CDNs were designed to meet the needs of all of the players in the value chain—especially the content provider that wants control and to ensure fresh, quality content delivery, and the ISP that wants to conserve bandwidth. CDNs typically charge content providers a fixed fee based on the volume of content flowing through their network. The CDNs, in turn, purchase bandwidth and rack space from hosting providers to place their cache servers near major peering points. The major CDNs include market leader Akamai, Sandpiper Networks (recently merged with Digital Island), and firms that specialize in international content delivery—Adero and Mirror Image.

Akamai and Sandpiper have designed their networks to accelerate the delivery of content to content consumers around the world, but mainly in the United States today. Adero and Mirror Image, by contrast, are more focused on content delivery outside the United States. International content delivery poses some challenges, however. Bandwidth can be very expensive outside the United States, because download times can be greater (and more costly) than in the United States, and because international markets can be difficult for content providers to manage. Adero and Mirror Image enable companies to obtain worldwide content distribution through a single service provider. Adero and Mirror Image move greater amounts of content overseas so it can be picked up locally

Figure 3-6. *Selected Service Providers and Software Vendors*

Function	Content Hosting	Distribution-Replication and Synchronization	Content Delivery/ Caching	Traffic Management/ Load Balancing	User Profiling and Authentication	Filtering	Web Site Analysis
Service Providers		Akamai					Web Side Story
	Sandpiper/Digital Island						
		Mirror Image					
		Adero					
		iBeam					
		SkyCache					
		Edgix					
	Exodus						
	Intira						
Software and Hardware Vendors		Inktomi		Allaire	Funk Software	Symantec	Accrue
		InfoLibria		ArrowPoint	Novell	Secure Comp	Andromedia
		Novell		Cisco		N2H2	Marketwave
		F5 Networks	CacheFlow	HP QoS			netGenesis
			Cobalt	Holon Tech			WebTrends
			Entera	iPivot			
		RealNetworks	NetApp	Platform			
				RADWare			

Source: The Yankee Group, 1999

rather than from an origin server in the United States, greatly reducing bandwidth charges for international ISPs (see Figure 3-6).

Part 6. Conclusion: Looking Ahead

Content delivery is all about rapid and cost-effective delivery of increasingly complex, increasingly dynamic content. Hasty content consumers are quick to click to competing Web sites when content takes too long to download. In their need to ensure a quality user experience and to capture advertising revenues, content providers will put increasing focus on accelerated content delivery as well as increased control of and reporting on that content. ISPs will look to minimize costs. And Net sourcers and content delivery service providers will seek to address the need for speed by continuing to offer new and enhanced content delivery services.

Ultra-distributed content delivery will become increasingly important as content providers seek to push more and more content to the very edge of the network to gain the speed described above. But what will the optimal path be, and what path is right for the company?

We believe two models will prevail: Net sourcers that offer value-added content delivery services atop extensive networks and content delivery service providers that offer services across a variety of networks. At present, we believe the CDSPs are at an advantage because they can place their content closest to the user in local POPs. With increased attention to content delivery, we anticipate that Net sourcers will begin to add sites as well. The interesting aspect of this is that the ISP POP is about to become a valuable piece of real estate. CDSPs have proliferated because it is incredibly expensive, if not impossible, for companies to develop their own 1,700-node networks, and that is why Akamai has historically given its servers to ISPs that deploy them in their POPs. Further, now that Akamai and Sandpiper Networks exist to tie those POPs together, the POPs have suddenly become valuable.

We predict that in the near future, ISPs will begin to charge Net sourcers and CDSPs to deploy their servers in the POPs, increasing the cost and competition of both CDSP and Net sourcing services to their customers. The first suggestion of this new cost of real estate came as AOL renegotiated its agreement with Sandpiper this month, charging Sandpiper to place its servers within the AOL network. Even though AOL stands to gain by deploying Sandpiper servers, it certainly has other options as well—and it has partnered with a service provider that was willing to pay for access to AOL's customer base. In addition, the Yankee Group believes that the content delivery platform will emerge as a major element of the ebusiness infrastructure in the near future. Just as operating systems have formed the platform for applications accessed within the firewall, so will the content delivery platform form a foundation for ultra-distributed applications delivered outside the firewall.

One of the major challenges in developing the platform lies in the balance between applications run on the origin server and those run at the edge. Personalization today sits at the confluence of these two areas. The question is not whether various components should be run on the edge, but what elements and to what benefit and trade-offs? The holy grail of the Internet is speed—everywhere, all the time, for anything. And rich, dynamic, pervasive content deployed at the edge of the network, and the emerging content delivery systems that support it, will ensure that speed.

Chapter Summary

Mark Hoffman of Commerce One provided his outstanding vision and perspectives on "The Role of Content in Internet Initiatives" and The Yankee Group offered us a compelling perspective on "Managing Pervasive Content on the Edge of the Network." These perspectives evidence the sheer magnitude of the volume of content and the power that it has over the growth and future of the Internet. In the upcoming chapters we will review the strong community and commerce effects that content has when put into play in the context of the global ebusiness network.

CHAPTER

B2B Community Strategies

As long as businesses need customers, groups of prospective customers who are easily accessible and share common needs will remain attractive opportunities. Add in the opportunity to narrowly target the most likely prospects among these groups as well as the potential to garner additional information for marketing and product development, and you have the promise of a vibrant online community. This chapter focuses on the key opportunities for e-Marketplaces to become online community developers and hubs. Creating and building these communities offers a tremendous opportunity for both the stand-alone community developer as well as those entities that wish to develop a focused community as an adjunct to their primary enterprise.

E-Marketplaces as Communities

When one thinks about trade via an e-Marketplace, the tendency is to think about the physical exchange of goods. But most of what happens in a marketplace involves the exchange of a less tangible substance: information. This process is often more complex, and less efficient, than one might think. At each stage of the sales cycle, from presale merchant/ product selection to post-sale service and support, buyers and sellers draw information from many sources to make a transaction successful.

In simple terms, three types of information are needed to make a transaction successful:

1. *Product information*—What should the purchaser buy?
2. *Relationship information*—Whom should purchaser buy from?
3. *Transaction information*—What are the terms of the sale?

Buyers rarely rely solely on direct information? such as catalog listings or product sheets—in making a purchase decision. Such sources rarely reveal the common problems with a piece of equipment, or identify alternative products or vendors. To complete their information set, buyers typically turn to other buyers or objective third parties. See Figure 4-1.

One of the best ways to supplement the direct information provided by product manufacturers and vendors is to create opportunities for market participants to interact with one another. Today, many markets are enabling participants to make suggestions, offer comments, or engage in dialogues around products, services, and companies. By doing so, market makers ensure that buyers can obtain online the information they seek from their peers. Sellers benefit as well, by having informal opportunities to respond to buyer questions, and to hear candid feedback about their products and services. As with offline interactions, this communication, over time, has another important byproduct: the development of trust among participants.

Programs that enable users to interact as a group are commonly referred to as *online community* programs, and these programs are at once similar and very different from their consumer counterparts. As with consumer communities, the word *community* here signifies the distinctive nature of these interactions: not one-to-one, like the typical

Figure 4-1. *Portal Network*

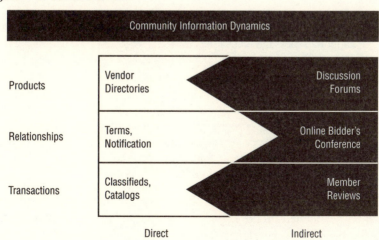

buyer-seller interaction; not one-to-many, in the way sellers reach buyers through advertising or other mean; but many-to-many, in the way only the Internet can enable. Like the markets they support, community interactions take advantage of marketplace dynamics to ensure that the right information reaches those who need it. Some examples of community programs in Net markets include the following:

- Technical discussion forums
- Interactive Webcasts
- User-created product reviews
- Virtual conferences and meetings
- Expert seminars
- User-managed profile pages

Some common market elements such as classified ads, job boards, and industry news can be either user-published or producer-published. Classified ads published by site editors appear static and dated in comparison with the interactive, user-created classifieds on, for instance, PlasticsNet. Interactive community classifieds allow market participants to recommend products, vendors, and other listings to the author of the classified ad. This makes the person posting the ad many times more likely to receive the product or service they seek.

It's becoming increasingly clear that competitive advantage in Net markets will not come from having latest commerce platform, but from offering value-added services participants want and need. Top 20 Net markets such as Altra Energy, HoustonStreet, and PlasticsNet, have embraced community programs as the kind of services that will ensure success:

- Altra Energy has discussion areas for members to discuss technical support issues and questions, as well as general discussion areas for each energy vertical.
- HoustonStreet's SquawkBox live discussion allows energy traders to discuss among themselves about industry topics and questions they may have about the HoustonStreet marketplace.
- PlasticsNet's 35,000 registered users generate thousands of classified advertisements every year. PlasticsNet also has searchable user profiles that allow users to submit contact information, Web links, and any personal or company information that they choose.

It's perhaps not surprising that early adopters like PlasticsNet, which was launched in 1995, understand the power of community: they have the benefit of experience. But the new wave of e-Marketplaces is learning from their predecessors. Competitors to PlasticsNet such as GE Polymerland have established buyer and supplier communities programs of their own. Even the recent coalition markets such as MyAircraft.com (a partnership between United Technologies, Honeywell, and i2) include community programs in their proposed offerings. Signs of future growth in this space include the appearance of companies like Participate.com, which specializes in creating and managing online community programs on an outsourced basis for e-Marketplaces and other companies.

The Evolution of the Online Community

For eons in the physical world, communities have been and remain to this day vital to both personal and professional success. Whether formed for defense or social interaction or to facilitate trade and commerce, communities have always been the center of human activity.

Up to now, however, communities have been generally limited by the physical ability to interact. Communities developed in physical spaces where people could converse, exchange information, organize, undertake common activities, trade, and do commerce. The village square, the town hall, the inn, the universities, palaces, legislatures, and meeting halls all provided framework for interaction between two or more people. From these physical places, communities developed and often flourished.

Certainly the ability to write and exchange correspondence allowed the development and maintenance of relationships beyond the constraints of a single locale but always on a small scale. The interjection of tele-communications and rapid transportation clearly expanded the physical boundaries of many communities, but again the interaction generally occurred one-to-one, and occasionally one to a few.

With the introduction of the Internet and evolution of multimedia technologies, many of the constraints of the physical dissolve. We can now interact as a community one-to-one or one-to-many or many-to-many with great ease and with significant depth. We can converse in text, by voice, or increasingly in full audio/video formats. We can share insights, documents, and presentations on both a synchronous and asynchronous basis. Language translation capabilities coupled with the trend toward standardization on one language (English) for international commerce continue to facilitate communication on a global basis. In addition, the melding of economic markets coupled with (and enabled by) communication/information technology has set the foundation for a true worldwide community.

While used by many before, the analogy to Gutenberg and his printing press remains an apt one. With the printing press came the ability to
share thoughts effectively and efficiently over space and time. It truly
revolutionized the world. Yet this communication was essentially one
way: author to reader. With the Internet, we enter a whole new era of
interactive communication. Communication can be person-to-person,
back-and-forth and instantaneous. It can be light, superficial communication or reflect great depth (complete with documents, presentations,
and links). It is not just one to many but many-to-many communication.
It is the village square and more. It is the concept of community super-
charged, one whose only boundary (currently at least) is the planet earth
and its immediate environs.

Who Benefits from Communities?

Communities are built and sustained for mutual benefit. Benefits flow to
the community member, the organizer, and where commerce is involved
to the participating vendor.

Benefits to Members.   Communities represent the aggregation of
members, similar in one or more ways. Once established in sufficient
numbers, a community's critical mass justifies the assembly of a diversity
of resources that, individually, members may not be able to access. Content specific to the needs of a particular community (for example, research on a rare disease) can be assembled and certain commercial transactions enabled (including, for example, volume purchases on products
or services important to the community). The interaction of the community itself produces distinct benefits, including shared insights and
knowledge concerning a common concern.

Benefits to Organizers.   Online communities can be of substantial
value to freestanding community organizers (like AOL, Excite, and Amazon). The aggregation of large numbers of potential customers can generate substantial revenue flows for those community organizers who lis-
ten to and respond to the needs of their communities.

In addition, enterprises that are not primarily community organizers
may choose to organize communities as an adjunct to their current business focus. These too can benefit as well. Successful adjunct community
building can have dramatic impacts on both the top and bottom lines of
existing enterprises, especially as ecommerce becomes an increasing important revenue stream for many enterprises. Vibrant online communities
can serve to

- Attract new customers
- Strengthen customer loyalty
- Increase existing customer revenue
- Provide priceless market intelligence

Because the Internet dramatically facilitates communication among individuals, especially those separated by space (geography) or time (different work hours, time zones, and so on), the impact of an online community can be significant in terms of geographic reach, aggregation, and resultant commercial transactions. Online communities are not restricted by travel times, meeting hall sizes, weather, and so forth. In most cases, they are 24/7 operations. Correctly structured and member focused, a sponsored online community can become a substantial revenue generator.

Benefits to Vendors/Advertisers to the Community. By aggregating both the members and information about them, vendors can less expensively and more effectively sell their products and services. Instead of marketing to the many to access the few, the vendor can more precisely target prospects. They can choose to address those community participants with demonstrated interests and specific buying habits, often at the most likely time of purchase. For example, a member of a travel club may wish to purchase travel or accommodations for a trip as they research the same on the Net. Further, these targeted few may be more inclined to buy given the context of a supportive, focused environment, which facilitates vendor-related information (both pro and con).

The result for the vendor is generally lower marketing costs, along with the ability to more precisely target product messages and potentially to access collective member profile information, which can result in better product development and marketing strategies. These are a few of the benefits to vendors of a vibrant online community.

What Are Virtual Communities?

A *community* can be defined most simply as a group of individuals who interact. A virtual community is one that interacts using the Internet and in doing so magnifies the potential for impact in both the commercial and noncommercial realms.

Virtual communities parallel many of the more typical physical communities with which one may be familiar: a neighborhood, office staff, club, or association. While the technology is virtual, the application and the users are quite human. In fact, increasingly even the more traditional communities (chambers of commerce, service organizations, school PTAs) may themselves have a virtual dimension to them.

Given that interaction is a necessary requirement of a community, the question is begged: How does a virtual community interact? Typical activities of an online community can include the following:

Communication Elements

- *Chat rooms*—Real-time text-based conversations among participants viewable by all in the chat room at the time. This is the virtual equivalent of the talk around the water cooler. Chat rooms represent synchronous *some-to-some* interactive communication.
- *Threaded discussions*—A string of questions and answers/comments among two or more participants. A question or response can be posted at one time by an individual and responded to by others at a later time. The string of comments is visible to all that access the area for as long as the site posts the discussion. To the extent that the topic and the ensuing questions and answers are compelling to the community, these strings of discussion can become a valuable resource for the community in developing a body of community knowledge. Threaded discussions are similar to a transcription of a debate or discussion. Depending upon the general interest in the topic and the level of expertise of the participants, these discussions can be a significant asset to community members—especially if archived in a manner that facilitates topical searches. Threaded discussions represent asynchronous *some-to-many* interactive communication.
- *Bulletin boards*—Messages posted at any time by community members for all community members to read at a later time. The real life bulletin board is an apt parallel. This is an asynchronous "one to many" non-interactive communication.
- *Email*—Both among members and from member to community developer and community developer to member. While email requires no definition, facilitating it warrants mention. If the target community members, on the whole, do not have or do not choose to use preexisting email accounts, then providing email within the community can be important. Email is asynchronous "one to one; or one to some (using email address lists) communication.
- *Netzines, newsletters, bulletins, general Web site postings, and so on*—This is general published content about the focus area, often provided by the community sponsor directly.

Informational Elements

- *Directories*—These links to other Web-based resources can be organized by topic or activity. The better directories include abstracts describing the links to other sites and the information they offer. Directories can greatly facilitate research by the community member, especially on topics related to the focus of the community site.

- *Member ratings and other member-generated content*—These elements are of great value and can run the gamut in terms of format and content. Member-generated content should on the whole be facilitated and posted by site administration. As an example, member rankings and commentary on various products and services targeted to the community often attract substantial interest.

Commerce Elements

- *Product/service offerings and advertisements*—The commercial offerings accessible through a community site can be diverse. Policies as to the role and responsibility of the community site with respect to commercial offerings should be well thought out. Commercial offerings often include links to online catalogues, marketplaces, or other offerings.
- *Auctions/reverse auctions*—Either many buyers may bid on an offering from a single vendor in the traditional auction style or alternatively separate buyers may post their requirements for multiple vendors to respond in a reverse auction.
- *Exchanges*—Targeted vertical markets can support a bid/ask process; these environments work best with commodity-type products with price and quality easily compared by the buyer.
- *Classified advertising*—Both community-specific offerings as well as nonrelated offerings among members and/or vendors can be included.
- *Procurement functions*—These can be provided as both a facilitation to the member and an aggregator/pooler of purchase requirements in order to access volume pricing.

Prerequisites for Community

Virtual or not, communities generally share the "three I's":

1. *Interest*—A commonality of interest
2. *Incentive*—A rationale to interact
3. *Interaction ability*—The capability to communicate and interface with others

Interest. Whether it is a common industry, common profession, common hobby, or common heritage, communities generally share something that connects them as a group. We are all members of various communities as they reflect our interests and involvement.

For example, Tripod.com built its initial success by offering a resource for the 18- to 34-year-old Internet-proficient segment. With 33 interest areas (termed "pods"), the site addressed issues including work, money, home life, relationships, and health. Tripod's members were on the whole still in their formative years in terms of brand loyalty and thus proved most attractive to a trove of leading advertisers. In 1998, Lycos Network acquired Tripod for $58 million in stock.

At this point in the Internet growth cycle, it is likely that only those entities with dramatically large marketing budgets can afford to introduce a general community with no topical core focus, as did Tripod. Others will do well to identify one or more core elements or draws to their community and to emphasize these in their marketing and community building efforts. Each individual has a diversity of interests and priorities. Each of these in turn has varying degrees of intensity in their own hierarchy of needs. Baseball may be the epicenter of one person's experience, while another may be their profession or their role as a mother or father.

Communities can focus on a diversity of areas and may reflect a vertical or horizontal orientation. Horizontal communities generally stretch across multiple, otherwise unrelated groups and individuals. Vertical communities generally share a fundamental (often economic/commercial) relationship. Vertical communities can include a profession or an industry or part thereof (for example, the publishing industry, financial services, or electronics manufacturers). A horizontal orientation might include a topical focus (history, travel, baseball), an organizational function (information management, sales, manufacturing), cultural affinities (Irish, German, and Latino), or a geographic location (New York, London, San Francisco).

In the business environment, communities can be industry-focused vertical environments such as education, the chemical industry, or financial services. Alternatively, communities can be defined around an ecommerce function. These include exchanges, auctions and reverse auctions, aggregators, and procurement sites. The "interest" in this case may be the best price and quality for a particular category of goods or services. Increasingly, they can be hybrid communities incorporating both functional and topical elements (e.g., exchanges with a community focus targeting specific vertical niche or aggregation sites incorporating affinity group information). Communities can be oriented as business-to-business, business-to-consumer, or business-to-employee as well.

Incentive. Arguably, self-interest drives all our actions. Communities form out of need and are sustained only when they continue to meet and fulfill salient needs of the participants. Absent an underlying incentive to participate in a community, no interaction will occur. Internet communities often form for the purposes of exchanging information and knowledge and to facilitate commerce.

Interaction Ability.   As a prerequisite, members of a community must have the capability to interact with each other. That interaction most often occurs physically through the day-to-day routine of personal or professional life. Meetings, conferences, or other gatherings may set the environment for interaction for more formal communities such as professional associations or clubs. Alternatively, a community can interact through the mail with correspondence and newsletters or electronically via telephone, videoconference, or of course, the Internet. The easier it is for a potential community to interact, the more likely it will interact and the stronger it will grow.

Community Building Blocks

The four building blocks of a successful community are as follows:

1. Content
2. Applications
3. Services
4. Commerce

Community Content.   While clearly a community sponsor will have a depth of knowledge and resources in their respective areas of expertise, providing additional areas of information will add to the "stickiness" of the site, keeping the targeted user online in the online environment longer. Content can include the following:

- Interest-specific information (of the target industry, professional, or other interest area), including Web newsletters, journals, online learning and continuing education, and Web seminars and conferences
- News (financial, sports, and so on)
- Weather
- Horoscopes
- Health
- Online polls
- Other topical departments

Applications.   In addition to content, the site sponsor may choose to provide various online applications that further add to the utility of the site and its attractiveness to the user. Applications include the following:

- Address book
- Calendar
- Contact managers
- Collaborative work environments
- Portal/Start screen personalization tools (page settings, layout, color, content, and so on)
- Screen savers
- Other relevant software applications

Services. Providing services to the user can go a long way to promoting a vibrant online community, especially those services that facilitate communication among community members and between members and sponsor. Potential services include the following:

- Free email
- Chat rooms
- Threaded discussions
- Search engines
- Maps/directions
- People locator
- Site index
- Stock quotes
- Online greeting cards
- Yellow pages
- Bookmarks
- Free downloads (photos, music, and so on)
- News clipping services
- Free Internet access (where appropriate and in conjunction with a third-party provider)

Commerce. First and foremost, the site should facilitate commerce with the sponsor's organization or its affiliates. If an adjunct site to an existing commercial operation, the catalog product offerings, service offerings, and so on should be a central and easily navigated element of a successful sponsored community. In addition to the sponsor's commercial offerings, offerings should be added to increase the depth of the site as appropriate and to generate additional revenue. Potential commercial elements include the following:

- Catalog/product/service offerings
- General shopping

- Specialty focus bookstore/Resource center
- Classifieds
- Airline tickets
- Event tickets
- Auctions
- Special events/Sales
- Shopping directories/Links

The Web Portal: The Preferred Foundation for Community Building

Online communities have historically developed around one or more linked sites. The challenge with a standard Web site has always been keeping the member "on the farm." A community member may leave the site to obtain additional information, interact with others, or complete a financial transaction, often not to return. Once off the site, the community member is no longer an immediate prospect for commerce related to the community sponsor or affiliates. A focus on site "stickiness" has resulted in a concerted effort by many sites to build in as much content and functionality as possible to avoid the need for the community member to go elsewhere.

Portal technology is a strong complement to this strategy. Increasingly, portals have become the preferred structure for community building. Optimally structured, the portal can be more than just a point of entry to a content area. Portals allow the user to "bring along" both information and function while navigating the Web. A portal can be a combination Web guide and toolbox in one for the user. Common functional elements of portals include the following:

- A search engine
- Organization/categorization of information
- Interactivity
- Personalization capability

An apt metaphor for the portal might be that of the dashboard of your favorite vehicle. As you cruise the Web, peering through your "windshield" to the Web world, your portal dashboard provides the instruments and tools you need to navigate successfully.

"Ready-made" portal technology is offered by multiple sources, including:

- Epicentric.com
- PeopleNet.com

- Ibelong.com
- eSociety.com
- Wego.com
- essociation.com

Each has its own partnering or service provider strategy and should be evaluated based upon the specifics of your community strategy.

As an added benefit of the portal strategy, much of the content, applications, and services needed to round out a community are often available on a subscription/syndication basis from the portal technology provider. While some of these elements represent cost centers, other elements represent potential revenue sources through referral fees or commissions. Often the provider of the portal technology has established relationships with a litany of providers of content and applications. The portal provider in turn offers a menu of options that dovetail into their portal platform.

As an example, Epicentric provides a portal platform that it views as a "packaged solution." The package includes the following:

1. A portal framework
2. An extensive range of content
3. Integrated applications
4. A menu of commerce services

A single provider of the technology platform and syndication content/services and commerce can accelerate the speed to market as well as minimize the potential pitfalls of interface between content and technology. Accessing a menu of options on a "plug-in" basis via a single infrastructure can be very attractive.

Most importantly, such a strategy allows the community sponsor/developer to concentrate on its core focus and minimizes both external negotiations and workflow requirements on in-house IT staff.

Irrespective of the technology provider, an integrated module-based approach to building community functionality offers many obvious benefits and should be evaluated seriously in developing the strategic plan.

An interesting evolution in the portal arena has been the development of multiple portals within the same organization. According to Hadley Reynolds, research director at Delphi Group, "Recent research with organizations implementing portals shows that nearly half of them already have from two to more than five portals active in various business applications. This kind of development grows organically out of the ebusiness process as it laces business webs inside and outside the organization." Portals have been established for customers, partners, or employees in addition to separate business lines. The challenge, of course, becomes exploiting the promise of the portal without becoming overwhelmed by parallel development and maintenance efforts of multiple portals.

Epicentric recently responded to this apparent need with a portal server (Server 3.0) designed to support networks of portals. Michael Crosno (Epicentric's CEO) observed, "It's clear that businesses are becoming overwhelmed by the cost, complexity, and inefficiency of multiple portal initiatives. Portal networks solve these problems and create an entirely new level of business value for the organizations that deploy them." The Epicentric platform proposes to empower "end users or affinity groups to tailor every aspect of the content, layout, branding, and look-and-feel of their own custom portal. Advanced page building capabilities enable flexible, free-form page design as well as an abundance of templated portal layouts for banners, tabs, columns, and rows."

Figure 4-2 shows an example of a financial portal that consists of a portal network within a single organization.

A portal network can allow different groups related to the same organization (for example, divisions, product lines, partners, employees, customers) to leverage a centralized technology platform to customize a portal vehicle for their specific needs. Administrators optimally can provide complete portal building resources to end users, including the management of content and applications.

The organization benefits by forwarding the objectives of the individual groups while minimizing duplication of effort and resources. Strengthening of customer relationships and site stickiness are just two advantages of leveraging a flexible portal network platform.

Key Strategies for Successful Online Community Building

Be Member-Centric from the Start. Identify and serve the needs of the community participant. The greater the *relevant* content and functionality, the stronger the relationship with the community member/participant. It is vital to communicate with that community early in the community development process. Early-stage communication can take multiple forms, including focus groups, advisory boards, and researching the content and format of both online and traditional media addressing the target audience or segment. Research should include potentially competitive and complementary sites. Keep a pulse on membership. Ongoing market research should include both monitoring and active involvement in the activities of the community. Poll or survey community members

Figure 4-2. *Multiple Portals Constituting a "Portal Network" Within a Single Organization. Shown Is a Financial Portal.*

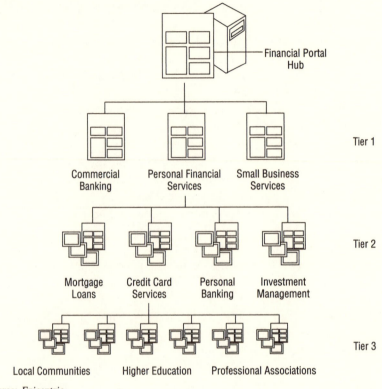

Source: Epicentric

as to their needs and preferences on a regular basis. Within the bounds of appropriate disclosure and operative legal parameters, develop member profiles as to preferences and activity. Use this information to assemble resources (informational and commercial) of interest to the community member. Also, use member profile information in growing membership in the community.

Define Your Focus. As with any undertaking, it is vital to understand your focus. This primary focus should be based on the needs of the community that the site is serving. Be clear in your internal planning and in what is to be portrayed to the outside. There is a diversity of focal points for a community. Irrespective of the chosen focus, the key is building from that initial core. Optimally, one should build a community, which first addresses the core focus of the community (in terms of content and functionality) and then widens its focus to include other needs and interests of the participant. Develop a clear plan with goals, objectives, priorities, and a time line. In particular, develop a strategic functionality statement. Define general need areas based upon your initial and ongoing market research. Don't let capabilities drive decisions. Just because it can be done doesn't mean it should be.

Involve the Community Member.   Involve the participant in the activities of the site; integrate the site into the regular routine of the community member and where appropriate their organization. Develop an active orientation to the community not a "passive reference only" perspective. The more involved the participant becomes, the stronger a linkage with the community he or she develops. As an example, online polls can involve the participant by eliciting the thoughts and opinions of community members. The member is involved both through the input process and subsequently should he or she seek to find out the results. Of course, the findings of the polls provide content, which may be of interest to all, irrespective of whether or not the individual participated in the poll. Build a feeling of investment in the community whenever possible. Provide opportunities for input from community members and use it in the evolution of the community. Through involvement, one truly becomes a member of a community. While involvement online can take many forms, those entailing person-to-person communication tend to build the strongest loyalties. Integrate a market research dimension where possible to community communication functions including bulletin boards, chat rooms, and discussion groups.

Weigh Carefully Internal Staffing versus Outsourcing.   There are multiple options in terms of structuring the personnel and resources necessary to build and maintain a community. The following represents more ranges on a spectrum rather than discrete strategies:

- Use your own IT staff.
- Bring in outside expertise only for start-up and for strategic consultations.
- Maximize outsourcing of both development and ongoing support.

The attractiveness of each of these options varies somewhat based upon where you are standing. If your head count and internal expertise are sufficient, you may choose more of an in-house strategy. Limited funding may suggest an internal approach as well, although always be cognizant of the "penny-wise, pound-foolish" adage. If community building is an important strategy for your organization, the appropriate investment should be seriously considered. Evaluate outsourcing such activities as hosting, data collection, and site feedback. Databases of email addresses, online surveys, and member profiles can often be most efficiently managed on the outside.

Consider Buying versus Building Technologies.   The community building arena is active and growing more so. The choices of platforms and related technologies and options continue to grow as competition in the solution provider area grows. Similarly, technology sophistication is rapidly evolving. Take advantage of these trends and evaluate the various sources of technology available externally. In choosing among external options, consider the following:

- *Integration with existing legacy systems in your organization.* If this is a relevant concern in your organization, research compatibility closely. For associations, member data and online conference registration are just two of the areas which might be evaluated.
- *Scalability.* As with all technology decisions, consider the future. Growth in community members and/or activity should be welcomed, not feared. Make certain your technology strategy allows for anticipated growth.
- *Speed of implementation.* Turn-key solutions or at least integratable application modules can dramatically shorten the time to introduction.
- *Support capabilities.* Ongoing support of your chosen platform and any separate components is critical. Consider not only the level of expertise but also the availability of the same. For example, do you need to consider diverse geographic locations to be supported and does the external organization have sufficient head count to support all its customers?
- *Insights into your market.* Clearly, your technology partners should be proficient in the latest technologies. Optimally, they should also understand somewhat the nature of the community that you are organizing. Have they had experience with similar communities to yours? Can they bring along any insights that can push you more quickly up the learning curve?

Minimize the Need for the Participant to Go Elsewhere for Function or Content.   The more needs that are met by the site, the less rationale for leaving it. Maximize both the number and duration of visits. Make the environment as rich and compelling as possible. The more community needs addressed the better. Jupiter Communications reports that online consumers can sustain only ten significant relationships with Web sites at any one time.[1] With an estimated 9.5 million Web sites

---

[1] Jupiter Communications, Licensing and Syndication: Weighing Distribution Against Dollars, as cited in *Epicentric Syndicated Services: Syndicating Content, Applications, and Commerce.*

existent as of 1999, there's a lot of competition for eyeballs on the Web.[2] Parallels in the physical world might include the shopping mall or large department store. Through a diversity of offerings, the shopping experience evolved. Instead of visiting a single specialty shop and leaving, the modern-day mall creates an environment at which one can spend an afternoon or a full day. In addition to multiple merchandise offerings, the mall meets other needs including dining and often social needs (especially among teenagers). In like manner, the most vibrant online communities may start with a core offering but expand from that and complement the initial core focus with both additional unrelated content (weather, stock quotes, search engines, directories) and functionality (email, calendars, meeting options, and so on).

Make It Personal. Personalization opportunities should include the ability to add and delete content, services, and applications as the needs and preferences of the member change. Much of Tripod.com's initial success, for instance, was based on its focus on personalization. It offered simple, easy-to-use templates to post anything from a personal Web site to a favorite recipe.

In the physical world, the drive to personalize has driven the entire home improvement industry. Leaders like Home Depot offer the opportunity to paint your rooms, put in new kitchen cabinets, and renovate your bathroom. The optimal online community offers options in like manner. Personalization options can include the aesthetic such as color choices for the look and feel of your navigation bar and screen frame, a choice of graphics and the addition of personal photos to your screen frame. Content personalization can take the form of weather reports for home or other important locales, selected stock quotes, or news about favorite sports or teams. Personalization can be looked at as the distillation of an individual's demand curve for his or her online experience. The more options provided to the member, the more he or she can fashion their own space to reflect their needs and preferences. The more personalized their experience becomes, the stronger the attachment to the community grows and, in turn, the greater the barriers to switching to another community. Each personalization option or functionality added (and used) by a community participant can be looked at as a brick in the wall against competitive sites. The more bricks, the stronger and higher the wall.

---

[2] Netcraft in Iconoclast Internet at a Glance, September 1999, as cited in *Epicentric Syndicated Services: Syndicating Content, Applications and Commerce.*

Facilitate Communication Among Members. The need to socialize is a strong drive in humans. Capitalize on this! Facilitate communication among members as much as possible. Through email, chat rooms, discussions, and so forth, build communication among members to answer the need to socialize. In the process, identify, archive, and store topical communications as appropriate. Topically oriented threaded discussions, as an example, can become a significant resource for any site and its members. Threaded discussions can reflect the technical or other expertise of community members and when organized and made searchable can constitute an important resource and draw to a community site.

Promote the Segmenting of the Wider Community into Smaller, More Comprehensible Interest Areas. Envision your online community as a city, and create neighborhoods and business districts. Enable community members to converse, sharing thoughts and content within these nooks.

Promote Member-Created Content. Enable members as much as possible to crystallize their insights, perspectives, and experiences and to communicate the same with others. The summation of these contributions provides a perspective distinct from commercial published sources and advertisers.

- *Decentralize content creation and publishing.* Empower members and groups with the tools to develop their own resources and share them. Successful communities reflect a depth of information and resources. Developing and maintaining that depth can most feasibly be accomplished by enlisting community members.
- *Facilitate clarification of content by enabling communication with the publisher/source of the content.* In turn, facilitate the evaluation of content credibility by enabling topical communication among members about published content.

Open the Door to the Outside. Facilitate access to other sources information, products, and services beyond your site. Don't restrict access to external sources; rather, assist the member in organizing, processing, and evaluating this information. Ultimately, it is the long-term value to the member that will build loyalty to the site.

Evaluate Syndicated Sources of Content. Content syndicators can provide a key flow of content to augment that internally developed. Given the cost and effort necessary to identify, contract for, and maintain relationships with individual content providers, syndicators can play a valuable role. Relationships with a few syndicators may be much more efficient than with dozens of individual content providers. In addition, familiarity with the community's technology platform can be important in accessing content. A strong relationship with a content syndicator can mitigate many a problem in this regard.

Associate, Ally, Partner.   Consider alliances for applications, service, or content resources that members value but which might prove to be expensive or unfeasible to create internally. As an example, consider offering free Internet access to members; in conjunction with a third-party provider, you may wish to provide free Internet service to your community. Providers like 1stUp.com offer free dial-up service through community builders and affinity groups. Such an offering likely would be most appealing to individual consumer/nonbusiness participants, presuming that most businesses (and their employees) will seek higher quality (for instance, DSL) service.

Trends and Future Directions

Personalization versus aggregation is the yin and yang of Web community development. One underlying benefit of ecommerce is the aggregation of needs so as to facilitate economies of scale in fulfilling them. Those needs may be for information or goods and services. This initially focused the Internet more on a broadcast (one-to-many) orientation. One could access information much like the reader of newspaper or order goods in a similar manner to a catalog. However, increasingly, personalization of the Web experience has become the norm. As we spend more and more of our time in the Web environment, we want to personalize it, as well as make it more efficient relative to how we do things. We want to minimize Web surfing and searching. More and more, we have begun to develop default sources for information and commerce for certain areas of activity.

In community building, this trend to personalize must be acknowledged and embraced. Clearly, a vital underlying element of a community is "sameness." Nonetheless, the capability to personalize your online environment will grow increasingly important. As discussed earlier, the development of the Web portal is a prime illustration.

The increasing popularity of portals will most likely ultimately result in completely personalized portals. Just as you decorate your home, choose your car, lay out your office or desk, pick your clothing, and so on, the portal (or some derivative of it) will become your Internet presence and living/working environment on the Web with tools of your choosing (such as software applications), your preferred links, and so forth.

Interested commercial entities will need to look at how their solution dovetails into your personal portal—the competition among some entities will be to become your default source of information or commerce for particular topical arenas.

Increasingly, applications including software (constantly updated to the latest versions) will most likely be "rented/licensed" and delivered online directly to these personal portals with a pay-as-you-go option. In like manner, much of your memory requirements may also be served remotely via online storage with a link to the personal portal.

The Educational Opportunity. As discussed elsewhere in this chapter, the Web experience has become and will continue to grow to encompass much more than commercial transactions. In fact, it is the growing content and community of the Web that set the context for the burgeoning commerce. An important and growing element of that content and community is education. Education in its many forms will become increasingly Web-centric. Degree-oriented educational programs, employee training, and customer-oriented training and education will be key areas of online activity.

Elements of online education are worthy of consideration even by those organizations that do not have education as a primary focus. The key goal for commercial entities will be to develop *education-based relationships.* (See Figure 4-3.)

The core of this strategy is to develop or expand relationships with a targeted community not by selling to them directly but rather by providing education and/or training in the firm's area of expertise. Optimally, these educational offerings are low-cost or complimentary and easily accessible to the targeted community. When accomplished effectively, the sponsoring firm establishes itself as an "expert" in the field, while at the same time approaching the members of the targeted community in a less aggressive, less commercial manner. The targeted community benefits by receiving quality education at little or no cost. In addition, a two-way sponsor-participant relationship can be developed in the context of learning that does not have the inherent stress of a "sales call" with its operative caveat emptor warning.

It is acknowledged that relationships are likely to follow between sponsoring professionals and educational participants and that these relationships may evolve to commercial transactions. Indeed, such com-

Figure 4-3. *Three Phases of Building Education-Based Relationships*

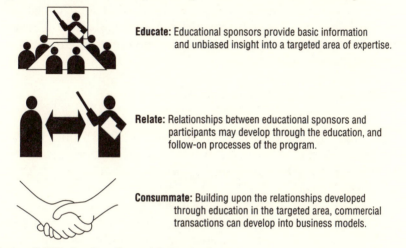

Educate: Educational sponsors provide basic information and unbiased insight into a targeted area of expertise.

Relate: Relationships between educational sponsors and participants may develop through the education, and follow-on processes of the program.

Consummate: Building upon the relationships developed through education in the targeted area, commercial transactions can develop into business models.

Source: © 2000, American Group of Companies, Inc.

mercial relationships can be productive and beneficial to both parties, provided that they remain distinct from the educational component of the program. In developing any such program, the primary goal is to educate participants in an unbiased manner, with insights from professionals in relevant fields of expertise. The "educational sponsor" should work to develop programs that address the needs of a targeted community in the areas of expertise of the sponsor while maintaining educational integrity. The sponsor can accomplish this solely with its own staff or alternatively work with third-party educational institutions, or training organizations.

Nonetheless, the sponsor should optimally do more than simply provide the funding for these programs. Rather, the sponsor should maintain a central and high-profile role in the delivery of the educational information.

The Development of Education-Based Relationships

With respect to potential application providers, industry leaders in the e-learning environment include Blackboard.com and DigitalThink.com. Both have applications worthy of review. Many others have branded versions of the leaders. DigitalThink reflects a corporate orientation applying their e-learning platform primarily for "boosting employee efficiency, fostering customer loyalty, and improving sales channel performance." Blackboard tends to reflect more of an academic focus in promoting the integration of "courses, communities, information services, academic resources, and content." Both arguably have application in the online community building arena. It is worthwhile noting that Blackboard.com recently added a fully integrated portal application to its platform.

Building an Online Community ASAP

Online communities represent attractive groupings of prospective customers. Well-structured and supported communities can offer dramatic efficiencies in targeting commercial offerings. In addition, communities can provide invaluable market intelligence for both sales strategies and product development.

The development of a successful virtual community follows the basic approach to any innovation. For this reason, I developed the ASAP process in conjunction with Desander Mas to identify and facilitate the sequential stages of activity—the steps in the process—which culminate in an innovation. In this case, the process is applied to the development of a new online community. For convenience, we can define the steps of the development process utilizing the acronym, *ASAP,* shown in Figure 4-4.

In practice, the ASAP process entails the following:

Assess: Define the community to be developed, its nature, its context, and your goals with respect to it.
- Be member-centric from the start. Identify and serve the needs of the community participant.
- Define your focus. Be clear in your internal planning and in what is to be portrayed to the outside. Build from a well-defined initial core.
- Understand the three prerequisites for community and how they apply to your community; the three Is are
  1. Interest
  2. Incentive
  3. Interaction ability

Figure 4-4. *ASAP Process*

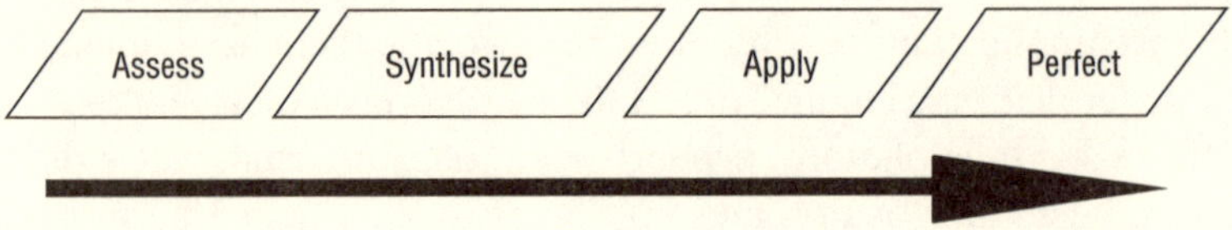

Synthesize: Generate alternative strategies for configuring the community and then select among them based upon your insights from the assessment stage.

- Decide on the directions for the four key building blocks of a successful community:
  1. Content
  2. Applications
  3. Services
  4. Commerce
- Select and configure the appropriate technology platform for the online community. Strongly consider a portal format.
- Consider buying versus building technologies given the pace of technology and the widening options available.
- Weigh carefully internal staffing versus outsourcing, since there are multiple options in terms of structuring the personnel and resources necessary to build a community.
- Evaluate syndicated sources of content, especially outside of your core focus.
- Minimize the need for the community member to go elsewhere for content or applications by maximizing both in your community.
- Make it personal by maximizing the opportunities for the member to personalize their Web experience in the community.
- Facilitate communications among members.
- Consider building in an educational element to your community, especially through the integration of an established e-learning application.
- Associate, ally, or partner to gain needed content, applications or strategic advantages.

Apply: Implement your selected strategy in a manner that acknowledges the obstacles and considerations that might impact its effectiveness.

- Involve the community member in the activities of site to encourage a strong linkage with the community.
- Promote the segmenting of the wider community into smaller, more comprehensible interest areas.
- Open the door to the outside by facilitating access to information, products, and services beyond your site.
- Promote member-created content to provide a perspective distinct from commercial published sources and to enrich the depth of site resources.

Perfect: Promote the evolution and growth of the site by proactive action.

- Actively monitor site activities to identify trends in member preferences.

■ Review progress in site evolution based upon the initial assessment and goals.

■ Respond to changes in the environment, which require site modifications.

■ Most critically, involve the members in the growth of the community. Use archived member profiles as well as active solicitation of the members in the evolution process.

Chapter Summary

The foundation of every successful e-Marketplace is firmly grounded in its ability to build communities and develop marketplaces for exchange of information. Communities represent one of the most significant drivers of commerce in the Internet era. E-Marketplaces are evolving into more than digital marketplaces. They are becoming digital workplaces where communities gather to collaborate and to conduct business. The impact of communities can be significant. One of the biggest challenges faced by Net market makers is not only the building of these online communities but the ongoing maintenance and support of the communities. For these critical communities to thrive, the e-Marketplace must have an organizational mandate to support the communities. Dedicated personnel will need to be assigned to the role of community manager to assure the support and growth of the communities that form around the e-Marketplace.

The following chapter will discuss e-Marketplace commerce strategies with an emphasis on dynamic commerce models.

CHAPTER

E-Marketplace
Commerce Strategies

E-Marketplaces are quickly becoming relentless vehicles of efficiency, streamlining the information exchange and commercial trade between buyers and suppliers. The economics can be leveraged among buyers, sellers, and the e-Marketplace itself. If a product or service offering for example, is entirely information-based, an e-Marketplace can expand to handle not only buying and selling but also manufacturing, distribution, sales, and marketing. Already, the physical markets for bonds and stock trading are evolving, with the rapid progress of electronic communications networks like Instinet and Archipelago, where trading is 100 percent digital. Also, watch for e-Marketplaces to evolve for books, music, software, education, and even consulting services. The time will come when e-Marketplaces for these information-based goods will evolve to take over most of the industries' noncore activities. The information costs associated with the purchase and sale of physical goods represent at least 50 percent of the price a buyer pays. That 50 percent is up for grabs, and the exchanges are grabbing it.

According to Forrester Research, ecommerce flowing directly between pairs of trading partners will expand to $2.7 trillion in 2004. In addition, the Gartner Group/Dataquest has estimated total ecommerce at $7.3 trillion in 2004. Firms in every industry will continue to invest heavily in their extranets to increase customer value and build deeper connections with channel partners. Today, most online markets are still in their infancy, but trade through these markets will grow at a compound rate of 200 percent. B2B trade isn't growing up in the high-tech hubs like Silicon Valley—it's developing in the industrial hubs like Cleveland and Detroit.

Community Ebusiness

Online marketplaces provide tremendous efficiencies as well as opportunities to solve the remaining procurement challenges. Not only will existing buyer-supplier relationships thrive in these ebusiness communities, but new relationships are much easier to initiate. Buyers with demand are efficiently matched to partners with supply, and both are assured that the relationship is initiated at the right price, with the right lead time, the appropriate level of quality, and so on. The interaction is so easy that relationships can be created around a single transaction. No longer will companies spend countless days searching for the right supplier or the best sales opportunity. When the need arises for a one-time spot purchase, that need can be quickly and easily fulfilled. When a long-term relationship is required, the partner can be identified and the relationship initiated through the same process. This eliminates huge headaches for both buyers and suppliers.

It is estimated that the average cost of a purchase order ranges from $80 to $150. Companies like Commerce One are automating the procurement process, which significantly reduces overhead for both buyers and suppliers and brings the cost of a purchase order down to $10. Consider many of the inefficient markets that exist today. Traditionally, purchase orders are created on the buyer's computer, printed out, and then faxed to the supplier. In turn, the supplier takes the purchase order off the fax machine, manually enters the information into his or her order entry system, prints out an order confirmation or invoice, and faxes it back to the buyer.

Today, with Commerce One e-procurement and e-Marketplace software, the exchange of business documents takes place seamlessly and automatically. With a couple of mouse clicks and a few keystrokes, a buyer can select a product from an electronic catalog, enter the quantity, and click to send the purchase order. The purchase order is received by the suppliers system, which automatically verifies that the product is in stock and immediately sends an order confirmation to the buyer. Because there is no printing, no faxing, and no order reentry involved, big savings are realized.

Similarly, companies may carry vast amounts of inventory even when a surplus exists because the supply and the demand cannot be matched efficiently. Online marketplaces promise to meet the challenge with capabilities like auctioning, bid management, and spot purchasing.

Simple business communication within the e-Marketplace is also much more efficient. Because everyone is connected to the same service, the need for point-to-point integration with each trading partner is eliminated. Buyers and suppliers have centralized access to transaction details and other vital information.

Overall, to be successful, an e-Marketplace must do the following:

- Be open to all buyers and sellers.
- Match the right buyers to the right sellers.
- Provide relevant content that accurately represents goods and services.
- Support various transaction types.
- Provide business services and practices that are flexible enough to adapt to the differing needs of customers and market segments.
- Maintain a technological infrastructure that enables companies to seamlessly conduct business with anyone, anytime, anywhere.

Supplier Networks

A major manufacturer or a group of manufacturers, like Covisint, that have formed an industry consortium typically initiates a supplier network. These e-Marketplaces are often established as separate or joint ventures so that they can focus their efforts solely on the establishment and management of the e-Marketplace without being encumbered by the bureaucratic culture of the parent organization. Moreover, as a separate entity, they open their e-Marketplaces to a broader range of buyers and sellers with the goal of becoming the definitive e-Marketplace in a given industry or region.

These e-Marketplaces are initially adopted by the founding manufacturers and their suppliers, which often number in the thousands or tens of thousands. Depending on the e-Marketplace, the suppliers may pay a subscription fee to access the marketplace, as well as transaction fees for using it. E-Marketplace operators may provide the access software at a reasonable cost to encourage buyer and supplier participation. In the case of Commerce One e-Marketplaces, any buying or selling application may be used, which further increases the number of trading partners who can participate, even very small suppliers with a single computer, an Internet connection, and a browser!

The Internet flattened corporate organizational structures. Similarly, e-Marketplaces are leveling the playing field for buyers and suppliers.

For the past twenty years, large companies have been using electronic data interchange (EDI) networks to automate business transaction between trading partners. EDI networks are private networks that are very expensive to set up and manage, and they require a dedicated team of experts with specialized knowledge to keep them running. In short, only the Fortune 500 companies can afford these systems. Given the high costs of setup and maintenance, only preferred suppliers are connected to the network. This leaves the majority of suppliers out of the club, so to speak.

Not only does the supplier network provide a framework for the technical integration of supplier content, it also addresses the business process issues associated with various goods and services. For example, the sourcing and procurement processes are very different for printing than they are for computer equipment or temporary staffing—in the case of temporary staffing, the first step is to screen résumés; for computer equipment, a list of detailed technical specifications may be the only thing required; for printing, you often need to solicit details of the supplier's skills and equipment. The supplier network proactively addresses many of these business process issues.

Suppliers in an e-Marketplace offer a broad range of goods and services, including temporary staffing services, computer equipment, printing, office supplies, maintenance and repair parts, and more. A few of the early members of supplier networks include Adecco Staffing Services, Boise Cascade Office Products, Compaq, Corporate Express, Dun & Bradstreet, GE Supply, Harbinger, Motion Industries, Requisite Technology, and TPN Register.

Vertical E-Marketplaces Target Specialized Communities

As the number of buyers and suppliers in a trading community grows, participants with common requirements tend to converge into smaller communities. For example, the majority of commonly used administrative goods and services are purchased without significant differentiation across industries. However, within certain industries and geographical regions, there is a need for specialization around content and supplier capabilities. E-Marketplaces satisfy these needs, aligning with specific industry requirements. The e-Marketplace provides the technology and a professionally managed ecommerce framework, and the founding companies provide the domain expertise and buyer-supplier relationships for their industry.

Trade Alliance is an example of an e-Marketplace in Singapore that plans to address the needs of a geographic market—first Singapore, then 15 other Asian countries, including China and India. Trade Alliance is also addressing vertical market interests such as the food and paper and pulp industries. The company recently launched two vertical e-Marketplaces called ePaperAlliance and eFoodAlliance.

Trade Alliance, a joint venture of The Sinar Mas Group and Nissho Iwai Corporation, is using Commerce One solutions. Sinar Mas is a major regional player in food, paper, and agribusiness, and Nissho Iwai Corporation is one of the world largest trading companies. The Sinar Mas Group is spearheading the eFoodAlliance e-Marketplace, and Nissho Iwai Corporation is spearheading the ePaperAlliance.

Many other horizontal and vertical markets are being established, as described in Chapter 6.

Collaboration Hubs

While today's EDI networks and ERP and supply chain applications can help buyers forecast demand and suppliers manage their inventories, e-Marketplaces hold the promise of deepening those relationships. Construction marketplace Cephren, for instance, made a project bidding and collaboration tool its first service out of the box. Cephren is focusing on collaboration as an integral part of ecommerce for its architecture, engineering, and construction industry e-Marketplace.

Collaborative commerce is the use of an online business-to-business exchange to facilitate the flow of business processes in addition to transactions. Business partners can exchange information such as inventory data by using a Web server as an intermediary. In many cases, collaborative commerce simplifies data interchange by eliminating the need for special client software at each customer's site. By using Web servers as hubs for collaborative commerce efforts, companies are seeking to exchange proprietary data, jointly manage projects, and cooperate on the design of new products. Collaborative commerce may also speed up cycle time for interaction between trading partners. Collaborative commerce requires that data such as product pricing, inventory, shipping status, credit, and financial information be shared among business partners.

When marketplaces move beyond basic transactions and into mission-critical collaboration, the question of public versus private exchange becomes an issue. Clients of marketplaces want the ownership of customer data that impacts pricing decisions. E-Marketplaces offer the opportunity to deepen relationships between all trading partners while reducing cycle times throughout the supply chain.

The Ability to Match the Right Buyers to the Right Sellers

To match the right buyers to the right sellers, traditional purchasing models based on catalogs and contracts are being supplemented with new, Internet-enabled models. While catalog- and contract-based purchasing may work well in relatively stable pricing environments, these models don't work well for commodities with volatile pricing or for situations where a relationship doesn't already exist. However, this is changing. New, more robust content management solutions can support price changes in real time, which is important to the success of any e-Marketplace. In addition to catalog- and contract-based purchases, e-Marketplaces support new Internet procurement and sourcing models like spot purchases and buyer auctions.

E-Marketplaces are also becoming increasingly popular for direct purchases where the buyer creates a bill of materials (BOM) that specifies many or all of the components that will be used to manufacture or create a particular part, product, or solution. This buying model is particularly advantageous to buyers because it allows them to attribute components and costs easily to a particular project. In November 2000, Commerce One and SAPMarkets released the industry's first direct procurement application that supports the creation of a BOM.

Finding new buyers or suppliers is a costly and time-intensive exercise; however, e-Marketplaces are simplifying the process and reducing costs. On CommerceOne.net, for example, a buyer can get access to a directory of suppliers and vice versa. The buyer can interact with an online catalog and find out which suppliers carry a certain product and at what cost. If the quantity or transaction volume is high, the buyer may opt to run a reverse auction to attract suppliers.

Clearly, interacting with an e-Marketplace can be far more efficient than ordering catalogs over the phone and then thumbing through them or walking one's fingers through the yellow pages. Again, efficiency is the driving force.

Auctions

Close cousins to plain-vanilla buyer-supplier transactions are auctions and reverse auctions. Both bring dynamic pricing to the selling process.

Sellers take the lead in auctions, putting products up for sale and letting buyers bid up the price. The market mechanism works very well when a seller needs to liquidate excess or used inventory. For example, IronPlanet.com processes used construction equipment through its auction site.

Following are various types of auctions:

- English auctions start with the price low and bid it up.
- In Dutch auctions, the price starts high and drops by fixed increments until a buyer steps forward. Multiple, identical items may be offered by the seller with or without a minimum bid, and buyers can view all other bids. The first person to bid automatically wins, since by default that person's bid is is the highest.
- In private auctions, the bidders' identities and bid amounts are not shown during the auction.
- In a reserve auction, the seller defines the lowest price he or she is willing to accept; however, this amount is hidden from the buyers. If the reserve price is not met, the seller is not obligated to sell the item.
- In Vickery auctions, there is a single item for sale. All bids placed are hidden from the view of other bidders. The highest bidder wins, paying the second-highest successful bid price.
- In Yankee auctions, a seller offers multiple identical items with or without minimum bid. Bidders can bid any amount at or above minimum bid for a specific quantity. Buyers may be able to view all bids. A winner pays exactly the price of his winning bid. In a Yankee forward auction, the bidders who have placed the highest bids at auction close win. In a Yankee reverse auction, the bidders who have placed the lowest bids at auction win.

Price is not always the basis on which auction bids are selected, however. In fact, often the midprice bidder wins. Auctions are often structured with multivariable bidding that may specify terms and conditions, quality, and delivery terms, among other things.

eBay is proof that auctions are popular for business-to-consumer (B2C) and consumer-to-consumer (C2C) applications. B2B auctions are also very popular; however, the marketplaces, products, and players are different. For one thing, B2B auctions involve very large amounts or products—for instance, a million bolts in the case of an automobile manufacturer. B2B auctions also involve large sums of money—a multimillion dollar auction is very common. Also, B2B auctions provide much greater control for the originators than a B2C auction. They can control the participants, how long they last, and so forth. These types of auctions are not the focus of an e-Marketplace like eBay.

Commerce One e-Marketplaces often "go live" with auctions first. For one thing, it takes less time to run an auction between a manufacturer and a group of bolt suppliers than it does to set-up an e-Marketplace that hosts a million catalog items and supports tens of thousands of trading partners. More to the point, auctions often prove to be more profitable than hiring liquidators. Where a liquidator may get ten to thirty cents on the dollar, auctions can yield 50 percent or more.

Auctions in a B2B e-Marketplace may be open or closed as determined by the supplier. In an open auction, the auction may be advertised on the e-Marketplace or in an email sent to buyers who have previously requested participation in such an auction. In a closed auction, the seller preselects buyers and invites them to participate.

Commerce One Auction Services software conveniently manages users and groups, so a very complex, multimillion dollar auction can be set up in a matter of minutes using a simple graphical user interface. Policy decisions, such as the highest price a buyer is willing to pay or the lowest bid a seller is willing to accept, still may take days or weeks, depending on how a company makes such decisions. In the case of a closed auction, the supplier can use a mouse to select groups of buyers or specific buyers (users) who will be invited to participate in the auction. The invitation is automatically generated by the system detailing the time and duration of the auction, as well as the item(s) for sale and the name of the seller, which is sent via email to all invitees.

Reverse Auctions

Auctions are also being used by buyers to streamline the Request for Quote (RFQ) and Request for Proposal (RFP) processes. In this case, the buyer may specify a particular purchase and allow suppliers to bid on it. Typically, the lowest bid wins in a reverse auction; however, some auctions, such as Commerce One Auction Services, support very complex auctions of all types so that businesses can better align the auctions with their business practices. For example, sales terms may be determined by price, delivery, quality, service, or some combination of them all. The entire bid process can be easily controlled.

In addition to defining which elements are most critical, buyers can also determine what information will be visible to the suppliers who choose to respond. The buyer may choose to let suppliers see information like the current bid. Multiple bids may be accepted right up to the closing moments of the bid process. Buyers may choose to have open reverse auction where any supplier can respond, or a closed reverse auction where the bidders are limited to those who meet some defined criteria. A bidder's list may be automatically generated from the supplier registry based on such criteria. Either way, the appropriate suppliers are notified automatically, and they can choose to respond and submit their bids or not. Buyers then review supplier responses online and make the award or allow additional rounds of bidding.

Spot Purchasing

Spot buying allows companies to purchase quickly from suppliers with whom they have no previous formal relationship. Even if there is an existing relationship, there may not always be a contract or detailed pricing arrangements. A great example is maintenance and repair. A company may have a parts supplier that is used regularly, but the company simply cannot anticipate what parts will be needed and when. In fact, many of the purchases may only occur once. In this case, a contract is not required. The company just needs to get the goods or have some service performed quickly.

E-Marketplaces fully support spot purchasing by allowing buyers to search the available inventory of a supplier from online catalogs and quickly place an order. If the item or service is not available at favorable terms via suppliers' published catalogs, the buyer may choose to launch an online auction. By analyzing spot purchasing trends, a buyer may make a decision to formalize a supplier relationship and include frequently ordered items in an online catalog.

Catalog Aggregation

By far the most basic and widespread market mechanism is catalog aggregation. Here, e-Marketplaces bring together catalogs from a wide array of industry suppliers, giving buyers a convenient, one-stop shop. The first commercial marketplaces on the Web were aggregators that pulled together product catalogs from many companies.

SciQuest.com is a leading business-to-business e-Marketplace for scientific products used by pharmaceutical, chemical, biotechnology, industry, and educational organizations worldwide. SciQuest.com offers its customers extensive laboratory products and supply chain management expertise, exclusive product listings, a robust portfolio of e-procurement solutions, as well as a cost-effective sales and marketing channel—all to help reduce customers' procurement costs while increasing researchers' productivity.

According to Scott Andrews, SciQuest.com's chief executive officer, "The concept here is not just to process orders, but to help our customers solve problems within the context of doing their normal work." SciQuest offers its no-cost services to buyers, which mainly include individual scientists and purchasing departments of large laboratories. Basic capabilities of the site include a sourcing catalog that includes some 8,000 suppliers, the majority of which don't even offer products today via SciQuest. In addition to the sourcing guide, SciQuest offers a used-equipment auction and a service that helps companies dispose of chemicals in compliance with federal guidelines.

Buyers have traditionally negotiated contracts for high-volume, repetitive purchases. Contracts are also used to lock in pricing, as well as negotiate volume discounts from suppliers. Typically, buyers have catalogs or contracts in place for suppliers with long and established relationships. While spot purchases and buyer auctions are valuable purchasing models, a full-service marketplace needs to support traditional catalog and contract purchases as well.

E-Marketplaces increasingly are providing aggregated buying a value-added service to buyers. For example, an e-Marketplace may negotiate a discount for its community based on its buying power. Perhaps one or more very large companies connected to an e-Marketplace already purchase pencils from Acme Pencil Company and are currently receiving a 5 percent discount on all purchases. By becoming part of the e-Marketplace and extending the same discount, or a better one, to all buyers in the e-Marketplace, Acme Pencil Company may be able to significantly increase its sales.

Further, if the e-Marketplace is connected to other e-Marketplaces, Acme Pencil Company may be able to increase sales another order of magnitude. Commerce One e-Marketplaces are beginning to open up their communities to other e-Marketplaces. PeopleSoft and BT recently announced bidirectional transactions between their two e-Marketplaces with Credit Suisse First Boston as the buyer, for example. If Acme Pencil Company participated in both trading communities, then it would have visibility in e-Marketplaces that are physically located in the United Kingdom and the United States, but which both serve trading partners worldwide.

Content and Support for All Goods and Services

An important element for the success of any online marketplace is the quality and accessibility of its content. Users naturally congregate to sites that offer rich content and intuitive search tools to easily access the content. In ecommerce applications, it is imperative to make both the buying and selling processes as painless as possible. Therefore, e-Marketplaces must gather sufficient content, normalize the content so it is easily searchable by buyers, and provide a means by which suppliers can differentiate themselves.

All Goods and Services

E-Marketplaces host electronic catalogs that feature all types of goods and services, including MRO, production, nonproduction, administrative, and capital goods. Registered suppliers can upload their catalog content to an e-Marketplace-hosted catalog, provided the supplier has become a member of the e-Marketplace. A robust solution will support all types of goods and services.

Full Range of Content Management Support

Good e-Marketplace software will include support for the full range of content management strategies. It will enable marketplaces to centralize content, allow suppliers to host content on their own sites, and allow buyers to create customized catalogs.

One of the most compelling value propositions an e-Marketplace offers suppliers is the ability to publish once. A supplier can upload his or her catalog to an e-Marketplace, where it can be accessed by a number of buyers. In the case of Commerce One software, once a catalog is updated, price changes can occur dynamically, which means that the suppliers don't have to upload the entire catalog or re-create content just to change a price. Moreover, once a catalog has been published to one Commerce One e-Marketplace, it can be made accessible to other Commerce One e-Marketplaces instantaneously—with no systems problems and no software problems. This, of course, assumes that a supplier would want to participate in another e-Marketplace, among other things. It would not make sense for a supplier of jackhammers to participate in a dental e-Marketplace, for example.

Suppliers can also tailor their messaging to a buyer's profiles and preferences, significantly reducing the cost of acquiring and retaining customers. Normalizing content does not mean that suppliers can't differentiate themselves. Let's say that two suppliers offer power supplies. They look the same, and they cost the same, but one is approved by Underwriters Laboratory and the other is not. If the buyer is looking for standards compliance and is doing business in the United States, he or she will most likely choose the UL-approved power supply.

Good content management simplifies the buying process. If a purchasing agent is a large corporation in charge of procuring office supplies, he or she will likely prefer to customize an electronic catalog to include only those products that are directly relevant. In the case of an e-Marketplace, this provides the buyer with some distinct advantages. The buyer can poll the e-Marketplace for all suppliers of blue ballpoint pens, for example, click on the supplier or suppliers the buyer wishes to purchase from, and immediately he or she has created a customized catalog of blue ballpoint pen suppliers. Or, if the buyer already buys MRO from Acme Office Supply, he or she can specify that in the search and still create a catalog of products the buyer commonly buys from the company.

Supplier Registry

In addition to offering catalog content, the e-Marketplace offers access to multiple online supplier registries. If an item or service you require is not listed in a catalog, you can optionally search for a list of suppliers that are capable of offering that item or service. Buyers then create an online auction and invite the suppliers on the list to participate or initiate a straight buy transaction directly with the buyer online. Buyers can directly search these supplier "white pages" at any time to locate new sources for an individual item or an entire commodity.

Self-Guiding Search

Most search engines pursue one of two search strategies to locate an item or commodity—aggregation or indexing. Leading search engines on consumer oriented sites such as Yahoo! and Excite return an indexed list of Web sites where the content may be found. While this approach decentralizes ownership of the content to the supplier, the user is faced with a multistep search and different search engines and user interfaces at each supplier's Web site. The content aggregation approach, on the other hand, centralizes content from suppliers into a central repository offering a uniform interface and search technology.

E-Marketplaces support a unique combination of both approaches to help the user source goods or services with the least amount of effort. Users aren't required to know the particulars of a classification schema or catalog hierarchy; they simple enter natural language descriptions of the good or services they require, and the search engine guides them to the right place. Search results include a list of relevant items, along with pointers to specific parts of the catalog that contain major groupings of relevant items. Results can be sorted and further refined based on additional criteria. If an item or commodity is not listed on the provider's e-Marketplace, the search can optionally return a list of suppliers that have indicated their ability to service that request in their registration profile.

With the vast range of products and services offered by participating suppliers, and the industry leading search capabilities of its self-guiding search engine, the e-Marketplace adds value for a wide range of businesses.

Transaction Routing

E-Marketplaces provide full end-to-end transaction delivery services to participating buyers and suppliers. From content loading to purchase orders, these transactions flow quickly and easily from buyer to supplier and so on. For transactions that span company-maintained systems as well as the e-Marketplace, participants only need one set of mappings to be able to communicate effectively with the entire community.

Multiple Delivery Protocols

Several industry standards that define transaction flow, electronic business documents, document exchange, and system interoperability are available today at varying levels of maturity. These standards are essential to the realization of a global ecommerce system in which anyone using any computer and software in any country can participate. Companies must be able to conduct business on their own terms and yet be able to connect to other businesses.

The first step was system interoperability. At the base level, TCP/IP (Transaction Control Protocol/Internet Protocol) enables users with dissimilar computer systems to share information. Another important protocol was HTML (Hypertext Markup Language) that enabled users to graphically display data as Web pages. HTML does not aptly address the needs of ecommerce, which is why XML (eXtensible Markup Language) is becoming popular and will ultimately replace HTML. XML has been described as a smarter version of HTML, because XML is capable of realizing the differences between numeric values such as dates and prices, whereas HTML is incapable of the same in its original form.

XML allows for different date formats, currencies, and numeric expressions, which are imperative in international applications.

Value-Added Services

In addition to the core services listed in the preceding sections, e-Marketplaces will offer value-added business services to its members in the future, including:

- Financial services
- Advertising
- Aggregated buying
- Marketplace benchmarks and performance indicators
- Transportation and logistics support
- Supply chain planning
- Collaborative design

Successful B2B ecommerce requires more than a Web browser and a credit card. Businesses require credit approval, payment and clearing-house functions, logistics management, quality assurance and testing, insurance, and other business services. E-Marketplaces must provide a wide range of high-quality business services, either directly or through third parties. These services must be tightly integrated into the ecommerce infrastructure so their use appears seamless to the end user. Moreover, the services eliminate a lot of manual labor. Take credit checks for example. Let's say a supplier gets an order from an unknown buyer and decides to run a credit check. If credit checking is not a service offered by the e-Marketplace, the supplier will probably contact the supplier, fax a form, run a credit check, and then inform the buyer that his or her credit and order are approved.

Now imagine the same scenario with credit-checking services integrated into the e-Marketplace. The new buyer places an order with the supplier. The supplier's system recognizes this is a new buyer and automatically queries the e-Marketplace for a credit check. The e-Marketplace either runs a credit check or may have a repository of information that links the buyer with the buyer's excellent credit rating. Still without human intervention, the e-Marketplaces forward the credit information to the supplier, and because it meets or exceeds the supplier's acceptance, the supplier's system accepts the order and automatically generates an order confirmation.

Obviously, the future lies in the second option.

By offering services above and beyond transaction processing, marketplaces will evolve into key business partners with the buyers and sellers they serve. Value-added services will a major source of revenue for e-Marketplaces to make money in the future.

E-Marketplace Commerce Trends

The B2B ecommerce frenzy is here, and it is poised to become even more frenetic as the network effect kicks in. Dot-com start-ups or technology suppliers in procurement or supply chain management executed the first dot-coms, but there's been a shift in recent months. Industry powerhouses are starting to partner to create their own marketplaces.

Buyers with inefficient purchasing processes will find themselves at risk as more efficient competitors lower prices and increase profits. Suppliers outside the e-Marketplaces will be bypassed, and those with inefficient processes will be quickly exposed as the transparency afforded by the e-Marketplaces uncovers inventory gaps, price oddities, and product line inconsistencies.

The e-Marketplace imperative will make buyers and sellers transparent, exposing weaknesses as well as revealing strengths. To succeed in this more open environment, the transparent corporation will need to be both agile and collaborative in interactions with their trading partners.

A new "cooperation model" will emerge that will require openness between departments, external trading partners, contractors, alliances, and suppliers. This model will operate across a *Value Trust Network* that will provide the security, collaboration, and commerce tools, as well as the neutral governance to the business community. Once these Value Trust Networks are in place and operational, the next phase will be interconnection of multiple Value Trust Networks either directly or through intermediaries such as e-Marketplaces.

Emerging e-Marketplaces are moving into four community segments based on the complexity of the products they exchange or the process they employ, as well as each market's fragmentation, or number of channel players within a particular industry. Figure 5-1 depicts the online trading community segmentation. To survive, each of these four models will need to move into providing value to the communities that they serve above and beyond the exchange of product and services.

The Defense Department has long used extranets for collaborative development efforts. Now supplier trade in the aerospace and defense industries is migrating to e-Marketplaces, as evidenced by Exostar, an aerospace and defense e-Marketplace founded by BAE SYSTEMS, Boeing, Lockheed Martin, and Raytheon.

Figure 5-1. *Four Models of Online Trading*

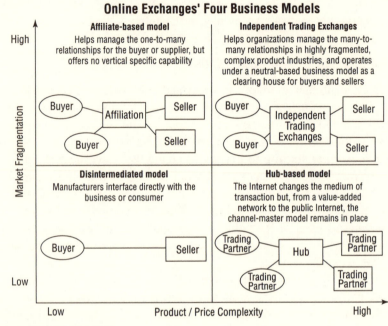

Online Exchanges' Four Business Models

Source: AMR Research 1999

The commodity nature of utilities makes them ideal for trading via online exchanges. Recent federal mandates will force innovation in these concentrated industries as wholesale trading of electricity and gas moves to the Internet. Twenty-one utilities and energy companies, including PG&E, recently launched an e-Marketplace called Pantellos. More recently, another group of utility and power companies announced Enporion.

Forrester Research predicts that the petrochemical, shipping and warehousing, paper and office supply, and medical and pharmaceutical industries will be largely online by 2003. Envira will be formed by 14 chemical and petroleum companies.

In early 2000 the automobile exchange Covisint, created by the merger of GM TradeXchange and Ford AutoXchange, was formed by executives from General Motors, Ford Motor Company, and Daimler-Chrysler. Later, automobile manufacturers Renault and Nissan Motors joined the exchange. The Covisint name represents connectivity, collaboration, visibility, and the international scope of the exchange. The e-Marketplace will create a central source for auto parts and related components that includes suppliers and dealers. Commerce One and Oracle have been selected as the technology providers. Soon after the exchange is up and running, company executives expect to spin it off as a separate company. Alice Miles, president of Ford's B2B Consumer Connect division, said, "Covisint will provide the language for manufacturers and suppliers to talk with each other. With complete confidence and security, buyers and sellers—regardless of their size and position in the supply chain—will soon have away to communicate with each other in real time."

Electronics marketplace PartMiner.com provides sophisticated sourcing tools to help companies uncover hard-to-find products. The site also allows sellers to liquidate their unused inventory via the PartMiner marketplace. The two-way flow that PartMiner has achieved, with companies participating equally as buyers and sellers, is a hallmark of a mature marketplace.

Commerx, which runs several marketplaces including early player PlasticsNet.com, has found that what buyers really want in their marketplace is a hub that makes it easier to integrate with their key suppliers, according to Commerx CEO Tim Stojka. PlasticsNet sees making the bulk of its revenue in the future from selling sophisticated software and marketplace services to companies to set up private partner exchanges, while allowing them to tap into its more open, public exchange when the need arises.

The Ventro marketplace is expanding into more verticals and has learned not to ignore its suppliers. Supplier transaction fees are the main revenue source for Ventro. Buyers conduct basic transactions for fees, so ensuring supplier stickiness is crucial. Ventro has deployed a series of sales and marketing tools to help suppliers target buyers via the marketplace. Online tools help sellers quickly and easily update their product catalogs on a daily basis. Ventro has also begun building reports out of its transaction data to help suppliers assess marketplace performance.

Altra, the energy marketplace, has built a risk management system right into its marketplace, so traders can determine, even in an anonymous environment, whether or not they should risk doing business with a new supplier.

Consumer packaged goods giant Procter & Gamble Co. is working with vendor I-many Inc. to build a contract portal to help it use the Web to manage complex incentive contracts with its trading partners. "Marketplaces tend to degrade the nature of commerce down to a pure price auction," says Tim Curran, I-many's vice president.

Priceline.com, which started as a reverse auction for highly perishable goods in the travel industry—namely, airplane seats and hotel rooms—has expanded into product categories such as cars, groceries, home equity loans, and refinanced mortgages. In addition, Paper-Exchange is the preeminent digital marketplace for buyers and sellers of pulp and paper, boasting a membership of 2,400 corporations from more than 75 countries. It has a growing staff of over 55 employees as of year-end 1999.

Trading Edge Inc., a fixed-income securities dealer, launched BondLink, a virtual exchange that brings together buyers and sellers of corporate bonds. Investors seeking to buy or sell bonds access the Trading Edge servers and post a bid to buy or an offer to sell a particular security, which is immediately transmitted to all other traders on the system.

NECX, a computer products reseller in Peabody, Massachusetts, provides online purchases at its NECX Global Exchange. Buyers can view prices on computer components from dozens of companies and check inventory availability. Online auctioning capability is combined with a staffed trading exchange on the NECX trading floor.

HOTS, is an Australian food services marketplace. This independently operated e-Marketplace facilitates trading among the hospitality industry in Australia, New Zealand, and the Asia-Pacific region, including food and liquor distributors, breweries, hotels, and restaurants. By building an open Internet trading hub, the HOTS site has been able to expand its target customers from the hospitality industry to other businesses that buy food and liquor.

E-Steel is an exchange that debuted in September 1999. Buyers log in and create inquiries, specifying details, terms, and suppliers for the steel they wish to buy. They then receive responses from those suppliers. Alternatively, buyers can search for certain types of steel, offer bids, and negotiate with suppliers in real time. Sellers can choose to just post the specifications for their products, or they can search buyer inquiries to find the most likely customers.

Businesses around the world are in a race to seize first-mover advantage in their industry or geographic region. Expect to see further consolidation in the e-Marketplaces, for a given industry supply chain can't create e-Marketplaces ad infinitum. There will be an increase in mergers and acquisitions by the e-Marketplace providers. In addition, many industries have not yet automated, so new players will be coming in at the same time others are going out of business. The future of e-Marketplaces will bring consortiums or partnerships between vertical players and more broadly based horizontal players that are in multiple industries. That's why major players are establishing global e-Marketplaces that can support both.

Chapter Summary

The B2B e-Marketplace landscape is exploding. Large manufacturers, consortiums, and Net market makers are now in a race to establish the definitive industry or regional portals. Increasingly, these e-Marketplaces are becoming communities of collaboration, rather than simple transaction processors.

Value-added services will differentiate e-Marketplaces as this industry continues to develop, which will create exciting and profitable niches that can be exploited. The value of an e-Marketplace rests in its ability to improve the efficiency of business processes throughout the supply chain.

The following chapter reviews in detail the opportunities and issues of globalization. Going global with your e-Marketplace strategy requires a review of your business model from multiple dimensions. The companies that understand the global opportunities and capitalize on them will be at the forefront of their industries.

CHAPTER

The Global Economy

The Internet has forever changed how the world communicates. Now ecommerce is changing the way the world does business. The global B2B opportunity is huge. How big is huge? According to Credit Suisse First Boston Technology Group, the global B2B economic activity represents approximately $47 trillion per year in transactions. Of all B2B commerce, 65 percent, or $31 trillion, is transacted electronically; 40 percent, or $12 trillion, of electronic transactions are moving through a third-party marketplace. The average transaction fee recognized as revenue is 3.5 percent, or $400 billion, in third-party global B2B transaction revenues. This chapter reviews the multidimensional issues that need to be addressed to capture the global opportunities.

We, the People

Almost every country has embraced the Internet, according to an interconnectivity map produced by the Internet Society. Nua Limited, an Internet consulting and development company, estimates that by 2005, more than one billion people will be using the Internet—about 700 million of them outside the United States. While the Internet got its start in North America, the greatest growth in Internet use during the next few years is expected to occur in the European and Asian-Pacific markets. North America, which currently represents 43 percent of the online population, will account for just 30 percent of that population by 2005, according to a forecast by Computer Industry Almanac. A third of online users will be in Europe and 25 percent in Asia. Internet use in Latin

America continues to grow, with approximately 10 million Latin Americans online today—a number that's expected to jump to 65 million in the next five years (Jupiter Communications). Internet user growth will be slower in Africa, India, and some remote parts of Asia where high costs and a lack of infrastructure hinder technology progress.

We, the Builders of the New Economy

According to *The Industry Standard*, the global ecommerce market is exploding, with sales expected to reach $1.3 trillion by 2003. The ability to conduct business—selling products and services to a worldwide market regardless of language, country, or currency—is a vital and growing need in today's Internet-based economy.

The world's most influential companies are in a race to establish the definitive B2B e-Marketplaces—in Asia, Europe, the Middle East, North America, South America, and Africa. These e-Marketplaces have several objectives. Clearly, the companies that establish these marketplaces want to lower their own procurement costs while profiting from transactions that take place on that e-Marketplace. They want to establish recognition as early leaders in the global economy. At a higher level, these e-Marketplaces are being established on the basis of national competitiveness. If any economic power fails to embrace new economy business practices, it will adversely affect national competitiveness.

Transforming the world economy will be a time-consuming and complex process, and yet the global business cycle is moving toward Internet time. Global e-Marketplaces go from concept to operations in ninety days or less. Unfortunately, the world cannot transform all its commerce-related and regulatory practices at the same speed. A world economy, even an electronic one, cannot emerge without governance.

Founders of global e-Marketplaces realize that it will take effort and negotiation to achieve the global business and world economic policies that are necessary to realize the new economy. These global e-Marketplaces are being established by the players who already have global business experience and the power to influence their local governments. This chapter examines some of the players, the role of governance, and the factors that influence global ecommerce.

Vertical and Horizontal Markets: Friends or Foes?

By 2005, it is conceivable that every country and every industry will have more than one global e-Marketplace, and within those very large marketplaces, vertical or regional e-Marketplaces will also proliferate. Can the number of e-Marketplaces continue ad infinitum? Clearly not. Will competitive issues arise? Yes, which underscores the need for governance.

Government Involvement

The rise of e-Marketplaces is akin to the rise of global industries. Take the computer industry, for example. The computer industry is fiercely competitive, not just in the United States, but on a global basis. In the United States, organizations like the Federal Trade Commission govern what is anticompetitive practice and what isn't. The FTC is now extending its reach to e-Marketplaces to ensure fair play. Internationally there are similar challenges. Although it may be technologically possible to achieve the new economy, the laws and practices that govern international trade will have to evolve to meet the needs of a digital population. The Internet industry leaders are taking a proactive approach to these issues with industry leaders like Commerce One and the Global Trading Web addressing government involvement head-on, with the goals of expediting global online trade practices and influencing the direction of these trade practices. This is an effort that will take involvement at local, national, and global levels.

Achieving a consensus on world trade policies requires the mutual agreement of all parties to a set of rules that will govern it. Cultural differences between and within countries can mitigate this process, which is why local involvement by global e-Marketplaces is essential. Those individual country representatives must be able to understand both the needs of their geographies as well as the needs of the global economy and be able to translate that into a set of international rules that best addresses the needs of both.

The Language of Global Ecommerce

XML (eXtensible Markup Language) is the language of global ecommerce, but unfortunately, it is not a human language. Allowances will need to be made for differences in human language, culture, and practices. To compete effectively in the global marketplace, businesses must communicate in the language of the customer, not the company. For most readers of this book that means the world speaks more than English, and therefore, if you hope to achieve or maintain success internationally, it's time to adopt international standards.

First, a word about terminology and three words that are frequently misused or misunderstood outside the "language community." *Internationalization* (referred to as I18N) is the preparation of code and data structures to enable software to operate in the unique requirements of foreign languages. An example is the ability to accept the double-byte format required for Asian characters. *Localization* (referred to as L10N) refers to the adaptation of software to operate in a foreign language. *Globalization* implies operation concurrently in a number of user-selected languages, including all cultural and formatting idiosyncrasies.

Globalizing content means ensuring that the content is more than simply translated. The content needs to be localized and personalized to the community, the sectors, and the individuals. The fundamental elements of globalizing content include adapting it to suit the local language, culture, and currency as a starting point. The purpose of globalization and localization is to make it easy for customer and trading partners to do business.

The Internet is enabling an information-rich global economy, yet most of the content is still in English. In the battle for international market share, companies can gain a significant competitive advantage by localizing their Web content to reflect local languages and cultures. Localization, if done correctly, can also translate to significant revenue increases.

Ecommerce is driving the need for localization, because transactions, as opposed to static Web content, are directly attributable to the bottom line. Customers in any community are more likely to buy from an e-Marketplace with which they can easily interact. That means the company Web site or e-Marketplace must present content in the local language and be able to process—or at least support—foreign currencies and customer support, among other considerations.

The Internet has always been presented in any-to-any terms. Despite the fact that it is technologically possible to link virtually any entity to any other, there remain several barriers that separate both people and businesses internationally. Language is only one of those barriers. Others include culture, local laws, customs, time formats, date formats, and currencies—all of which directly relate to ecommerce. Any breakdown in communication, whether technological or cultural, can translate to lost sales.

One could argue that the Internet is Americanizing the world. After all, most dot-coms are in the United States, most Internet users are in the United States, and most Internet innovation comes from the United States. However, all that will change very rapidly. Ninety-two percent of the world's population represents nonnative English speakers, according to the *World Almanac*. Clearly, if you want to make it easy for trading partners to do business, you must allow them to conduct business on their own local terms.

Globalize or Else

Smart companies are taking action, making Web globalization a priority. In a recent study, Forrester Research, a Cambridge, Massachusetts-based market research firm, found that 32 percent of the companies it surveyed had plans to globalize their corporate Web sites. In the past, Web globalization wasn't a budgeted item, but it is now.

Selling in the local language makes potential customers more receptive to sales pitches, which translates to increased revenue, says Forrester Research. The company asserts that foreign visitors linger twice as long as they do at English-only URLs and that business users are three times more likely to buy when addressed in their native language. Further, Forrester says customer service costs drop when instructions are displayed in the users' native language.

A few statistics underscore the trend toward Web globalization. International Data Corporation (IDC) a Framingham, Massachusetts–based research firm, estimates that 50 percent of today's Internet users are non-English speaking, and the percentage will increase to 70 percent by 2004. If the global ecommerce market explodes tenfold between 1997 and 2002, from 13 billion to $1.2 trillion as Coopers and Lybrand expects and non-U.S. ecommerce rises from 14 percent to 37 percent by 2002, as forecasted by IDC, the value of non-U.S. ecommerce alone will account for more than $444 billion.

In addition, language translation is only the beginning. Foreign supply chains, local laws, privacy policies, and commercial practices must also be supported. It can seem overwhelming to take on the localization issues on a global basis for e-Marketplaces, but there are companies that provide real solutions at least to some of the most pressing immediate issues of language, culture, and currency support in foreign markets. A number of companies provide machine-generated translation services for content, including Lernout & Hauspie, eTranslate, IBM, and AltaVista, this is still in its early stages of development and requires a watchful human eye on the translations to assure accuracy and localization. Companies such as Idiom and Lionbridge provide translation services and human translation services combined with integration services for a full ecommerce solution. Many of the larger Web services and consulting companies such as marchFIRST, Scient, Viant, Arthur Andersen, and EDS claim to provide a full service in this area, but of 152 such companies surveyed by Forrester, none had a complete set of tools. The most comprehensive set of tools is available through WholeTree.com, whose strategy is to partner with these established providers to ensure an integrated solution. WholeTree.com provides Input Method Editors for Asian and Middle Eastern characters, solutions to track changes simultaneously in all languages, customer support systems enabling monolingual personnel to communicate in up to 50 languages, and automatic globalization tools for Web site generation.

The Global Trading Web, Globalizing Ecommerce

The Global Trading Web exemplifies how technologies, business practices, governance, globalization, and localization can be executed in the context of e-Marketplaces and the new economy. The Global Trading Web, founded by Commerce One, is now the world's largest global online B2B trading community. It connects businesses via regional e-Marketplaces strategically located in the Americas, Asia, Europe, the Middle East, and Africa. As of September 2000, the Global Trading Web comprised 80 global e-Marketplaces that represent trillions of dollars in aggregated spending. It enables companies to connect business with anyone, anytime, anywhere.

The Global Trading Web is an open community of global, regional, and vertical e-Marketplaces engaged in intermarketplace B2B ecommerce. Linked together, these e-Marketplaces cooperatively provide a common infrastructure that is similar to the Internet and the telephone systems. As the number of users increases, so does its liquidity.

The Global Trading Web provides economic and global trading efficiencies through online aggregation. Each e-Marketplace has access to the products, sources, and services of others, extending the market of buyers and suppliers bidirectionally. These ad hoc partnerships enable e-Marketplaces to share economic advantages such as access to trading partners and value-added services to eliminate redundant development efforts, speed time-to-market, and increase return on investment. Individual e-Marketplaces become more efficient by aggregating demand, managing supply chains, developing trust models, and providing a common platform that enables companies to seamlessly route business documents throughout the marketplace.

Through the Global Trading Web, local markets in different parts of the world can be addressed in their native languages and according to their cultures, laws, and business practices. Each regional entity is given the freedom to adapt its e-Marketplace to serve the unique needs of its local audience.

The flexible nature and open architecture of the Global Trading Web enables each global partner to operate its business independently, encouraging localized content, services, and development. Each operator may set its own pricing and economic model, as well as offer unique business services to its constituencies. In return, each e-Marketplace contributes tools and principles that can benefit the entire Global Trading Web community.

The Global Trading Web also provides first-mover advantage. It accelerates the development of regional and vertical e-Marketplaces by providing technical and document interoperability, guaranteed service levels, and common business services. Buyers, suppliers, and e-Marketplace operators typically establish a Global Trading Web presence in approximately three months.

Interoperability Through Standards

The Global Trading Web is based on open architectures and widely disseminated industry standards. XML is the key underlying technology, which provides for document interoperability, accurate transaction processing, and scalability. Using a common data model, the Global Trading Web maps documents, which enable trading partners to seamlessly conduct ecommerce. Commerce One SOX, an XML schema language, and xCBL, a document framework, provide a common development platform from which fully interoperable XML documents can be created and exchanged among trading partners.

Seamless document exchange is important to any trading entity. Without it, trading partners must agree to the format of a business document, such as a purchase order. If one company places the date field on the upper right-hand corner of a page and another places it on the upper left-hand corner of the page, these business documents may be unreadable by their respective ecommerce systems. By providing a standard method of document exchange and leveraging the "extensible" nature of XML, document interoperability is guaranteed. Moreover, xCBL is designed to be the *lingua franca* for XML documents. That means companies currently using EDI (electronic data interchange) can map to xCBL and vice versa. This level of interoperability taken to a global international scale translates to support for foreign languages and currencies, among other items.

For the first time in history, a paperless system of world trade is possible as enabled by XML technologies and proprietary innovations as demonstrated by the Global Trading Web. XML allows trading partners to seamlessly exchange documents regardless of any differences in computers, software, or connectivity methods. Further, XML allows parties to automate the processing of certain documents, which further reduces the time and costs associated with some international business functions that now take days or weeks. Given that XML is an Internet-based technology, it enables parties with sophisticated ecommerce and ebusiness structures to engage in transactions with any other party, including those with mere access to a browser.

Increasing E-Marketplace Value Through Value-Added Services

CommerceOne.net provides the key point of entry to the Global Trading Web, centralizing certain functions to maintain consistency and highly reliable operations. It enables high e-Marketplace efficiency through infrastructure, content, community, and meta services.

Infrastructure

The infrastructure services route data and documents to the appropriate e-Marketplaces, as well as facilitate easy navigation through directory services. The services include document normalization, XML interfaces, and community management.

Content Syndication

GlobalTradingWeb.net provides products and services to facilitate content syndication and reuse throughout the Global Trading Web. The content syndication and reuse service can be provided to the global e-Marketplace operators and/or brokered to affiliate marketplace partners. E-Marketplaces can syndicate their content throughout the Global Trading Web to other markets in remote geographic locations. This is particularly appealing for vertical markets looking to reach new communities.

Business Services

CommerceOne.net provides services essential for conducting business over the network. These business services provide added value to all participating e-Marketplaces, sellers, and buyers. Some of the key services areas include trading directories, format directories, and international trade facilitation.

Trade Facilitation

The Global Trading Web's combined business and technology model enables e-Marketplace operators, buyers, and suppliers to "publish once" and reap the benefits of a leveraged economic community. Participants can reuse content, speed time-to-market, and benefit from highly integrated services without having to make unnecessary technology investments.

Global e-Marketplaces and their respective communities can realize both economic and global trading efficiencies. Each e-Marketplace has access to the others, which extends the market of buyers and suppliers bidirectionally. Moreover, e-Marketplaces may be able to share economic advantages such as volume purchasing discounts and value-added services to eliminate redundant development efforts, speed time-to-market, and increase ROI (return on investment).

The global interoperable e-Marketplaces play an important role in the Global Trading Web. They aggregate demand, manage supply chains, develop trust models, and provide a platform that companies within their respective marketplaces can use to route business documents and establish enterprise e-Marketplaces. Through the Global Trading Web, businesses of all sizes can enable their employees to source, buy, and sell goods and services on a global basis in real time.

The Players

This section describes some of the global e-Marketplaces that compose the Global Trading Web. These represent horizontal, regional, and vertical marketplaces. Regardless of the initial focus, all of these e-Marketplaces have aggressive plans for expansion. The horizontal e-Marketplaces plan to add value-added services and smaller vertical e-Marketplaces to expand their reach. Many of the vertical e-Marketplaces intend to set the standard in their industry for global trade. All of these e-Marketplaces may interoperate with each other, share services and trading communities, and partner to achieve greater levels of efficiency.

Artikos (Mexico)

Grupo Financiero Banamex-Accival ("Banacci"), Mexico's leading financial group, and Commerce One, Inc. (NASDAQ: CMRC) jointly established the Artikos e-Marketplace, the first of several e-Marketplaces in Latin America. Banamex conducted the first reverse auction, executing a $1 million purchase order for automatic teller machines (ATMs). The reverse auction saved Banamex nearly 10 percent on the 50 ATMs acquired from NCR, Diebold, and Unisys-Siemens. Artikos plans to work with Net market makers in Latin America to establish additional vertical and horizontal portals in the region.

Asia2B MarketSite

Asia2B MarketSite is a joint venture including Beijing Enterprises, i-CABLE Ventures, Jardine Internet, New World China Enterprises Projects, SUNeVision, Swire Net Ventures, and WI Harper Group. The seven companies have an approximate trading volume of 20 percent of Hong Kong's gross domestic product. Asia2B MarketSite will anchor the Hong Kong and mainland China hub of the Global Trading Web, providing B2B trading opportunities for many industries, including aviation, automotive supply chain, building materials, computer and components, fixed and wireless telecommunications, hotels, medical and health care products, retail, shipping, and logistics.

BT MarketSite (UK)

BT MarketSite was established by British Telecom (BT) to provide an e-Marketplace and ecommerce services to U.K. businesses. By rationalizing the supply base and improving the internal process for purchasing, BT MarketSite has already reduced the average cost of a purchasing transaction from £70 ($113) to £50 ($80). BT estimates that the cost per transaction will fall again to £5 ($8) as a result of the use of BT MarketSite. BT currently handles 1.3 million purchasing transactions of indirect goods each year.

Cable & Wireless Optus (Australia)

Cable & Wireless Optus is streamlining the buying and selling of goods and services throughout Australia and New Zealand. The company is also using the e-Marketplace to automate its internal procurement function, as well as to offer a range of advanced ecommerce services. Since launching the e-Marketplace, Cable & Wireless Optus has realize a 75 to 90 percent reduction in purchase order processing time that by September 2000 saved 10,000 employee hours.

Citigroup (United States)

Citigroup's e-Citi unit, a global leader in electronic financial services and ecommerce, is launching a business-to-business e-Marketplace providing ecommerce services to Citigroup's worldwide corporate customers. The virtual marketplace will link corporate buyers and suppliers to the new

Citibank Procurement Connection e-Marketplace, which will process procurement transactions and host vendor catalogs, as well as market-specific applications addressing the needs of particular industries. In addition to linking buyers and sellers, Citibank Procurement Connection will benefit participating enterprises through distinctive financial service features, such as immediate online executable currency exchange rates, financing, procurement card capabilities, digital certificates, electronic business-to-business bill payment and presentment, and electronic payments linked to a company's accounts payable processing.

Citibank is demonstrating how business services can be successfully deployed into several e-Marketplaces globally. Through its alliance with Commerce One, Citibank will become the primary financial services provider on the Commerce One Global Trading Portal, which will enable all buying organizations trading on Commerce One.net to take advantage of Citibank's broad array of financial services. These services will also be made available through the Commerce One Global Trading Web.

Com2B.net (Taiwan)

Com2B.net is a Taiwanese joint venture, partially owned by Compaq Taiwan, that is establishing the e-Marketplace for exchanging goods and services among businesses worldwide. The e-Marketplace will comprise many industries, including retail, telecommunications, automotive supply chain, computer and components, cable, stainless steel, semiconductor, and mechanics. All of these combined will represent approximately 10 percent of the trading volume of Taiwan's gross domestic product.

CommerceOne.net (USA)

CommerceOne.net is the U.S. e-Marketplace for exchanging goods and services among businesses worldwide. Buyers and suppliers can access the e-Marketplace for comprehensive ecommerce transactions and value-added services that streamline the buying and selling process to save time and reduce costs. Through CommerceOne.net, trade is accelerated, technology barriers are eliminated, and costs are reduced for all trading partners.

Concert

Concert is an AT&T and British Telecom global venture that is establishing an e-Marketplace that enables its business customers to exchange goods and services worldwide. This venture will provide global connectivity and support for BT customers who are currently using BT MarketSite within the United Kingdom. The Concert portal will support direct, indirect, and ad hoc spending among trading partners.

Covisint

General Motors Corporation, Ford Motor Company, and DaimlerChrysler have formed a business-to-business integrated supplier exchange through a single global e-Marketplace. Covisint intends to provide trading partners visibility across the supply chain. The e-Marketplace will create a unique environment for collaborative design and development, enable e-procurement, and provide a broader marketplace of buyers and sellers. It will bring a wealth of supply chain expertise and experience, ranging from IT to procurement to product development. The goal is to eliminate the inefficiencies and redundancies of supplier relationships through integration and collaboration. This will result in lower costs, easier business practices, and a marked increase in efficiencies for the entire industry.

Deutsche Telekom Marketplace (Germany)

The Deutsche Telekom Marketplace is expected to streamline the buying and selling of goods and services between businesses throughout Continental Europe. Deutsche Telekom manages catalog content and trading communities, among other services.

Enporion (Energy and Utilities)

The Enporion e-Marketplace was founded by Allegheny Energy Inc., New Century Energies, Minnesota Power, Northern States Power, and PPL Corporation. It will seamlessly link buyers and suppliers, reducing cycle times, lowering inventories, and reducing transaction costs. Suppliers will enjoy seamless interfaces with buyers, exposure to new markets, and more standardized processes. Buyers will gain access to new suppliers and lower operating costs.

eScout

eScout.com is the leading ebusiness resource for small to midsize businesses and community banks across America. Through a group of online services, eScout will guide independent businesses to success by empowering them to buy, sell, learn, grow, and access business solutions right from their desktop. As of September 2000, eScout had 5,900 members and was processing 2,000 transactions worth $400,000 per week.

Exostar (Aerospace and Defense)

BAE SYSTEMS, Boeing, Lockheed Martin Corporation, and Raytheon Company recently established Exostar as neutral electronic marketplace that increases the efficiency of supply chain transactions and improves design collaboration across the aerospace and defense industry.

Metals and Mining

The mining and metals procurement marketplace will create a platform to bring together mining, minerals, and metals producers and suppliers. It is anticipated that the e-Marketplace will transform the procurement practices by standardizing and streamlining transaction processes, as well as improving inventory management. The new virtual marketplace will utilize a common catalog of products in multiple languages and will allow participants, regardless of size and location, to access and trade with a large pool of suppliers both locally and around the world. In 1999, the estimated procurement spending of the industry was approximately $200 billion.

Metique

Metique is a global procurement e-Marketplace for the metals and mining industry jointly established by Ispat International N.V., one of the world's largest steel producers, and Commerce One. Metique's initial commercial transactions were completed by Ispat Inland Inc. and one of the company's most valued suppliers, Graybar Electric Company. Through Metique, companies within the metals and mining industry can dramatically reduce their procurement costs, and their suppliers can increase revenue from both existing customers and new customer acquisition.

NTT MarketSite (Japan)

Commerce One, Inc. and NTT Communications launched the first MRO (maintenance, repair, and operations) e-procurement marketplace for Japan to enable buyers and suppliers to conduct open transactions via the Internet. NTT Com began using the marketplace for its own MRO procurement in February, achieving 60 percent cost reduction on processing.

Opciona (Spain)

Endesa, one of the world's largest utilities and telecommunications providers in Spain, Commerce One, and PricewaterhouseCoopers jointly own Opciona, the Spanish hub of the Global Trading Web. Endesa initiated transactions on the e-Marketplace earlier this year that involved the purchasing of over $3 million worth of electric material ranging from twisted wire and aluminum cable to power transformers. More than 15 qualified suppliers from all over the world participated in the bid-quote system, and the buying companies were based in Spain, Brazil, and Chile. E-Marketplace trading partners currently include Endesa's clients and partners and its international operations in Europe, North Africa, and Latin America.

Pantellos

Pantellos is an independent Internet e-Marketplace for the purchase of goods and services between the energy industry and its suppliers formed by a consortium of 21 leading North American energy and utility companies. As of this writing, members include American Electric Power, Carolina Power & Light, Cinergy, Consolidated Edison International, Inc., DTE Energy, Dominion Resources, Duke Energy, Edison International, El Paso Energy Entergy, FirstEnergy Corp, FPL Group, GPU, Inc., Ontario Power Generation, PG&E Corp., Public Service Enterprise Group, Reliant Energy, Sempra Energy, Southern Company, TXU Corp., and Unicom.

PeopleSoft

PeopleSoft Marketplace, built on PeopleSoft Internet architecture and powered by Commerce One, will deliver content-rich online trading communities that connect customers, suppliers, and employees. Tightly integrated with PeopleSoft ebusiness applications, these trading exchanges will allow enterprises to effectively manage their business processes and participate in frictionless commerce, dramatically increasing efficiencies in business-to-business and business-to-employee relationships.

PT Electronic Marketplace (Portugal)

Portugal Telecom, through its PT Prime subsidiary, is launching an electronic marketplace called the PT Electronic Marketplace that will link buyers and sellers throughout the Portuguese-speaking world (including Portugal, Angola, and Mozambique) and Morocco. Portugal Telecom's own purchasing department will be the first customer for the PT Electronic Marketplace, with its more than 1,000 suppliers and 70 billion PTE in annual aggregate purchases (the second-largest buyer in Portugal after the government).

SESAMi.NET (Singapore)

SESAMi.NET was established as part of a joint venture between Singapore Telecom Group (SingTel) and National Computer Systems. The e-Marketplace serves all major SingTel Group companies for the procurement of goods and services, as well as other Asian businesses. As of September 2000, SESAMi.net had 1,500 customers and was processing $400,000 in transactions a month.

Swisscom (Switzerland)

The Swisscom Electronic Marketplace will link buyers and sellers throughout Switzerland and central Europe, accelerating trade and reducing costs for all trading partners. Swisscom will offer online procurement solutions designed for the needs of large companies. In the future, the new online marketplace will be extended towards vertical markets or communities, including small and medium enterprise communities. Together with other Swiss partner companies, Swisscom plans to introduce additional value-added services such as logistics and auctions.

Telco Exchange

BellSouth and Commerce One are jointly creating an e-Marketplace that will link buyers and sellers of goods and services across the telecommunications industry worldwide. The e-Marketplace will initially offer procurement management functionality, reporting, and analysis capabilities. The exchange will support BellSouth's overall strategy aimed at transforming its $16 billion global supply chain and reducing ongoing costs by $1 billion over the next two to four years. BellSouth and its affiliated companies will be the first to automate the purchasing of goods and services throughout the e-Marketplace.

TD MarketSite (Canada)

TD MarketSite is the first business-to-business electronic marketplace and trading e-Marketplace of its kind in Canada. The Toronto Dominion (TD) Financial Group will use the e-Marketplace to offer new ecommerce services, as well as to cut costs on internal procurement. The initiative will be run as a distinct operation within TD Bank Financial Group, with the support of a sales and marketing department.

Trade Alliance

Trade Alliance is a $30 million joint venture between Sinar Mas, a major regional player in food and paper, and Nissho Iwai Corporation, one of the world's largest trading companies. Trade Alliance is initially offering two e-Marketplaces, eFoodAlliance and ePaperAlliance. eFood Alliance is the premier marketplace for the food industry in Asia, bringing together buyers and sellers in the $500 billion global food industry. ePaperAlliance is the first business-to-business pulp and paper exchange in Asia, serving trading partners worldwide. Trade Alliance expects to launch more vertical trading marketplaces over the next few months and intends to expand its operations to 15 Asian countries including China and India. It reported the successful completion of $500 million in transactions on its first day of operation.

Trade-Ranger

A group of fourteen leading energy and petrochemical companies worldwide have launched an independent industry procurement exchange. Founding partners include Royal/Dutch Shell, BP Amoco, Conoco, Dow Chemical, Equilon Enterprises, Mitsubishi Corporation, Motiva Enterprises, Occidental Petroleum, Phillips Petroleum, Repsol YPF, Statoil, Tosco, TotalFinaElf, and Unocal.

Summary

The global e-Marketplaces that make up the Global Trading Web serve as an early indication of how e-Marketplaces will evolve in the future. Notice that most of these global e-Marketplaces are being established on regional capabilities; however, they all intend to support massive global trading. Some of these e-Marketplaces will extend the parameters of their regions. Trade Alliance, for example, will initially focus its efforts on Singapore but will soon expand to India and China. After that, the company plans to extend out to 12 other Asian countries.

These e-Marketplaces will also expand vertically. Trade Alliance currently serves two vertical markets and plans to support many others. Conversely, some e-Marketplaces are being established as global vertical sites like the Boeing e-Marketplace that serves the aeronautics and aerospace industries. The Global Trading Web will continue to grow, attracting Net market makers, enterprise e-Marketplaces, and other global trading partners. In short, it is delivering on the vision of open, interoperable global ecommerce.

CHAPTER

Global Knowledge
Networks Take Flight

We've arranged a civilization in which most crucial elements profoundly depend on science and technology. We have also arranged things so that almost no one understands science and technology. This is a prescription for disaster. We might get away with it for a while, but sooner or later this combustible mixture of ignorance and power is going to blow up in our faces.

CARL SAGAN

To play and win in this hyper-accelerated network economy, organizations need to access vast amounts of information from all across their organizations, as well as across the entire value chain of their industry. It is not only this access to information that is critical, but as Carl Sagan points out in the preceding quote, information without understanding is a formula for disaster. Information has always been a critical factor for successful organizations to compete and thrive. Now in today's ebusiness-accelerated world, information quickly converted into knowledge at the point of highest business impact is a matter of survival.

This chapter reviews the emergence of knowledge exchanges and knowledge networks that will be purpose-built to blend information access with human intelligence networks to produce collaborative analysis and knowledge creation on a global basis. Later in the chapter, Gideon

Gartner, the founder of Gartner Group and Giga Group and a visionary leader in the IT knowledge provider industry, will provide his perspective to this discussion of the emergence of knowledge networks.

If Carl Sagan is right, then all of this access to information without understanding could indeed blow up in our faces. There will undoubtedly be casualties along the way as this new economy takes form. But there is hope for the forward-thinking and agile companies that leverage this powerful resource of knowledge. Information can be captured and converted into useful knowledge and ultimately into power. Others prognosticate about the impending doom that will strike from "info wars" between competing firms and the hackers and—worse—the crackers of this new seemingly open access society. The bottom line is that information is more critical than ever and needs to be treated as a strategic business asset. The information needs to be harnessed, secured, and deployed rapidly at the point of highest business impact.

The twenty-first-century enterprise will be shaped by the collective performance of *global knowledge workers* collaborating through *global knowledge networks*. Technology will enable the integration of content, community, and commerce into new forms of *knowledge exchanges* and *knowledge providers*, which when combined, will become the foundation for the development of knowledge networks that provide virtual workspaces and marketplaces that empower the twenty-first-century enterprises.

Our culture, businesses, and educational institutions will transform through the global access to information. This ubiquitous access to global knowledge will launch an era of mass innovation and creation that will rival any developmental era the world has ever seen. The keys to the new networked society are not in the hands of an elite group of technologists, capitalists, or governments. They are openly available to knowledge workers around the world. This knowledge access will shift the traditional power base in some industries. The traditional boundaries of capital, geography, and access to knowledge and resources no longer apply in this new era of creation. Individual knowledge workers will be as valued as teams of knowledge workers. Knowledge workers will be united into new virtual organizations that are formed around shared vision and objectives. The twenty-first-century enterprise will not be a fixed organizational structure, but one that is agile. The emergence of the digital enterprise, one that unites knowledge workers from both inside the enterprise and external to the enterprise, will become the norm for the networked society.

The Foundation for the Knowledge Network Is Forming

A new era of knowledge access and application is emerging. Business-to-business enterprise application integration (EAI) solutions in combination with business intelligence and knowledge management solutions are breaking through business barriers as companies take bold steps to connect to their customers, suppliers, and partners. Businesses are connecting to share information, collaborate, and integrate at a business process level. The global infrastructure for the emerging knowledge network is quickly forming—first with the foundation of a standardized global telecommunication network, followed by a universal data and rich media network that is provided via the global Internet, and finally via communication, collaboration, and EAI solutions, which are being introduced at a breakneck pace. The pioneers in this new era come from a variety of companies, ranging from software giants such as IBM and Microsoft to new entrants and reinvented companies like Extricity Software, TIBCO, STC, New Era of Networks, Scriptics, Cohera, and TSI International Software—just to name a few. Companies are starting to share information all along the value chain, ranging from catalogs to inventory levels to demand forecasting to complete supply chain integration.

As the global knowledge network forms, organizations will no longer be bound by their physical constraints. A new digital enterprise model will emerge. A digital enterprise will be able to rapidly identify opportunities, form knowledge worker teams from both internal and external resources made up of employees, partners, and customers, and collaborate across a knowledge network. Members of these knowledge networks will draw upon the most advanced knowledge workers, resources, best business practices, technologies, and a global network of business partners. These knowledge networks will bridge the limitations of geography, time, and talent.

Many companies will form their own knowledge network, protecting it and nurturing it as intellectual capital and using it for competitive advantage. Others will collaborate with e-Marketplaces that evolve into *knowledge hubs*. These knowledge hubs will be the connecting points for many disparate and fragmented knowledge points that together will form a powerful knowledge network. These knowledge networks will form around vertical industries and value chains and also around horizontal areas of interest and commerce.

The technology challenges are being met. The real challenges lie in the human nature elements of forming such a utopian network. A lingering concern that lies just below the surface of e-Marketplace growth and expansion is the possibility that the megacorporations will use the rising industry consortiums to channel their procurement power and supply chains into *global private networks* where only those that belong to the club can participate. This would potentially form a polarization between the private network "clubs" and the neutral independent e-Marketplaces, which would be left to serve the more fragmented industry players. However, even companies that choose to build their own private knowledge network will want to be connected to these global knowledge hubs in order to gain access to others' pools of knowledge as well as their own. The best defensive mechanism that an independent exchange or e-Marketplace can do is to start building their knowledge systems and knowledge networks while the consortia are busy trying to build their management teams and reach consensus on direction. Most of the consortia are playing catch-up to the independent exchanges and building out the basics of transaction and trading engines.

Regardless of which way the power base swings, the knowledge networks will ultimately emerge, and those that "get it" and can master the new way of doing collaborative business will enjoy the benefits.

New Economy Knowledge Providers

As the realization hits the visionaries leaders that *the transaction business is the fuel for the knowledge business*, then the resources will begin to be deployed to begin the transformation of enterprises into digital knowledge enterprises and e-Marketplaces will transform into knowledge hubs. Islands of knowledge will be interconnected into knowledge networks that form to meet customer demand, solve industry pain points, or capitalize on new innovative opportunities.

There are knowledge producers and knowledge consumers at every level of a value chain.

The Information Silos Problem and Knowledge Hubs

The collective power of organizational intelligence is one of the most powerful assets that a company has, yet it is also one of the most difficult assets to quantify, capture, retain, and deploy. The information resides in information silos throughout the organization. These information silos have been a problem for years (see Figure 7-1).

The IT industry has provided solutions to address this problem that stress the integration of these information silos. The solutions fall into the category of capturing business intelligence (discrete data) and using

Figure 7-1. *Information Silos*

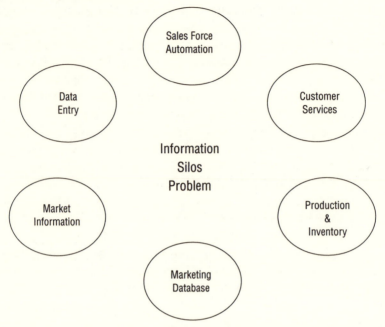

knowledge management solutions that put this business intelligence into context for decision support. E-Marketplaces are prime business entities to evolve into knowledge hubs, shown in Figure 7-2. Since much of the critical data is related to customer demand, product availability, and key trends, the e-Marketplace is a natural knowledge capture point for an industry. Ultimately this knowledge capture could be far more valuable to the e-Marketplace and its members than the transactions that pass through the exchange part of the operations.

Knowledge Management

What is knowledge management? Gartner Group, a Stamford, Connecticut-based IT advisory firm, offers this explanation: "Knowledge management promotes an integrated approach to identifying, capturing, retrieving, sharing, and evaluating an enterprise's information assets. These information assets may include databases, documents, policies, and procedures, as well as the uncaptured tacit expertise and experience stored in individual worker's heads."

The integration of information sources is at the heart of knowledge

Figure 7-2. *Knowledge Hub Models*

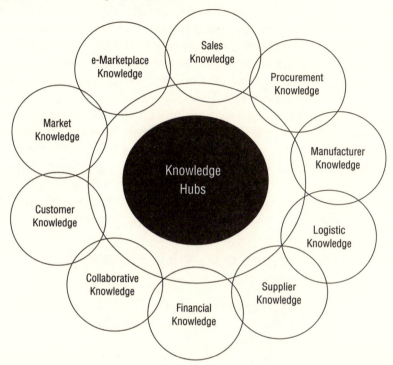

management. (See Figure 7-3.) This is also a central theme in the foundation of knowledge networks.

The Internet and knowledge-management systems are combining to offer a virtual workspace for collaborative communication and workflow. E-Marketplaces can capitalize on this opportunity by taking best-of-breed solutions and combining them to support the business process flow and the communities that are formed around the e-Marketplace. Through the integration of email, groupware, and collaborative-computing software,

Figure 7-3.

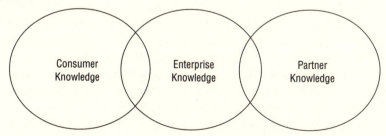

document management and workflow, databases, and text-search and retrieval engines, e-Marketplaces can provide not only a marketplace but
also a collaborative workspace for members. This will have much more
lasting impact and secure the e-Marketplace with a more long-term place
in the overall value chain of the industries supported.

Using a robust relational database as the foundation of the knowledge management system is a good place to start. This provides the
fundamental repository for the captured data and the ability to search
and retrieve the information. It also provides a reliable foundation for
capturing information at multiple levels. Transaction-based ecommerce
systems require a database so the investment can support both the transaction flow as well as the information flow. An Oracle relational database
with Oracle InterOffice and ConText, integrated with a Web interface can
offer a foundation for a knowledge management system.

The Relationship of Time to the Value of Knowledge

Setting value on knowledge is always a tricky game. Knowledge is most
valuable at the exact moment that it is needed for critical business requirements. Knowledge is also valued by the timing that it is received
in advance of the competition.

Forrester Research points out in a recent report on ebusiness networks that companies can use information as a competitive advantage
by being first to have access to that information. But that advantage
decays quickly as the information becomes more widely distributed. (See
Figure 7-4.) The key is to not only have access to the information but
to rapidly turn the information into knowledge and apply that knowledge
to the highest points of business impact.

As e-Marketplaces offer knowledge services, setting value for these
services will be determined by the timeliness and impact of this knowledge on the person purchasing this knowledge. The value will go up or
down depending on the critical nature of the knowledge. So, in order to
provide a pricing model for knowledge services, it will require a sliding
scale of pricing based on timeliness and importance. General market data
will be priced toward the lower end of the scale, while customized
knowledge on a critical purchasing decision, for example, that combines
the latest data with analysis from experts will command a higher value.

Information combined with expertise is the key to the successful
models that deploy the new knowledge solutions. Capturing the information is the first step, followed by rationalizing the data so that it can
then be shared by the appropriate people both internal and external to

Figure 7-4.

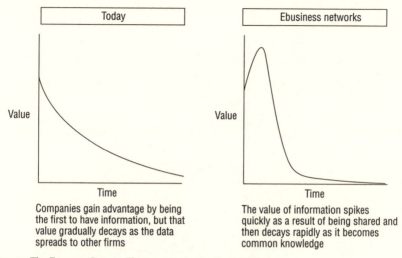

Companies gain advantage by being the first to have information, but that value gradually decays as the data spreads to other firms

The value of information spikes quickly as a result of being shared and then decays rapidly as it becomes common knowledge

Source: The Forrester Report: Ebusiness Networks, April 2000

the enterprise. Then expertise must be applied to the information so that it can be put into context and converted into knowledge. In a controlled environment of an enterprise, these steps are difficult to actually put into practice. The complexity increases exponentially when you look at applying this process across an entire industry value chain. Given this complexity, it is most probable that even the largest industry-backed consortia with money, resources, and expertise will not be able to create a seamless frictionless system for their industries. What will most likely occur is that specialized knowledge providers will emerge to address specific portions of the information gathering, and these knowledge providers will be integrated together into a knowledge network.

Start with specific business opportunities or issues and then expand the knowledge management strategy from there. Knowledge management is a major undertaking. Take it one step at a time. Make sure that what is built is scalable and has open APIs (application program interfaces) that will allow the system to grow and interact with other systems.

A full review of an industry value chain with an eye on mapping the information flow that leads and supports the transaction flow would determine the key *knowledge impact points* that could be rapidly applied to opportunities. An integrated system or an integration of knowledge providers could be designed to capture information and covert it into knowledge. These knowledge systems could address opportunities of consumer behavior and transaction analysis, Web automation, collabo-

Figure 7-5.

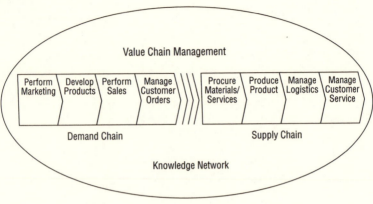

rative business process, improved productivity, and cost reduction. Such knowledge systems could be used as a major competitive advantage.

The modern value chain should be viewed from an holistic viewpoint taking a customer-centric external perspective on the enterprise, allowing for interaction within an enterprise as well as external to the enterprise. (See Figures 7-5 and 7-6.) The "new economy" value chain calls for operations that are focused on core competencies and linked to partners and outsourced service organizations that combine to offer new customer value.

Figure 7-6. *Manage Logistics*

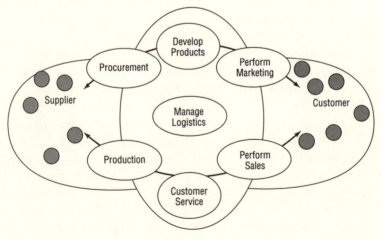

Several knowledge delivery providers and networks will emerge to serve this new knowledge network as follows:

Knowledge providers—Knowledge providers can be individuals or teams made up of both inter- and intra-enterprise members of a value chain. Traditional and emerging knowledge providers such as research and analysts firms and content service providers (CSPs) will also play a key role in the new business and operational models of providing knowledge at the point of impact to the knowledge network.

Global knowledge networks—Interconnected knowledge providers will be linked together either directly or through intermediaries such as e-Marketplaces acting as *knowledge hubs* to form *knowledge networks*.

Global production networks—Digitally connected production teams, resources, and partner organizations that collaborate, design, produce, and deliver products and services at a speed and customer focus that have never before been possible.

Global Resource Planning Networks—MRP (manufacturing resource planning) and ERP (enterprise resource planning) have helped provide information capture and decision support primarily within an enterprise. Global resource planning (GRP) networks and solutions will become the next wave aimed at productivity and business process optimization. However, these systems will be built with a clear recognition of the power of the Internet and the fact that companies and even industries will operate in a partnership mode to produce value. This is in contrast to the rather myopic, internally focused manner that typified the last century.

The Three C's of Knowledge

The knowledge and creation process follows the three C's of knowledge. Namely:

Capture—The first step in building a knowledge exchange is to capture the knowledge from multiple points including the e-Marketplace, customers, employees, suppliers, and trading partners. Ultimately, the value of transaction flow through an e-Marketplace will be surrounding information and knowledge that it generates. With this in mind, you should build a knowledge repository.

Creation—The next step is to take that information and create value in the form of market intelligence, decision support, demand forecasting, fulfillment forecasting, and new product or service development. Add

CAPTURE	CREATION	CONVERSION
Information	Knowledge networks	New education/
Resources	Production networks	training systems
Best practices	Knowledge products	Rapid production
Knowledge workers	Knowledge services	systems
Market data		Global distribution
Customer		systems
requirements		E-solutions
		E-services
		New revenue streams

expertise to information and create knowledge. Mine the information repository on an ongoing basis. Information is truly the gold in the Internet gold rush. Rich sets of knowledge management tools are available to provide this capability. However, it is what is done with the knowledge that will differentiate the e-Marketplace from the competitors.

Conversion—Finally, once the knowledge has been captured and creation of value has been accomplished, then the conversion stage should occur whereby this value is converted into a return for your stakeholders, customers, employees, and partners. For example, conversion could take the form of increased revenues, increased productivity, improved decision support systems, cost reductions, improved efficiencies, or increased customer satisfaction.

Knowledge Tools for a Knowledge Economy

In the knowledge economy, it would seem apparent that knowledge workers are the greatest assets that a nation, an industry, or a company has. With this recognition, the emergence of more advanced knowledge tools to support a knowledge-based society is a key trend that is starting to occur across multiple industries on a global basis. Unfortunately, educational institutions still are not taking the lead on this opportunity, and the private sector is picking up the slack by educating the supposedly educated graduates. The speed of knowledge creation and transference is moving at an accelerated pace. This acceleration causes traditional means of knowledge transfer to be obsolete and nonscalable to the mass market of knowledge workers. Unfortunately, classic educational institutions are based on the foundation of physical classrooms and memorization rather than collaboration and the development of thought process. Given this situation, it is no wonder that the private sector has to teach the skills required to succeed in business and also teach the process of thinking.

Forward-thinking companies such as Cisco Systems are leading the way in partnering with traditional educational institutions to offer new innovations in learning. Through programs such as the *Cisco Networking Academy*, Cisco is working with a wide range of educational institutions (high schools, vocational schools, colleges, and universities) to provide students an online curriculum with extensive hands-on activities. Graduates of the Academy program are prepared to sit for the Cisco Certified Networking Associate (CCNA) exam, pursue other education or training opportunities, or move directly into the workforce.

The opportunity for e-Marketplaces and information intermediaries to evolve into knowledge creation and transfer hubs is enormous. Tapping the power of collaborative education through a combination of digital and physical experiential learning is powerful and hopefully will become a part of the fabric of the new economy.

The following is a perspective from one of the leading visionaries and business leaders of our time, Gideon Gartner. Mr. Gartner provides his vision for where he sees e-Marketplaces evolving. His vision provides insight into the role that knowledge networks play in the evolution of business and e-Marketplaces.

Perspective

Gideon Gartner

What Is the Future Significance of the Content Component of B2B?

The thesis of this discussion is that the B2B application space, which until now has been focused on goods exchanges and transaction systems, will evolve to embrace the exchange of knowledge. In fact, intra-enterprise knowledge exchange systems have been evolving for some time now (with mixed results, but inexorable forward progress overall). Soon, the time will come for interenterprise knowledge exchange. Knowledge exchange, as compared with information exchange, is the exchange of information in context, which is usable for decision making as well as for learning (for example, best practices will be exchanged between willing enterprises, affecting the development of professionalism and management skills). Such knowledge must also possess value.

Content Is Still King

Yes, content is already big and getting bigger. An Internet cliché repeats, ad nauseam, that a basis for Internet success is effective implementation of the "Three C's"—Content, Collaboration, and Commerce. Some wags now add a fourth, Context, as if to acknowledge that raw content is insufficient. Indeed, most content today is still underfiltered and underorganized, leading to relatively difficult retrieval by potential clients, resulting in lower value (and therefore more difficult revenue models). The problem is both technological and process-related. Interestingly, the technology is rapidly improving; it is the process side, which involves creative intermediation, that is lagging.

Entering the Knowledge Exchange Wars

Entering the knowledge exchange wars implies being conversant with the field of knowledge management (KM). Two broad views of what KM encompasses are fundamental and must be addressed by businesses, albeit via separate but overlapping strategies. The first and most common view is that within enterprises, reuse of knowledge must be promoted with supporting processes and with strong cultural enhancements to encourage universal support of these processes within the organization. Many benefits would result, the most obvious being a catalog of "best practices" that, if considered by the entire organization, would presumably promote efficiency. The second view is that any KM approach, whether intra- or interenterprise, must deal with the disease of information anxiety, which is caused by cancerous infoglut—unfortunately exacerbated by expanding technology plus the flood of misinformation. It should be noted that not only do organizations have an inherent interest in using KM to address reuse/best practices and infoglut/misinformation, but so do individuals, especially individual professionals who represent their businesses or who want to enhance their own careers.

The Infoglut Phenomenon

The preconditions are in place right now to elevate demand for KM solutions in the areas of reuse/best practices and in dealing with infoglut/

misinformation. After all, it can be surmised that every business executive and individual professional suffers today from lost opportunities and from the traumas of information anxiety. Therefore, remedies may enjoy great market acceptance (in fact, there is growing institutional recognition of KM). The situation unfortunately will become worse before it gets better: Even if available information is growing at only a nominal exponential rate, the phenomenon of compound growth renders staggering amounts of absolute future volumes of information (especially relative to our fairly fixed capacity to absorb any fraction of this information).

This infoglut pollution, comparable to that from exhaust or noise, creates overload that is debilitating, crowds our ability to think, and causes stress. Ironically, for many information providers, the glut has become hugely profitable, as channels such as specialized magazines, other media, think tanks, and information services have proliferated. Of course, this just further exacerbates the glut, creating enormous redundancies. Conflicts between narrow specialists with parochial views often further confuse the information consumers. The blatant misinformation (discussed below) which intelligent consumers need to deal with is today broadly suspect when it goes beyond raw information, analysis, or what often masquerades as knowledge—even from traditionally important sources (Wall Street being a notable example).

The range of KM solutions to these problems will at least partially depend upon technology. Very sophisticated retrieval or text-mining engines will continue to be built to exceed today's search standards for "recall" and "precision." Other solutions to the glut problem will likely employ technology to intelligently abstract a hit from a search and in fact synthesize multiple hits. When one adds to these developments various administrative functions such as permissioning, security, classification, and more, a "knowledge server" concept emerges. A knowledge server can be viewed as a "black box" between content and the consumer.

With assistance from these knowledge servers, the user organizations that exploit such technology effectively can be considered "e-knowledge" participants; e-knowledge would simply be the application of electronic technologies to the creation, classification, synthesis, analysis, storage, retrieval, and display of knowledge. But processing knowledge electronically still won't do the whole job; the human factor is needed to certify and calibrate the original sources, add value through analysis, and ultimately make recommendations that are customized to the consumer's environment—as help desks do today.

The Human Factor

The human factor will be an essential component of most successful e-knowledge activities. Obviously, people will be required to design and implement the processes that each organization employs to manage knowledge. But importantly, people will be crucial to commercial enterprises that offer services to knowledge consumers of all stripes. One should note that the IT industry's information provider sector (not to be confused with traditional consulting activities) has grown in the past 20 years from insignificance to a multibillion dollar industry.

The Knowledge Exchange Mechanism

Credit is generally given to Gartner Group as the corporate catalyst for the growth of the information provider sector. Today, a dozen or so other public participants exist and are growing rapidly. The Gartner model has been copied and enhanced by new firms employing the Web more or less intensively, but in almost all successful versions of the information provider model, employment of live people has been essential.

While the IT industry is the most successful example to date of the knowledge exchange mechanism, there will be many other successes. The fundamental epiphany that brought about the model's success was that written content should be tightly integrated with available expertise (personal advice and decision-support assistance), and that when effectively implemented, the bundle of content and expertise (plus some other deliverables thrown in to encourage user loyalty) could be priced, for once, at rates that approximated or exceeded the cost to produce the bundle and that proved the client's perception of value. This simple phenomenon—bundled content plus expertise—will hold true for future-generation models, as it has in the past two decades.

For example, while analysts employed by information providers offered this expertise in most implementations to date, there has recently been substantial experimentation with the use of expert networks as a source of expertise. While most experiments are attempting to prove the expert network concept, most have not yet figured out how to effectively qualify the experts, or how to intimately couple their expertise with supporting content.

The Need for Intermediation

The essential variable in making the expert network idea work is dealing with the propensity for generating misinformation from relatively uncontrolled knowledge sources, such as most of today's expert networks. Recall that misinformation is a causative factor of the dread "information anxiety" disease. The Nobel Laureate in Physics Murray Gell-Mann, who conceived of the quark, has been an articulate proponent of theories that justify the need for intermediation in the knowledge field. In fact, he aptly called the information explosion the "misinformation explosion." He reacted to the reality of infoglut (amplified by the massive capacities and speeds of the digital age) by observing that content is too often misinformed, poorly organized, or irrelevant. He called for a reward system that would encourage numerous and even competing processors (not originators) of information to act as intermediaries—in essence, to interpret what is produced by others. In physics, Gell-Mann recognized the rewards that awaited scientists who achieved results from experiments, even if later proven wrong. But what about the importance of continuously clarifying, synthesizing, evaluating, and so forth? Little if any reward is generally forthcoming for these essential activities. This state of affairs will likely change rapidly in the future in many fields, as the stakes in dealing with raw, unevaluated knowledge rise in the face of rising knowledge volumes.

The Problem with Disintermediation in the Knowledge Space

There is an absolute need for knowledge intermediation. Its effective visioning and implementation holds a fundamental key to knowledge management and knowledge enhancement breakthroughs. While this idea may seem obvious, note that it's counterintuitive with regard to the Internet, where present day disintermediation trends prevail. The problem is that disintermediation does not hold in the knowledge arena. Take, for example, the more sophisticated argument in favor of disintermediation— that the Internet will be a strong price-deflation mechanism. This is because if in fact there will be the conventionally viewed disintermediation between production and consumption, this will therefore release resources from intermediation into production, increasing the supply of goods and therefore reducing price levels.

If this is true, then the knowledge space is surely the converse of this, for the following reason: In the knowledge model, substantial intermediation is a key assumption and a strong differentiator. Might it not then follow that such increased intermediation, which requires capital and labor, will then absorb resources from production, decreasing the absolute supply of such valued content thus increasing price levels? This logic, if correct, supports the view that not all content will be exposed to the "content wants to be free" mantra. Rather, unique content (timely, relevant, creative, and so on) will command pricing which will presumably be proportional to the increased value.

Current dot-com expertise and network models offer too little, if any, intermediation. The managed expertise of a large number of experts requires not only up-front development of optimized processes, but employment of a controlled, internal group of trained professionals who will provide intermediation in a variety of forms, the enumeration of which is beyond the scope of this discussion and which, in any case, will vary substantially by industry and by business model.

Section Summary

Gideon Gartner's vision of the future of context-based content and the emergence of knowledge networks presented in this section offers an excellent perspective for setting a winning e-Marketplace success strategy based on the value of capturing, creating, and converting information into valuable knowledge services. The gold in the Internet gold rush can be found in the information that surrounds the transaction flow of the day-to-day business process. This powerful truth will hold the promise of new business models for those that grasp the opportunity and drive toward knowledge-based value delivery.

In the following chapter we will further explore the new value creation for e-Marketplaces and the business models that lie behind these emerging businesses.

C H A P T E R

E-Marketplace Business Models

The focus of this chapter is on value creation and building a solid, sustainable e-Marketplace business model. It explores various e-Marketplace business models, with perspectives on both private e-Marketplaces and industry-backed consortia models. We will start by reviewing which e-Marketplace models are viable for which type of industry and market that they serve. The following are some general trends and practical rules of engagement for developing an e-Marketplace or expanding one. As with any rule there are exceptions, and these guidelines are provided as general trends to be aware of in the strategic planning process.

Vertical Industry E-Marketplaces

Vertical e-Marketplaces address specific industry pain points. Taking a horizontal cross-industry approach can be far more difficult to administer and to reach critical mass. The long-term success of a vertical e-Marketplace is in the deep domain expertise of the senior management team. The business model will evolve, so it is critical that there be a seasoned team of industry-experienced professionals at the helm. A strong management team will be able to influence a percentage of the industry to support its e-Marketplace. This critical mass is a fundamental success factor for any e-Marketplace.

Interactivity Breeds Liquidity and Interdependence

The e-Marketplace model should be operationally interactive with the community that it is serving at as deep a level as possible. If the e-Marketplace is purely a transaction exchange for spot buying and selling, then the member loyalty will be transitory and may not provide enough long-term sustainable revenue to support the operation. Services such as exchange services, auctions, and catalog aggregation are necessary to attract and retain the member base, but additional value-added services should be developed quickly with the key customers that are providing the liquidity to the e-Marketplace. Once these true value-added services are developed and are operational for both the member and the e-Marketplace, then the switching costs will be higher for the key members if they consider leaving to explore other digital markets. Declining margins on transaction business is a reality in the commodity trading side of the business. The margin uplift comes in the form of real value-added services and long-term annuity models that will drive the profitability of the digital marketplace.

Liquidity Is Key

The liquidity of an e-Marketplace is determined by its ability to achieve critical mass. Prior to joining an e-Marketplace, companies should consider the points described in the following.

Size the True Market Opportunity

Size the market opportunity carefully. Look beyond the gross top-line numbers that are presented about an industry. The revenue for an e-Marketplace is in the distribution and operational sides of the business, where significant savings or efficiencies can be met by the presence of a well managed e-Marketplace. The rule of thumb on industry size is to look for an industry with a market size of at least $10 billion. But do not be misled by just the market size. As has been pointed out by a number of analyst firms, a $30 billion market size industry may be less attractive than a $10 billion industry. This would be the case if the $30 billion industry was a commodity product industry that only supported a 5 percent margin for the distribution and sales channel. This would then represent a $1.5 billion total market opportunity for the transaction oriented digital marketplace to address. In contrast, if the $10 billion industry supported a 50 percent cost for sales and distribution, then the smaller $10 billion market would represent a $5 billion market opportunity for the e-Marketplace.

Fragmentation Versus Consolidation

There are generally opportunities for e-Marketplaces in both heavily fragmented industries and for highly concentrated industries. Generally, the fragmented market opportunities lie in the distribution and reseller side of the business, where there is a large volume of players and a wide geographic spread between them. These fragmented markets are prime targets for independent exchanges that maintain trust and neutrality and can bridge the boundaries of geography and time and provide price transparency to the member base. Independent e-Marketplaces need to bring together a major portion of a fragmented market into a single marketplace. This plays well to the cost efficiencies for the members, as well as the time efficiencies for the members to do price and product comparisons and transactions.

Large, well-funded consortia are owned by the concentrated power base of the industry, and they provide the consortia e-Marketplaces with instant critical mass and liquidity, which is usually a large and powerful group of manufacturers and suppliers. They also provide a safe venue for the large equity players to start jointly solving industry supply chain problems. This tight operational partnering provides a very high switching cost for the members. It also provides strong potential for long-term annuity business models for the consortia.

The "Club" Factor

When reviewing market sizes and opportunities, be aware that every industry has a "club," and there are those that belong and there are those that do not. These clubs are figurative, of course, but nonetheless very real and represent significant economic power within their respective industries. These clubs are built on years of trusted relationships that will not be replaced by the introduction of a disruptive technology, even one as big as the Internet. They will, however, be transformed by the Internet and e-Marketplaces. The truth is that most of the large volume trading that is going on through e-Marketplaces today in the B2B space is between parties that know and trust each other. The typical non-club member exchange that is doing business today without tapping into this club community is primarily picking up opportunistic trading (spot trading for emergency components of supplies) or problem products such as excess, obsolete, or refurbished systems. Until the private e-Marketplaces can bridge the trust and relationship gap, they will be subject to building their business model around spot buying and excess, obsolete, and re-furbished systems. This is not always a bad place to be. In certain mar-kets, like the semiconductor market, this can represent a billion-dollar opportunity for an e-Marketplace player. Going into the game, you should know which submarket to address and then build a management team with a deep vertical knowledge of this market and position the company to be the leader in the chosen vertical market.

Attracting Members

E-Marketplace liquidity depends on locking in a critical mass of key trading partners. This is particularly difficult for the independent "neu-tral" digital markets. A balance must be struck carefully between locking in key traders and maintaining an unbiased neutral business.

Equity discussions come up early on. There are ways to balance the equation by always keeping any major trading partner in a minority share-holding position and by having a diversified shareholder base. There are also some interesting equity models that are being discussed around the idea of having dynamic equity participation. The premise of the discussion is that a block of equity is divided up and used to fund the company. Then there are remaining blocks set aside for management, key employees, mergers and acquisitions, and so forth. However, there is one block that is provided on a dynamic basis to the primary volume traders through the e-Marketplace. This block has a term of one year and is renewed for an additional year based on volume of business. This way, the high-volume loyal members are always rewarded for their continued support of the long-term growth of the company.

For many e-Marketplaces, even those that provided healthy equity participation to key trading partners, there comes a time when the key traders band together and either challenge the exchange for more equity or leave and form their own e-Marketplace in which they own 100 per-cent of the action. It is a difficult balance that must be struck and further highlights the point made in this book that e-Marketplaces must move quickly to higher levels of value than just the transaction business.

Moving from Secondary Source to Primary Trading

Most e-Marketplaces begin as a secondary source for members who are trying out the new venue either as a buyer or supplier or both. The goal is to move these members up the value chain as quickly as possible to the point where the e-Marketplace becomes a primary extension of the customer's business. To do this, the e-Marketplace must address real value-added services, channel conflicts, and provide a model that is significantly better than the existing model being used by the customer today.

As discussed in Chapter 7, information, and ultimately knowledge exchange, is a key area to add value and lock in loyalty from the members. Other key areas to review are the community-building aspects of the e-Marketplace covered in Chapter 4.

The Internet offers a new level of business integration that will accelerate new hybrid business models. The Internet is not the entire answer, but in this generation of ebusiness, there is an openness to try new ideas and to innovate. They say that innovation is born out of necessity. Perhaps that is part of the situation that the business community is facing today. Innovative new hybrid business models are forming from the necessity to adapt or die. They are also forming out of a global sense of hope and innovation that will ultimately result in the interconnection of e-Marketplaces. There have been very few historical occurrences that have rallied people from multiple industries, cultures, and countries from around the world to stop and work together on a common set of goals and opportunities. E-Marketplaces represent this type of cooperative global effort.

Table 8-1 lists a sample of the emerging business models that are forming around the e-Marketplace opportunity. One of the most exciting opportunities in this new era of digitally connected businesses is the ability for companies to partner to create new forms of value. E-Marketplaces represent one of the most fertile grounds for this new form of value creation. E-Marketplaces are not only the connecting point for buyers and suppliers, they represent the connecting point for communities, supply chains, and entire enterprise-to-enterprise value chains. E-Marketplaces represent the nexus point for innovation.

The idea of blending together different companies into new hybrid business models that can create new products and services is an exciting concept. It has been done in varying degrees over the years with companies cross-selling and up-selling to each other's customers. This type of blended service offering model will surely take hold in the first phase of the e-Marketplace evolution. Where the model really becomes interesting is when two or more entities collaborate and create products and levels of service that are uniquely innovative and either answer customer needs or create customer demand for items they did not even know they needed.

The hybrid revolution will probably be more of an iterative evolution as business bands together to solve industry pain points and meet customer demand. Let's review a few examples of what this new hybrid

Table 8-1. E-Marketplace Business Models

Types of Business Models	Types of Products and Services	Benefits
Buyer aggregation	Commodity products and services	e-procurement; price transparency; lower product costs; less rogue spending; shorter procurement cycle
Supplier aggregation	Commodity products and services	Global sales channel expansion; increased revenues; fast inventory turns for FG; obsolete and excess
Integration solutions	Blended products and services	PCs with value-added services
	Buyer/Supplier	Cross-sell, up-sell opportunities; higher-margin business
Integration services	Integrated business process	Collaborative business services
	Integrated collaboration services	Design, source, make, deliver, sell
	Workflow automation	Faster time-to-value; expense control
	Demand optimization	Better market intelligence
	Financial, professional services	Leveraged resources
Integrated systems	CRM, ERP, EDI, KM, SCM	Time-to-value acceleration; leverage partners
Integrated operations	Warehouses, logistics, freight	Improved working capital
	Freight consolidation	Fixed asset savings
Translator models	Interconnection services	Value chain integration
Direct model	Company-specific products/services	Direct to customers; no middlemen sales

world looks like in practice. The example shown in Figure 8-1 demonstrates how companies can work together to deliver customer-centric value through tight business and operational alliances. It demonstrates how a manufacturer can use the Internet to tap into a partner network of companies to provide a virtual and physical return and maintenance authorization process for repairing customer machines.

Figure 8-1. *Building a Digital and Physical Value Chain*

A manufacturer that needs to repair a customer's machine will use partners on the Net for ...

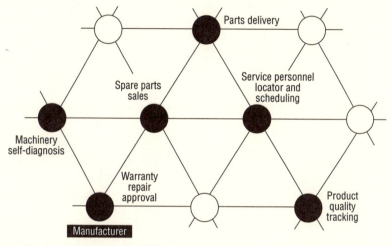

Source: *The Forrester Report, April 2000*

Firms Will Tap Process Specialists Across an Ebusiness Network

With the advent of e-Marketplaces, industries are now in a position to create mutually new forms of value through collaboration. For example, the recent deregulation of the financial services industry made it legally possible to offer services that had been restricted for years. A bank can now offer insurance services and securities trading. Similarly, legal firms can now offer accounting services, banking, and insurance services. In the future, we expect to see the emergence of new hybrid services that combine the core competencies of different industries. The Internet offers a new level of business integration that will accelerate these new hybrid business models.

Table 8-2 shows an example of a community bank. It outlines under the "old model" the existing bank services offered today. The "new model" demonstrates how the bank can now combine additional value-added offerings to service its existing customer base and expand its base to customers who are looking for a more complete set of financial, investment, and protection-based services.

Figure 8-2 illustrates how the traditional role of the bank as a trusted service provider can evolve to a new, more expanded role of trusted adviser. A bank can now leverage its position as a trusted financial

Table 8-2. Community Bank Example

Old Model	*New Model*
Consumer Services	
	Consumer banking services
Checking	Consumer insurance services
Savings/Money markets	Securities trading services
CDs/IRAs	Legal services
Lines of credit	Accounting/Tax services
Commercial Services	
	Traditional banking services
Business checking	Small business integrated services
Business savings	Midmarket integrated services
Merchant credit accounts	Large company integrated services
Business loans	Legal services
	Accounting and tax services
	B2B financial services

Figure 8-2.

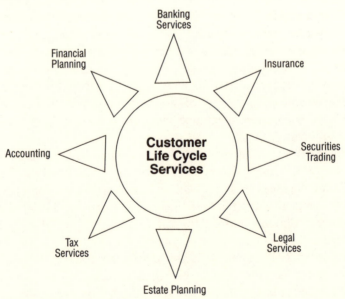

service provider to offer a complete set of services that provide the customer an entire life cycle of value. The bank customers can now expand their relationships with the bank to not only receive financial services, but they also can receive value in the form of protection services through insurance offerings, investment services, legal services, accounting, and estate planning. This expanded set of service offerings provides a long-term value-based relationship with the customer. It also dramatically increases the switching costs of the customers should they consider moving to another bank. This same business strategy can be applied in many different industries.

The Role of Exchanges

Exchanges were one of the first models to emerge in the B2B space, particularly for commodity products and services in which global market, distribution, and support structures already existed. Exchanges are two-sided marketplaces in which buyers and suppliers negotiate prices, usually with a bid-and-ask system, and in which prices move both up and down. The prices of perishable items such as food, or intangibles such as electric power, are sometimes volatile, particularly when a true market price is hard to define; however, an e-Marketplace provides a dynamic bid environment in which real-time pricing is always available. Also, exchanges work well for brokers who make high margins by buying low and selling high to purchasers. Altra (energy), PaperExchange.com (paper products), GoFish.com (frozen fish), Arbinet (telecommunications bandwidth), e-Exchange (IT industry), and eHitex (global-high technology industry) are some examples. Case studies of e-Exchange and eHitex follow.

Private E-Marketplace Exchange Case Study: e-Exchange.com

E-Exchange is a global online exchange founded in 1998 by seasoned executives from the high-technology industry. It is targeted to buyers, sellers, and market makers of goods and services within the information technology (IT) industry, with the goal of increasing liquidity, lowering prices, and reducing workflow costs. Business-to-business ecommerce trading solutions will be rapidly adopted by the IT industry because business imperatives demand it. As a result of evolving business processes, IT departments must be able to connect a large number of buyers and sellers or connect to a large community, easily enable product searches and price comparisons, and process large transaction volumes.

E-Exchange has two essential elements necessary for the rapid deployment of an exchange that can quickly achieve liquidity: management experience and the right IT contacts. E-Exchange initially focused on developing membership in the European and Asian markets that accounts for a significant percentage of the overall industry trading. International Data Corporation (IDC) estimates that the market for new IT products will exceed $570 billion worldwide in 2000.

E-Exchange supports existing business practices such as direct negotiation among multiple parties, while incorporating enhancements such as global reach, anonymity, and real-time access to information. In addition, e-Exchange provides features that support existing business relationships, expand opportunities to interact with new partners, and mitigate counter-party risk. E-Exchange is designed to be neutral, without bias toward any particular type of industry participant. It is committed to the regular upgrade of its service platform and is implementing a number of additional value-added services in the areas of third-party logistics, shipping, and finance.

E-Exchange "went live" in November 1999. The high-profile launch in Australia attracted more than 600 resellers, including heavy hitters such as Ingram Micro and Compaq, onto the site in the first day. Similarly, leading Taiwanese manufacturers and distributors, including First International Computers, Inc. ("FIC"), LEO Systems, Inc., RITEK Corporation, and Tantung, signed up as a result of the recent launch in Taiwan. In addition, Computex Online, the Taipei Computer Association's online channel resource, is using e-Exchange's service platform to enhance its member services and expand its global reach. South Korea has already signed up key industry players such as Lucky Goldstar, Hyundai, and Samsung.

During June 2000 the e-Exchange twice exceeded $1 million of trade in a single day, with the remaining daily average being $243,000. Following the June launch in Australia, e-Exchange hosted $871,000 in transactions by the end of July. Active posting of buy and sell orders now average in excess of $100 million daily.

The number of registered members had grown to over 6,300. In the same time frame, e-Exchange hosted 4,998 transactions, involving 62 selling members and 217 buying members, with an aggregate value of over $25 million. The size of transactions ranged from $20 to $757,600 with a mean value of $4,874 and a mode value of $3,575. These transactions comprised of trades executed in Singapore, Hong Kong, India, the United Kingdom, Taiwan, Bangladesh, Cambodia, South Korea, and the Philippines.

Positioned to Leverage Large Vertical Market Opportunity. According to IDC, end-user IT products will exceed $570 billion worldwide in 2000. E-Exchange's management estimates that with the trading between participants vertically within the channel the total market size is excess of $1.1 trillion, of which $730 million is accessible to e-Exchange. E-Exchange further estimates that the IT industry distribution channel has over 200,000 manufacturers, distributors, and resellers worldwide.

The IT products market is characterized by short product life cycles and rapidly declining prices. Traditional purchasing methods in the IT products industry are inefficient, costly, and time-consuming for both the buyer and seller. Traditional procurement of IT products does not allow for the efficient handling of complex specifications, rapidly changing requirements, and time-sensitive supply methods. E-Exchange believes that the proprietary service platform it has developed provides a solution to the existing inefficiencies in the IT products market by allowing

- Buyers and sellers to find and negotiate with one another, easily and anonymously
- Buyers to efficiently manage an increased number of supplier relationships
- Sellers to derive increased volumes from their new and existing customers

Global IT Management Experience.   With extensive experience in both the manufacturing and distribution of IT products, e-Exchange's management understands the problems of the IT industry and the complexity of relationships among its participants. E-Exchange's management team contributes a balance of corporate and entrepreneurial skills, together with a sound knowledge of finance, marketing, and supply chain management. A strong management domain expertise has enabled the company to build a service platform that responds to the needs of its members.

Generating Liquidity.   E-Exchange has launched several initiatives to increase membership and create greater liquidity on its exchange. For instance, it actively pursues direct sales efforts, including building an internal sales force dedicated to telemarketing and participating in industry trade shows. In some geographic markets, the company intends to enter into revenue sharing and other forms of partnerships with experienced participants in the IT industry to increase use of the exchange.

Ultimately, e-Exchange expects to establish buying clubs and to pursue other marketing efforts that accelerate the growth of the exchange.

Value-Added Services Through Partnerships. E-Exchange is in discussions with a variety of globally recognized industry leaders to establish alliances in the logistics and procurement industries over a number of geographic markets and to drive adoption of its marketplace solution on a global basis. It has entered into agreements with several organizations including Citibank, a major logistics provider, and eccelerate.com that will provide financing, shipping, and accreditation services, respectively. E-Exchange plans to work with its partners to seamlessly integrate their customer interfaces and enterprise resource planning (ERP) systems that provide formats for computer-to-computer exchange of information used to automate corporate procurement processes. The company believes these partnerships will increase the value of e-Exchange by expanding its service offering to meet the full spectrum of its members' needs.

Multiple Revenue Streams. E-Exchange intends to derive revenues from a number of different sources. Ultimately, the company anticipates that its main source of revenue will be fees charged on transactions over the exchange. To initially promote liquidity, the company elected to waive these fees until the end of March 2000; however, initially the company had been charging a transaction fee of half of 1 percent of the gross transaction value. Over time, e-Exchange expects to generate revenue through fees charged on premium services such as customized search capabilities and editorial content, as well as advertising and click through links. e-Exchange also intends to package and sell, to the extent permitted by applicable law, market and usage information generated from the activity of its members on the exchange. This information includes data on pricing levels, transaction volumes, and supply-and-demand levels of specific products. The company further expects to generate revenues through revenue sharing arrangements with fulfillment partners. Finally, the company intends to generate fees from licensing its customized service platform to third parties seeking to apply e-Exchange's trading system to other industry verticals.

In May 2000 the company sold its first license to a South Korean consortium operating in the IT vertical for $250,000. In addition to these fees, e-Exchange has also taken a 10 percent equity stake, plus revenue sharing of any cross-border trade generated from this exchange.

Customized Service Platform. E-Exchange's customized service platform offers a powerful trading solution to all members of the IT industry distribution chain. As opposed to pure auction model, the e-Exchange solution supports traditional business practices such as negotiating the terms of transactions and permits multiparty negotiations. In addition, the e-Exchange platform offers new Internet-based enhancements and functionality such as automated searches and comparisons, real-time updates to product offerings and specifications, anonymity in dealings, and immediate access to global market participants regardless of geographic location. The company's customized service platform has been developed using the BroadVision system as a base. The company's database engine resides on its servers and is accessible by standard browsers. E-Exchange intends to leverage the knowledge and experience gained in building and running its IT exchange to enter other vertical markets in the future.

Business Strategy. The immediate business objective is to establish e-Exchange as the premier business-to-business ecommerce exchange in the IT products industry. In the medium term, its plan is to establish a series of global exchanges within other vertical marketplaces, by leveraging the e-Exchange service platform, technology, brand, and partners. E-Exchange will make direct contact with its members through direct sales and marketing team in order to "match" buyers and sellers and to promote trades. They intend to increase membership through a variety of marketing campaigns, such as telemarketing, direct and viral marketing, as well as online and traditional media advertising.

E-Exchange is also addressing the global market. In the IT industry, many parts and components are produced in Asia, whereas principal end-user markets are primarily located in North America and Europe. Consequently, to generate the necessary liquidity, it is essential for an IT industry exchange to establish a global presence and recruit members worldwide. E-Exchange is currently actively marketing e-exchange in the Singapore, Hong Kong, India, the United Kingdom, Taiwan, and Australia, and has recently opened offices in New York and Los Angeles. A key element of its customer service strategy is to provide a local solution to each market in which it operates by tailoring its services to suit regional conditions and by taking advantage of local industry knowledge. E-Exchange has recently acquired a 10 percent equity interest in a Korean joint venture to which it is licensing its global service platform.

Building a Robust Exchange from the Ground Up. A fundamental requirement for successfully conducting online ecommerce is to construct a secure, scalable, and robust service platform. E-Exchange has designed and constructed a service platform using hardware and software from high-quality suppliers such as BroadVision and Sun Microsystems, enabling secure transmission of confidential information over public networks. They are committed to maintaining a high level of system integrity and security to permit members to make trades on our exchange 24 hours per day, 7 days per week.

E-Exchange intends to be able to fulfill the entire spectrum of members' procurement, selling, and logistics needs by offering additional services, such as accreditation and ratings for members, financing for members' purchases and arrangements to facilitate payment, and shipping of products. E-Exchange anticipates introducing regular incremental upgrades and periodic major revisions to their proprietary service platform.

E-Exchange intends to leverage the knowledge and experience gained in building and running their IT exchange to enter into other vertical markets. The key value proposition they provide in entering other vertical markets is experience in establishing end-to-end solutions with third-party fulfillment providers. They are currently developing the next generation of their global service platform, which will be used to upgrade the services offered in the IT exchange and as a base for expanding into other vertical markets.

Industry-Backed Consortia—eHitex Case Study

eHitex, the High-Tech Exchange, is an e-Marketplace launched by some of the leading names in the global high-technology industry. Founding members include AMD, Compaq, Gateway, Hitachi, HP, Infineon, NEC, Quantum, Samsung, SCI Systems, Solectron, and Western Digital. eHitex will enable businesses to manage their supply chains more effectively, improve the delivery of products and services, and increase customer satisfaction.

Forrester Research estimates that approximately $600 billion in online business-to-business sales of high-tech components and parts will occur over the next few years, making it the world's largest e-Marketplace opportunity. EHitex's founding members are some of the world's largest buyers and suppliers of computer and electronics components and products. Individually and collectively, they have developed considerable expertise in efficient procurement and sales.

The exchange's end-to-end services will be open and available to all parties in the supply chain process, consumer and business electronics makers, contract manufacturers, suppliers, and distributors. All participants in this electronic marketplace will be able to manage a wide array of their e-procurement purchases and sales through this new exchange.

"The creation of such an exchange can improve supply chain efficiency tremendously through cost reduction, timely transactions, inventory savings, and higher-value services," said Dr. Hau Lee, professor of operations, information, and technology at Stanford Business School. "But most importantly, it will enable supply chain partners to fundamentally redesign their business processes and create new business opportunities from end to end. This is a major step toward a virtual economy for the high-tech industry."

In addition to delivering the traditional benefits of the Web, such as continuous global reach and open industry-standard interfaces, the new high-tech exchange is expected to:

- Lower manufacturing and purchasing transaction costs through process efficiencies
- Reduce levels of inventory throughout the entire supply chain by better matching supply and demand via the online marketplace
- Increase customer satisfaction by improving the ability to deliver products more quickly and predictably
- Provide expertise on supply chain "best practices" to help participants achieve better results from product design to customer delivery

eHitex will use best-in-class technology to deliver a variety of services to participants, including open sourcing, e-catalogs, auctions and dynamic pricing, supply planning, and logistics. It will acquire some of this capability from its founders, who have already developed services for efficient buying and selling over the Internet. The exchange will use this expertise to start delivering immediate value to all members.

eHitex went from concept to operations within ninety days. The founders plan to contribute resources and an initial total of $100 million to the new company and will have equal ownership in it. They also intend to use the exchange for their own supply chain activities, driving significant transaction volumes through it.

A full-time interim management team, composed of representatives from the founders, has been chartered to finalize the formation of the new company and launch the business.

Purpose. Though it started with the computer industry, eHitex will offer its services to telecommunications and consumer electronics, and extend its range of services to all participants. Starting with fundamental electronic transactions, the exchange will offer complete, end-to-end services from e-procurement through supply chain optimization and collaborative design services. It will offer services focused on procurement such as auctions, catalog management, information services, and administration (workflow, audience selection). In the near future, supply chain collaboration, advanced logistics, and collaborative product design services will also be available. The goal of the exchange is to bring savings and efficiency to every participant of the high-tech trading community whether they act as a buyer, seller, or both.

Principles.   eHitex is open and equally accessible to all buyers and sellers in computing and related industries, including original-equipment and contract-equipment manufacturers, suppliers, and distributors. Wherever possible, the exchange is committed to use open standards to link participants. It is also global, like the Internet and the high-tech industry it serves.

eHitex is an independent entity. Its founders act as shareholders only, not participating in day-to-day operations. No employee of a founding company serves on the Exchange's Board of Directors. Neither venture capitalist firms nor technology suppliers have equity positions in the firm. eHitex is exclusively of, by, and for the high-tech industry.

The exchange offers value, in the form of

- *Increased reach*—Access to new customers and suppliers and to alternative trading vehicles
- *Improved execution*—High-performance, nonstop Web-based access to an entire array of supply chain e-services with real-time interaction
- *Greater accuracy*—Improved demand and supply visibility to better meet customer requirements
- *Lower transaction costs*—Use of open, standards-based e-supply chain infrastructure, resulting in business process improvements
- *Simplification*—Improved communication and interactions among members of the exchange's community

Procurement Solutions.   eHitex offers procurement professionals a wide range of options for sourcing supply and buying contracted finished goods, electric assembles, and components, by simplifying the negotiation and sales processes and by streamlining RFQ (request for quote) bid processes. In addition, electronic procurement solutions dramatically reduce the time needed to secure products or bid contracts, and allow the company to reach far more suppliers, with far more competitive results. It offers a front-end procurement catalog and requisitioning tool with purchase order transaction capability. In cases of excess inventory liquidation, the exchange offers solutions that permit both rapid and low-cost approaches to liquidation, depending on the value of the inventory and the liquidity of the market.

The exchange also supports spot purchasing. Component or product shortages require quick solutions. If the market for a product is small or inefficient, a shortage will quickly drive up prices. The global reach of the High-Tech Exchange allows quick sourcing from suppliers world-wide, including even smaller suppliers. Inefficiency is reduced by including the maximum number of suppliers and by reaching them electronically, all at the same time.

Catalog-Based Procurement.   The High-Tech Exchange offers large and small suppliers the ability to post their products worldwide in online catalogs. While some of these suppliers may not be under a current contract with a company because of geographic issues, because of limited capacity, or because they cannot link through EDI (electronic data interchange), they are all worth a quick look when there is a shortage. For many smaller suppliers, such opportunities drive their participation in the exchange.

The primary advantages of catalog solutions for spot-market sourcing are as follows:

1. *Speed*—No extra time is needed to contact multiple vendors or even to set up an online auction.
2. *Cost*—Parts located in a supplier's online catalog may cost less than parts bought at auction.
3. *Comparison*—Online catalogs enable comparison shopping for common items with multiple suppliers.

When working with smaller or distant suppliers for the first time, carefully consider closing the transaction in escrow.

Catalog Services.   The High-Tech Exchange's Catalog Services are hosted or self-managed ecommerce applications to implement specific business processes, allowing member companies to manage orders and update their catalog content at the exchange using any Web browser. With these services, businesses can integrate directly to the exchange and provide their customers with real-time information on order status, pricing, and availability.

Catalog Services allow vendors to use real-time ecommerce functionality and secure Web access to electronic catalogs and databases, without the delay and cost usually associated with such systems.

Auction Services.   eHitex includes a large trading community of independent and franchised distributors, brokers, resellers, online resellers, white box makers, warranty service providers, and more. These are managed to ensure their integrity and reliability. The large variety of businesses in the bidding community results in better pricing. Further, the services enable businesses to set up auctions and reverse auctions that accurately mirror business rules.

All trading partners connected to the High-Tech Exchange are eligible for trading, whether buyers or suppliers. Usually, customers for Auction Services are large corporations. Once registered, a company is visible to all other participants in the trading community and can participate in auctions. In all likelihood, within a given company, conducting an auction will be limited to the designated, professional buyers and sellers. (The average employee is not expected to requisition items and would not have access to Auction Services.)

Open sourcing via auctions helps buyers drive down the cost of goods and services. On the other hand, sellers can promote special offers to preferred customers or liquidate merchandise among a large community of bidders. If a participant has preferred trading relationships already, forward auctions and reverse auctions can be conducted among a select group of participants—buyers or sellers. Otherwise, they can be open to all exchange participants. Either way, auctions improve productivity while reducing administrative costs and cycle time.

Buyers Benefit from Exchange Auctions.   Traditionally, buyer sourcing is handled by RFQs (requests for quote), RFPs (requests for proposal), or RFIs (requests for information) sent to suppliers via mail, telephone, fax, or EDI (electronic data interchange). This involves many manual tasks and hand-offs that can lead to mistakes or confusion. Using Exchange Auctions via the Internet, buyers reduce the cost of goods sourced by improving overall efficiency of the process and by establishing true market prices for products and services. Buyers benefit by sourcing from suppliers worldwide. Negotiation cycles are shorter. And buyers have new sourcing for hard-to-find or discounted items from surplus or excess inventory. Sellers can liquidate obsolete and excess inventory or undesirable merchandise cost-effectively. They gain access to a bigger market of buyers. Previously, this type of liquidation was handled by third-party liquidation services that sell items at supplier's cost. With Exchange Auctions, sellers maintain better control of unwanted merchandise because the seller directly defines the minimum price and terms. So, they realize sales prices of 20 to 30 percent above cost. A buyer can submit a purchase order for a trade in an auction to the seller. Subsequent documents such as invoices, as well as shipping and payment, can all be handled through the Auction Service. This way, the auction becomes a complete and seamless transaction between trading partners who may never have done business before.

Channel Solutions. The High-Tech Exchange gives sales and marketing professionals a new electronic channel, extending their reach to customers throughout the global high-tech buying community. Existing channels can also profit from the flexibility and efficiency of an electronic exchange to improve the speed and accuracy of their orders. The exchange's standardized transaction procedures and browser-based interface make it easy for larger and smaller firms to conduct profitable business with one another, without burdening smaller firms with expensive EDI solutions.

Large companies can use the exchange to receive orders directly from the Internet, opening up specialty markets and changing formerly unprofitable business into a welcome improvement to revenues, margins, and profits. In the special case of excess finished goods inventory (FGI), the exchange allows rapid and low-cost liquidation to a global customer base, while minimizing conflict in existing sales and distribution channels.

Refurbished, end-of-life, and lease-return computer products retain significant value. However, if these goods are sold through the same channel as current products, they may cannibalize sales or introduce price competition, reducing overall margins. When excess finished goods are likely to move slowly, or when it is difficult to assemble a reasonable number of potential buyers over the term of the auction, the exchange offers tools to create an online surplus catalog. Viewers of the catalog may be limited to those specified by the company (for example, brokers and specialty resellers) to limit interference with current channels.

The exchange's Auction Services offer a quick, simple method for liquidating excess finished goods with minimal impact on current channels. Auction buying communities typically include brokers and resellers who buy excess products and sell them in secondary channels that seldom overlap those for new products.

Escrow Services. Escrow is a Web-based service, backed by licensed escrow agents, that protects buyers and sellers in an online transaction by placing the transaction payment into a third-party escrow account. Escrow is required for all eHitex secondary market auctions.

Revenue Models. Revenues will come from transaction fees as well as value-added services such as consulting and information services. Exchange fees will be competitively priced—given the value of these services, the exchange expects strong participation.

eHitex will be a buyer's and seller's marketplace. In the same way as leading financial exchanges, the exchange will provide a confidential and secure way of transacting business for both buyers and sellers, to-gether with information and other services to support those transactions. eHitex is committed to integrate its systems seamlessly with its partici-pants' procurement, manufacturing, and logistics systems. The exchange has standardized on XML and is working actively with RosettaNet to standardize its supply chain interface.

The exchange uses open and adopted standards, such as RosettaNet, which have broad support from information-technology and high-tech supply chain companies. Eight of the exchange's founders are active RosettaNet Board members, and the exchange itself is working with RosettaNet to make those standards universal.

The exchange ensures confidentiality and security of participants' transactions by providing a trusted place for high-tech companies to transact business. Consistent with its "best-in-class" approach to tech-nology, eHitex is working with top security, authentication, and industry experts to develop an infrastructure that exceeds its participants' require-ments. The exchange will also offer options including anonymous trans-actions and bidder selection to ensure transaction confidentiality where requested.

Analysis of the Independent and Industry-Backed Models

As can be seen from the preceding review of the independent (e-Exchange.com) model and the industry-backed consortia (eHitex), they are both aimed directly at the same high-technology industry, with a focus on optimizing the procurement process as well as streamlining the supply chain process. On the surface it may seem that these two ex-changes are directly competing for a piece of the $570 billion annual IT marketplace. To some extent they are, but upon a closer look there are some significant differences in the models.

The e-Exchange raised approximately $20 million in funds pri-marily through private placements. The eHitex Exchange raised $100 million from 15 high-tech industry companies. E-Exchange.com is well positioned to support the fragmented distribution channel, with over 6,500 high-tech distributors across 50 countries that are now a part of the e-Exchange global network. eHitex is well positioned to begin sup-porting the 15 equity partners of their exchange who represent a com-bined purchasing community of $250 billion in annual spending on direct and indirect procurement. Both of these communities represent a signif-icant portion of the overall IT marketplace. The market focus is distinctly different for each of these models. It is possible that both can survive and thrive in the marketplace and perhaps even collaborate to solve industry pain points from the manufacturing through the distribution channel to the end users.

Leverage the Global Ebusiness Network

Winning in the twenty-first century will require mastering the art of global networking. The millions of individuals and companies that are connected and interactively communicating on the Web represent an emerging global ebusiness network that impacts business from multiple points including all levels of customer contact, demand forecasting, product/service design and production, procurement, logistics, and lifetime customer care. Winning in the networked economy is a new corporate imperative. Achieving this imperative requires a complex holistic strategy that addresses the company culture. These two case studies outlined in the preceding sections represent typical examples of the trend in the e-Marketplace industry to develop both independent neutral exchanges, as well as industry-owned and -backed consortia.

Can Independent Exchanges and Consortia Survive Together?

The consortia are shaking the markets up considerably—even just the press releases announcing the intent to form an industry consortium has shaken the valuations of many independent e-Marketplaces. Some consortia will stumble over their size and lack of ability to politically operate a cooperative business with competition. Others will in fact cooperate to solve real industry supply chain problems and leverage their aggregated power throughout the value chain. Independent exchanges are well suited to serve the fragmented portions of the value chain, which are represented by global distributors and resellers as well as the smaller suppliers. These industry players are fragmented by size and geography and will receive great leverage, cost efficiencies, and productivity enhancements through association with independent exchanges. Coexistence can very definitely be maintained by the industry consortia and the independent exchanges. In fact, if the business models are worked out properly, it will be possible for not only coexistence but also cooperation. The two seemingly competitive ventures could band together to serve their respective markets and sectors and support each other's value propositions. The market opportunity is huge. There is room for value to be delivered by both models.

Information Will Replace Inventory

The growth of global e-Marketplaces offers unprecedented transparency
to the industries that they serve. This transparency will have the economic impact of rationalizing prices and driving down the price that
participants will pay for an e-Marketplace to conduct a transaction. Inventory is the devil in the supply chain. Shortages and excesses in inventory can generally be tied back to lack of timely and accurate information exchange between the buying community and the supplying
community.

One of the single largest opportunities facing e-market makers today is to add value to their communities by capturing, creating, and
disseminating highly customized information. The transaction services
that many of the early e-Marketplaces are building their business models
on are a fleeting revenue model. The transaction services do have their
value in building critical mass and early moves toward liquidity. But the
long-term significance of the transaction is not the revenue stream that
it generates. The long-term significance is in the information that can be
captured related to the transactions. Once this information is captured,
knowledge services can be created about specific industry trends, buying
habits, demand forecasts, and so on. Ultimately this information will be
converted into revenue. Thus, the three C's of information—Capture,
Creation, and Conversion—provide a foundation for value creation. The
basic principles can be applied to any industry. The e-Marketplaces
should be fiercely focused on information capture, creation of knowledge
bases, and conversion of knowledge into revenue streams.

Developing an Ebusiness Infrastructure

Building an ebusiness infrastructure is a topic worthy of a book by itself.
This section attempts to provide an executive overview of the key business process, technology options, and success strategies that are being
deployed today. It will review perspectives from the technology community represented by STC, as well as the research and analysts community represented by Jupiter Communications (NetMarketMakers.com)
and a financial and technology perspective from Lehman Brothers.

Business Imperatives Should Drive the Ebusiness Infrastructure

The optimized business processes and corporate vision should drive the
technology decisions. Far too often, technology drives business and this
leads to a number of problems fairly quickly. Usually in larger organi-

zations, individual business units of a company are frantically installing technologies to solve their business problems or to chase new opportunities. More often than not, they adopt point solutions that do not integrate easily with one another, which results in a great deal of waste and redundancy. This is not conducive to building an ebusiness infrastructure. It leads to lost time and money and often to a very disjointed customer experience.

It is understandable why this occurs in large enterprises. Frequently the management of the business unit is frustrated with slow executive decision making. Or, they fail to get direction from the executive management team but proceed anyway because time-to-market pressures strongly suggest immediate action. Usually e-Marketplace go-to-market teams take one of three approaches: they build, they outsource, or they adopt a hybrid strategy:

- *Building "in-house"*—In this approach, the team takes the full infrastructure design, build, manage, and update responsibility in-house and executes either a build-from-tools approach or a combination of best-of-breed solutions. This is by far the most costly and time-consuming option, but for certain businesses, it may be the best choice. If the company's ebusiness infrastructure offers a significant competitive advantage because of its proprietary and leading-edge nature, or the company's in-house resources are far superior to anything commercially available on the market, this approach makes sense. These situations are rare, but they do occur.

- *Outsourcing*—In this approach, after reviewing the business drivers and mapping them to internal capabilities, the team then considers time-to-market. One option is to outsource the ebusiness infrastructure to a partner or a series of partners who can help to execute in Internet time. Keep in mind that this option still requires a fairly extensive IT and management oversight on the outsourced operations. It may also require some internal redundancy or mirroring of systems for company operational security.

- *Hybrid infrastructure*—A hybrid infrastructure combines the best of what the company does internally with an outsourced strategy to develop contracted partnerships. Hybrid models work best when the outsourced partner offers higher levels of security, faster time to market, and service-level agreements (SLAs).

Remember, even if a choice is made to outsource services, it is still a company's responsibility to manage and ensure that the services are being provided properly, updated, securely managed, and backed up. Many companies are developing some redundancy into these relationships as an added security level that these operations will remain stable. Also look carefully into the SLAs; find out what portions are being guaranteed by the company's direct relationship with the vendor and which in turn they themselves are outsourcing. Ask to see the SLAs that they have in place with their providers. They cannot give better SLAs than they are getting from their providers. Determine which portions of the infrastructure support the core business. Then determine which portions of the infrastructure are considered intellectual property, and balance the decisions.

Objectivity Is Critical

The above-mentioned infrastructure decisions are not new. They reflect the same decisions that the business community has been addressing for years. The difference today is that the decisions need to be made not from an internal business process point of view but from an external member of the "networked society" point of view. If the company infrastructure does not address their ability to interoperate with multiple global buying networks, supplier networks, and enterprise-to-enterprise collaboration, then there will be significant business sustainability problems. It is not overstating the situation to say that if the company has not already begun to implement a strategy that leverages its resources both digitally and physically and provides a major competitive advantage in the new Internet economy, then it may be obsolete. This is not to say that the company will die overnight, but if the business model does not change and the infrastructure stays internally focused, there is a risk of losing it all.

The good news is that technology is advancing at such a rapid pace that there are many opportunities to leapfrog competition with the right business and technology strategy. The bad news is that so does the competition.

The Right Management Team and Business Model Are Critical

Technologies are advancing rapidly and are being developed every day to answer business requirements. It is more imperative to have the right management team and a solid business model worked out before beginning the infrastructure design and execution. Bet on the right management team over the right technology or even business model every time. The right management team will know how to adjust both the business models and the technology platforms. The old adage that the best technology never wins is fairly true. It is the best management team and marketing engine that frequently drives success. However, today it is not practical to build business strategies without integrating a technology strategy into the plan. They are now one unified strategy and execution plan.

Perspective

NetMarketMakers

This NetMarketMakers.com section is intended as a guide for managers who are presently planning for entry into ecommerce, either as marketplace hosts or as enrolled tenants in one or more marketplaces. It details some of the pitfalls and offers constructive guidance for implementing the appropriate technological infrastructure as the enterprise prepares to enter this new and promising arena. Visit the companion Web site for this book at www.netmarketmakers.com/b2bstrategies. Here there will be updates to this book, as well as new additions to the topics covered. The NetMarketMakers.com Web site is a rich resource for the latest information on B2B e-Marketplaces.

The emergence of an "Internet economy" is unarguable: Explosive growth in net-based buying, selling, and customer service operations has radically realigned traditional buyer-seller relationships. Consumers now shop the world, enjoying unprecedented opportunities for price and product comparison, often completely bypassing the local storefront retailers who once defined their shopping horizons.

As sweeping as these changes have been, they are rapidly being dwarfed by the Internet's impact on business-to-business commercial operations. Sensing the potential for streamlining and automating product information transfer, price negotiations, order entry, shipping data, and billing and collection cycles, many enterprises are eagerly embracing the electronic marketplace model. The model calls for the aggregation of catalogs and other buy/sell information at a central online location, with open access to all enrolled users via the Internet. Some of the Internet entrepreneurs who are embracing this new marketplace model include Global 2000 companies, purchasing consortia, large distributors, franchises, trade associations, and third-party service providers.

The Internet will, perhaps, have its strongest impact on the conduct of business-to-business commerce. To date, commerce processes—the critical links between buyers and sellers—have remained basically unchanged. Faxes, phones calls, and endless paper trails continue to clog the communication channels between businesses, creating inefficiencies at every point in the commerce chain. Now, the Internet offers innovative new ways to streamline commerce processes, reduce costs, and increase revenue. The opportunities are so large that Forrester Research estimates that business-to-business Internet commerce will skyrocket from approximately $43 billion in 1998 to more than $800 billion by 2002.

As illustrated in Figure 8-3, the emerging Internet economy is forcing companies to shift their focus from internal back-office processes to external commerce processes that automate interaction and collaboration among customers, suppliers, and even competitors. With this shift come several related changes, including a move from EDI- to Internet protocol-based communication, an evolution from client/server to network applications, and a shift from ERP (enterprise resource planning) to a new generation of commerce management applications.

Enterprises are rapidly recognizing the opportunities inherent in this shift. Throughout the 1990s, companies primarily focused on reengineering internal business processes, using client/server computing technologies and integrated ERP systems to streamline back-office operations. Today, as the flurry of Y2K and ERP activity subsides, companies find themselves with a wealth of available IT resources and a stack of reports highlighting the importance of the Internet. These companies are

Figure 8-3. *Business Process Shift*

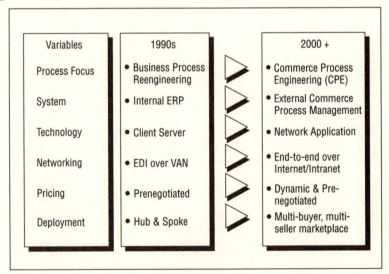

Business Process Shift

now asking themselves how they can "dot-com" their business models and avoid being "out-Amazoned" by their competitors. Today's challenge is to understand the competitive changes that will occur within the Internet economy, to anticipate the various new business models that will be developed and to adopt the right technology to support the rapidly changing landscape. Perhaps most importantly, businesses must understand how buyers and sellers will come together in new ways via digital marketplaces and exchanges.

For business-to-business commerce, the Internet tears down geographical boundaries, providing buyers with access to new suppliers and opening new channels of distribution for sellers. It dramatically accelerates the speed of commerce, increasing the rate at which companies must disseminate information and process transactions. In addition, it forms entirely new Internet-based markets by implementing new methods of dynamic trade, such as online auctions. In short, the Internet creates fundamental changes for all participants in the commerce chain.

Regardless of whether it is seen as opportunity or challenge, the Internet will reconstruct the commerce chain, changing market models at every point in the process and impacting all participants.

The Evolution of Business-to-Business Commerce Models

The emergence of the Internet economy has resulted in an accelerated evolution of commerce models. Early adopters (both buyers and sellers) have experimented with a variety of new business-to-business commerce models, technologies, and application designs. Examples have included online supplier catalogs, buyer-hosted e-procurement front ends, OBI (Open Buying Internet standard)-based systems, push technologies, and HTML parsing tools. At the same time, there has been a growing demand for new standards to facilitate the exchange of information, catalog content, and transactions between buyers and sellers. While the methods have been numerous and complex, the underlying goal has remained the same: to bring buyers and sellers together with an automated flow of information and transactions, while still supporting individual business and contractual relationships between trading partners.

First- and second-generation commerce solutions providers have fallen short of this goal. They have limited their focus to either the buy side or the sell side of the equation, without truly understanding how to bring buyers and sellers together. This lopsided view of the commerce process has usually resulted in one participant (the buyer or seller) inappropriately dictating proprietary solutions or standards to the other.

And, in most cases, this strategy did not scale. Perhaps the best way to understand the need for digital marketplaces is to examine the evolution of Internet commerce solutions to date.

First Generation: Sell-Side Solutions

Suppliers created first-generation sell-side solutions to lower the cost of sales by automating the order entry and fulfillment process. These solutions aimed to create an online "storefront" that stayed open 24 hours a day, offered the latest inventory, and enabled self-service ordering and tracking. In short, suppliers tried to capitalize on the Internet's potential by bringing their existing business relationships and processes online.

Unfortunately, suppliers soon discovered that most corporate procurement organizations (who control a majority of business-to-business expenditures) were unwilling to permit shopping across different supplier Web sites without regard to vendor relationships, pricing and financing terms, or prenegotiated company contracts. Additionally, customized supplier sites often required customers to learn unique passwords and procedures. While they found limited sell-side solutions unsatisfactory, corporate buyers recognized the power of the new online medium and soon began to explore new ways of applying similar techniques, utilizing their corporate intranets.

Second Generation: Buy-Side Solutions

Focused on cutting costs within a single enterprise, second-generation electronic procurement applications operated as a browser-based front end for back-office ERP and legacy purchasing systems. They allowed corporate procurement organizations to combine multiple supplier catalogs into a "universal" enterprise catalog and to deploy self-service requisitioning and order processing to the user desktop. Unlike supplier-hosted catalogs, these solutions allowed companies to deploy their proprietary processes and procedures while aggregating enterprisewide expenditures across a consistent supplier and product portfolio.

Second Generation: Buy-Side Model

The success of early buy-side procurement adopters, such as Raytheon Systems Company and Nippon Telegraph and Telephone Corporation (NTT), demonstrates the dramatic cost savings that can be realized with online solutions. By using a buy-side procurement application, Raytheon has reduced their cost per purchase order from more than $100 to less than $3. In November 1998, the Aberdeen Group released a report stating that organizations using buy-side e-procurement applications reduced their processing costs by an average of 70 percent per order. At first glance, the buy-side market appears to be fueled for meteoric growth. However, things are not always as simple as they seem.. Implementing leading-edge e-procurement solutions requires a detailed understanding of many new technologies, such as network application architectures, catalog content management strategies, ERP integration methods, and dynamic data interchange standards. Unfortunately, the resources and expertise to implement these systems are not within the reach of many of today's enterprises, especially medium-sized and small businesses.

So, while the implementation of stand-alone buy-side solutions may work for today's largest and most technically sophisticated companies, it does not meet the needs of the other 95 percent of buyers along the commerce chain. These companies cannot afford to aggregate catalog content, to link to individual suppliers, or to develop comprehensive Internet commerce applications themselves. Instead, they need a third-party "hosted" marketplace that brings together their suppliers and other, similar buyers into an organized trading community.

Next Generation: Digital Marketplaces

Digital marketplaces and exchanges offer the next generation of Internet commerce solutions. Unlike single-sided solutions, they are specifically designed to enable multibuyer/multiseller interaction and collaboration. They provide a common trading hub, where multiple buyers and sellers can come together and conduct commerce without compromising individual processes and relationships among the participants. Marketplaces can be created or "hosted" at any point along the commerce chain. Key examples of typical market hosts and models include:

- A large distributor who seeks to automate processes among several buyers, suppliers, or manufacturers
- A franchise or trade association that wants to aggregate its members' orders from approved suppliers by providing online procurement services
- A new market maker that is trying to replace existing distribution channels by offering online information and services to a specific industry
- A third-party service provider who wants to create a common marketplace by providing hosted procurement services to a specific set of suppliers and their customers

The formation of new digital marketplaces and exchanges will change the way we think about business-to-business commerce and will play a major role in the growth of the Internet economy. The Gartner

Group predicts that by 2001 70 percent of distributors who operate online will reap more than 80 percent of their sales through online marketplaces.

It is clear that that the formation of these shared marketplaces is necessary for Internet commerce to reach its full potential. A useful analogy can be drawn between Internet commerce and other, more mature services, such as electrical power and water utilities. There was a time when, if water was needed, a well was drilled. Water eventually moved to a shared network model, where a number of providers tapped a major water supply and delivered it to end users through a common network and delivery mechanism. A similar model is developing within electronic commerce, where many different distributors, buying groups, and new service providers are developing shared marketplaces, or portals, that deliver online commerce services to customers through the Internet and browser. Equally important, the creation of digital marketplaces enables innovative new methods of dynamic exchange. Many first-generation solutions are little more than Web front ends for traditional business applications. They have done little to advance commerce to the new Internet paradigm. Conversely, digital marketplaces create entirely new methods of commerce, such as online sourcing, auctions, and negotiations. They also enable trading communities to share common information and knowledge more easily.

While the specific business model and associated benefits will differ across marketplace models, a general set of core benefits can be recognized. The following list outlines some of the key benefits for each of the marketplace participants:

- Provides new marketing and distribution channel to customers
- Provides better customer service through online interaction
- Provides more complete product information to buyer
- Automates order and fulfillment processes
- Lowers overall operational costs
- Protects current role or creates new role within the commerce chain
- Establishes high "value-add" in digital economy
- Increases service levels to existing customers
- Leverages current information about customers
- Provides access to more information and suppliers
- Lowers up-front costs and risks
- Provides access to more information and suppliers
- Provides access to secondary and excess supply auctions
- Provides a more comprehensive solution

Figure 8-4.

Benefits of a Digital Marketplace		
To Seller	To Market Host	To Buyer
• Provides new marketing and distribution channel to customers • Provides better customer service through online interaction • Provides more complete product information to buyer • Automates order & fulfillment processes • Lowers overall operational costs	• Protects current role or creates new role within the commerce chain • Establishes high "value-add" in digital economy • Increases service levels to existing customers • Leverages current information and customers • Provides access to more information and suppliers	• Lowers up-front costs and risks • Provides access to more information and suppliers • Provides access to secondary and excess supply auctions • Provides a more comprehensive solution • Eliminates ongoing software upgrades & maintenance costs • Utilizes outsourced expertise

- Eliminates ongoing software upgrades and maintenance costs
- Utilizes outsourced expertise

Figure 8-4 shows further benefits of the digital marketplace for sellers, market hosts, and buyers.

New Digital Marketplace Models

Perhaps the easiest way to differentiate between marketplace-based solutions and sell-side/buy-side solutions is to examine the different marketplace models that are being inserted at all points in the commerce chain. They generally fall into three categories: procurement marketplaces, vertical marketplaces, and ebusiness portals. Each of these marketplace models supports different business models and functions along the commerce chain.

Procurement Marketplaces

Procurement marketplaces are buyer-hosted. They streamline corporate or group purchasing while empowering independent divisions, partners, or companies to maintain independent buying processes and supplier relationships. Key targets for this market include Global-2000 companies with multiple autonomous divisions, franchises, trade associations, and purchasing consortia.

Procurement Marketplace Model. Nippon Telephone & Telegraph (NTT) in Japan provides an excellent example of a procurement marketplace. They have built an internal marketplace to aggregate their enterprisewide expenditures for maintenance, repair, and operations (MRO) goods and related products. Because NTT is made up of several autonomous business units and subsidiaries, they required a solution that

Figure 8-5. *Procurement Marketplace Model*

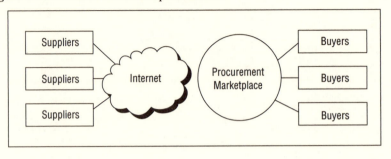

would allow them to easily create a central catalog of approved products, suppliers, and contracts. At the same time, they needed to enable individual operating units to establish their independent processes, workflow, and user profiles. A homogenous buy-side front-end did not meet these requirements. Figure 8-5 shows the procurement marketplace model.

A major hotel chain provides another basic example. This company wanted to aggregate procurement across both their owned and franchised hotel properties. They decided that the best way to do this was to host a centrally managed procurement marketplace, which would provide access to common suppliers, products, and in some cases, aggregated contracts. At the same time, they needed to enable the independently owned hotels to set up their own view of the marketplace, which matched their specific processes and buying relationships.

Vertical Marketplaces

Vertical marketplaces have sprung up in numerous industries and are, perhaps, the most widely understood example of new digital marketplace models. They generally focus on a single industry that is suffering a critical inefficiency in distribution or sales. They use the marketplace as a strategy to bring buyers and sellers together. Depending on the industry or market, they either automate existing distribution channels or break those channels by creating new exchanges. They thrive in fragmented markets that lack dominant suppliers or buyers. By exploiting a combination of technology and deep expertise in a particular industry, they can eliminate industry-specific problems, such as inventory levels, forecasting, or logistics, for both buyers and sellers.

Vertical Marketplace Model. Vertical marketplaces support industry-specific supply chains by providing new distribution channels for raw materials, secondary inventory, and supplies. Transactions are streamlined, information flows freely, inventory and sales costs are reduced—and the marketplace host generates revenue. Major distributors, resellers, and new market makers typically host these vertical marketplaces, and they tend to fall into one of three groups: virtual distributors, exchanges, and enablers.

Virtual distributors attempt to replace and improve some portion of the existing distribution channel. A good example is Chemdex, which has managed to eliminate as much as five hours a week from the process of product searching in the pharmaceutical and biotech industry. Rather than leafing through hundreds of vendors' catalogs, research scientists can turn to this marketplace, where the catalog data have been aggregated into a one-stop, online comparison-shopping venue. The online search cuts across all vendor catalogs—making the search easier for the researchers—while simultaneously reducing the vendors' cost to reach those scientists. In short, the virtual distributor cuts the cost to reach all customers, large and small, with product and price information. By integrating a catalog once into a marketplace, rather than separately with each customer, the marketplace enables a host of benefits for all parties involved.

Exchanges seize on loose and inefficient broker networks, using the Internet's ability to eliminate barriers of geography. The online solution creates effective transparency of distribution, price, and inventory. Another example, MetalSite, is a steel industry exchange that, for the first time, lets buyers post their demand for products while seeing the entire inventory currently available. The marketplace reduces cost, in time and money, since procurement extends beyond the enterprise to all marketplace buyers and sellers. The marketplace also enables small- and medium-sized companies to realize the benefits of reporting on purchases, which were previously available only to large enterprises.

Enablers facilitate the integration of an enterprise into a central platform. Bringing additional buying power into the marketplace spurs vendor participation, expands sources and selection, and reduces prices by increasing competition. These markets offer a tool that existing distributors or brokers can pass along to their customers. Collabria, for example, has created a market in the commercial printing industry among the corporate buyers of printing projects, print brokers, and commercial printers. Because print brokers know which local printers have idle presses, as well as which printers have the best prices and the capability to print a particular job, they add value and retain their place in the commerce chain. The online market enables the broker to speed up the matching process, while the sophisticated software offered in this online

Figure 8-6. *Vertical Marketplace Model*

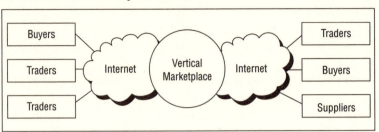

market—available on the customer's desktop through a Web browser—eliminates errors in the prepress process and sends the job to the printer electronically and instantly.

Figure 8-6 shows the vertical marketplace model.

Ebusiness Portals

Ebusiness portals, sometimes referred to as "horizontal" marketplaces, are hosted by trusted third parties and provide online buying and selling services to a set of identified clients. Typically, the goal of the portal provider is to extend their brand identity to the Internet and capitalize on new revenue-generating opportunities. They bring powerful assets to the game, by leveraging core competencies in facilitating commerce. There they can find plentiful business relationships and opportunities for branding or for positioning themselves as financial agents and trusted third parties in these growing online marketplaces.

Trusted third parties that often host ebusiness portals include large financial institutions, utilities, telecommunications companies, IT service providers, and commerce service providers. They provide the financial and operational benefits of online buying and selling to a specific customer base.

Ebusiness Portal Model. The world of online financing illustrates this trend. One major U.S. financial institution has recently initiated the development of a purchase card marketplace where its borrowers and other customers can buy and sell from each other. A credit card company has established a marketplace for its small business card holders. A large utility is using its market clout to establish and bring vendors into an industry-specific procurement marketplace for itself, along with smaller utilities. By pooling their buying power through a co-op, they cut both cost and time from the buying process.

Digital Marketplace Solution Requirements

Handling diverse user types, business processes, and trading relationships within a multibuyer/multiseller environment requires a significantly higher level of functionality and performance than offered by first-generation sell-side or second-generation buy-side solutions. To date, most new market makers have been forced to build their sites from scratch, using an assortment of technologies and development strategies. In many cases, companies have built their sites, only to discover that, while they look good, they do not scale, are difficult to maintain, and are nearly impossible to modify quickly as commercial activity requirements shift.

Today, for the first time, market makers are presented with a "build versus buy" scenario. While there are few, if any, offerings that provide a complete out-of-the-box solution, some software vendors are offering a comprehensive platform for developing and deploying digital marketplaces and exchanges. These platforms offer integrated application functionality and can be customized, configured, and branded to meet specific marketplace requirements. Before making a buy decision, it is important to separate the wheat from the chaff. Many software providers have attempted to repackage first-generation sell-side and second-generation buy-side systems into marketplace solutions. While this approach may work for demonstration, unknowing customers may find themselves with a solution that cannot effectively manage their complex marketplace scenarios or be scaled to meet their high-end performance requirements.

When looking at marketplace and exchange solutions, it is important to evaluate four key areas of design and functionality:

1. Performance and scalability
2. Application functionality
3. Flexibility and manageability
4. Customizability and extensibility

While it is outside the scope of this section to provide a detailed list of requirements for each of these areas, the following sections provide a high-level overview.

Performance and Scalability

Performance and scalability can be evaluated by looking at three key variables. First, can the application be effectively deployed across a limited-bandwidth network while requiring only that a browser be installed at the desktop? Second, can the solution be scaled to meet the peak user loads and transaction levels of the marketplace? Third, does the solution provide 24/7 reliability and fault tolerance?

Network Connectivity and Performance. Digital marketplaces must be capable of being deployed to a multitude of remote users over dial-up connections as slow as 28.8 Kbps. In addition, they must be able to work across a public network without sacrificing security or limiting access through tightly controlled corporate firewalls.

To meet these requirements, several key design features should be considered. First, the solution must run a true thin-client application, meaning that no software, other then a standard browser, should reside on the user's desktop. The client should be effectively downloadable at logon, even across low-speed dial-up connections. In general, this means that the client application should not exceed a maximum size of 500 KB. Solutions that utilize 1 MB-plus clients, which may work over a T3 intranet connection, are not viable in a distributed marketplace environment. (*Note:* It is not uncommon to find commerce applications with clients as large as 4 to 5 MB in size. These solutions are essentially client/server applications running over IP networks and are not considered true distributed network-based applications.) Buyers and suppliers from many different companies, all with varying security and firewall configurations, will need to access the marketplace. To work in these environments, marketplace software must run over or "tunnel through" standard HTTP ports and not be dependent on accessing specialized ports.

A final key factor is the amount of traffic that is passed between the client and the server when executing transactions. For example, in pure HTML-based solutions, the entire page is refreshed every time an action is taken. This can result in a huge amount of network traffic. In applet or dynamic HTML-based solutions, only changed data fields are passed to the server. In this model, the amount of data passed between the client and the server is significantly less, resulting in lower network traffic and faster response times.

Scalability and Reliability. Most client/server applications are designed for professional users within a single company, typically equating to no more than 1,000 simultaneous users. With the introduction of browser-based, self-service applications (such as e-procurement front ends), the concurrent user base can mushroom to several thousand if the enterprise is large. Marketplace software demands an even greater level of scalability. It must be able to support tens of thousands of concurrent users, while providing rapid response times and 24/7 reliability. In gen-

eral, the only way to effectively ensure this level of scalability and reliability is to design an application that supports load balancing across
multiple processors and machines. This is most effectively achieved by
utilizing new Internet application servers, such as BEA's WebLogic, Oracle's Application Server, IBM's WebSphere, or one of the other high-
end application servers.

As transaction volume increases, utilizing an application server will
allow the market maker to incrementally add processors and machines
without hitting a top-end limit. (*Note:* While many applications may
advertise their ability to run on these platforms, only a few utilize a true
component-based models capable of performing multiprocessor/multi-
machine load balancing.)

Additional benefits of running on an application server include the
performance and reliability achieved by running on multiple machines.
In a multinode configuration, the application server will automatically
distribute workloads to the most available machine, ensuring that optimal
performance is maintained. In addition, if one machine goes down, the
application server will automatically shift workloads to another machine—ensuring maximum reliability.

Broad Application Functionality

Unlike one-dimensional buy-side or sell-side systems, marketplace and
exchange solutions must support both the buying and selling processes
within the end-to-end commerce chain. This includes all commerce processes, from desktop requisitioning, cataloging, and purchase order management to acknowledgement, fulfillment, and online billing.

All transaction processes should be easy to use and should allow
both buyers and sellers to set up standard defaults, such as accounting
codes, shipping locations, and billing addresses. Transactions should
work in a symmetrical and integrated fashion, so that the commerce
process can be executed seamlessly between buyers and sellers.

For example, when a buyer generates an order, the system should
enable the seller to generate an order acknowledgment. If a supplier
sends an advance shipping notice, the buyer should be able to track the
location of the item in the shipping process. Finally, the solution should
provide open interface points for all core transactions (purchase order,
receipt, invoice, and so on), so that they can be easily integrated with
back-end systems or passed between trading partners. While it is unlikely
that any of the packaged software applications will explicitly meet each
market maker's functional requirements, the application design should
provide a strong set of baseline functions that can be easily customized

by the market maker. This approach will ensure that the market maker does not have to encode common application functions, such as requisition forms and receiving processes from scratch. While it is impossible to review all areas, other key areas of functionality to be considered include the following.

Catalog Management and Search. A key component of any marketplace application is the catalog search engine that drives a large percentage of marketplace processing. There are many different search metaphors and catalog tools. When selecting a solution, you should consider what types of commodities will be traded and what type of catalog search is most appropriate. Key factors include ease of catalog use, and support for multiple search modes and varied data formats, such as images and drawings. Because different marketplaces will have different search requirements, and because search engine technology is developing so quickly, ensuring that the platform separates the catalog from other pricing and processing functionality is extremely important. This allows other third-party search engines to be easily plugged in when catalog requirements or technologies change. It is equally important to ensure that the application provides tools for aggregating and rationalizing content into a single catalog view. These tools come in several different formats, but their underlying goal is to provide a flexible means of accessing and aggregating multisupplier content into a consistent catalog structure. Marketplace solutions should support both centralized and distributed catalog management.

Cross-Enterprise Communication. In all marketplaces, transactions need to move efficiently between buyers and suppliers. While in some cases, this information may be viewed online through the browser, it will usually need to be passed in one of many data formats. In general, marketplace solutions should be capable of supporting all common integration protocols, including fax, email, EDI, XML, and other digital data interchange formats. Solutions that are overly dependent on a single technology or pseudo-standard cannot effectively support diverse trading communities.

Dynamic Trade Functionality. Dynamic marketplaces should be designed with an understanding of the new online processes and interfaces that are possible on the Internet. In evaluating marketplace solutions, decision makers should look for baseline functionality in areas such as online quote and bid processing, online negotiations, and dynamic auctions.

Reporting and Analysis.   The marketplace system should provide integrated tools that allow buyers, suppliers, and market hosts to check on their outstanding transactions and activity. It should also provide some level of baseline reporting capability for analyzing marketplace expenditure and performance. In some cases, marketplace solutions may include more advanced multidimensional decision support systems. All of the query and reporting capabilities should be purely Web-based. In most cases, marketplace platforms will utilize best-of-breed reporting tools to meet these requirements.

Flexibility and Manageability

Digital marketplaces traditionally span large, diverse trading communities. Within a given marketplace, there will normally be a hierarchy of high-level tenants and associated users. For example, Company A may be a buying tenant within the marketplace. Inside Company A, there may be several different divisions, and each division may have several different types of end-users who are authorized to access the marketplace.

Considering the variety of buying tenants, selling tenants, and marketplace administrators that make up a given marketplace, managing this hierarchy of tenants and users becomes extremely complex. In many cases, it may not be possible for the market host or administrator to centrally manage every user. It may be more effective to take a decentralized approach, in which the marketplace host registers high-level tenants, and then empowers them to register and manage their own users. Regardless of the approach, it is essential that marketplace and exchange software provide intuitive and flexible tools for managing complex hierarchies.

Within each trading community, there will be a variety of user types, including customers, suppliers, and market administrators. In addition, some users will be experienced, while others may be casual or inexperienced. Normally, a single static interface is insufficient to support this diverse user community. Ideally, the system should present various interfaces that meet the different requirements and profiles of individual user types. For example, a casual requisitioner may see a wizard-type interface that offers limited options and functions. Conversely, a power or administrative user may see more of a windows-based interface that provides extensive systems management and administration features.

Supporting this type of dynamic interface is not possible using standard client/server architectures. Modern component-based applications, however, are capable of dynamically generating custom interfaces, based on individual user profiles. This type of dynamic interface generation is extremely useful when operating complex multibuyer/multiseller marketplaces.

User Registration and Administration.   To facilitate the rapid enrollment of thousands of users, digital marketplaces and exchanges should provide browser-based self-registration utilities that automate the process. These tools allow users to establish profiles, passwords, and other information that can be easily reviewed and approved by the marketplace administration. In addition, the registration process should automatically identify the tenant company that employs the user and set baseline permissions and profiles accordingly. These user registration tools will speed the enrollment process while keeping administrative costs to a minimum.

Finally, digital marketplace software must provide a high level of security, limiting access to enrolled users only. In addition to standard security protocols such as Secure Sockets Layer (SSL), the software should also support digital certificates and other encryption technologies.

Process and Workflow Management.   Early sell-side failures proved that buyers, not suppliers or market makers would dictate the rules and processes through which goods and services are procured. Therefore, it is essential that a marketplace solution give tenants the ability to establish their own "view" of the marketplace. Marketplace solutions support this fundamental requirement by allowing buying participants to establish their unique user profiles, permissions, and workflows. In essence, each buying tenant should be able to establish his own virtual procurement system within the larger marketplace. At the marketplace level, market hosts must be able to effectively establish and manage the high-level rules that dictate the marketplace structure. These rules must be transparently enforceable across all users.

It is important to examine carefully how user profiles, permissions, and workflow rules are established. Many systems rely heavily on third-party tools to handle some or all of these configuration processes. In many cases, these tools are not tightly integrated into the overall solution, making it difficult to change configurations once the marketplace is up and running. Ideally, all configuration activities should be done through the browser from within the core application, without reliance on external scripting languages or separate applications. Remember that the more difficult it is to configure and manage the marketplace, the more expensive it will be to operate.

Relationship Management.   Managing discreet pricing and contractual relationships between specific buyers and sellers is equally important. Business-to-business marketplaces cannot operate as open shopping malls, where buyers are free to browse across endless suppliers, shopping for the lowest-possible price. Early marketplace failures, such as Industry.Net, demonstrated that suppliers were not willing to put their products into the marketplace unless the market maker could, to some degree, protect their relationship with a buyer. Additionally, they showed that buyers would not transact within a marketplace unless the catalog represents their supply sources and their contracted prices. A viable marketplace solution must provide advanced features for managing customer-to-supplier relationships. This includes support for markups, discounts, and other pricing filters, as well as billing terms and other aspects of the buyer-seller relationship.

Usage Tracking and Billing. A key requirement for managing a digital marketplace is the ability to track usage and set up filters for capturing billing information. For example, a market maker may decide to charge a 1 percent fee to the seller, or he may decide to charge a fixed transaction fee to the buyer. Additionally, this charge may be directly reflected in the price of the product or aggregated and charged on a separate usage bill. In either case, the solution should provide the tools to capture this information and generate online bills for each marketplace participant.

Customizability and Extensibility

It is doubtful that any out-of-the-box solution will meet 100 percent of the functional requirements for a given marketplace. In addition, what is right today may not be right tomorrow. But perhaps more important than any other requirement in evaluating a marketplace solution is the ease with which it can be customized and maintained. Once again, the use of a new component-based network application architecture (as compared with client/server architecture) will give a marketplace solution the upper hand.

Customizing Core Objects. Component-based solutions typically deliver reusable objects that can be easily changed to meet specific functional requirements. Companies should carefully evaluate the openness of the solution by determining whether it is developed using standard development tools and open development standards. The most common component-based architectures are Microsoft's COM/DCOM and Sun's Enterprise Java Beans. To date, Enterprise Java Beans has provided a more comprehensive and scalable solution.

Marketplace solutions should publish all object libraries and APIs, as well as a customization methodology; enabling users to customize delivered objects or add new ones. When implemented correctly, component-based solutions are easy to upgrade, since custom-developed objects generally remain usable with upgrades to the core-delivered objects. Customers should take special care to evaluate these aspects of any marketplace solution. In the fast-moving world of the Internet, companies cannot afford to get caught with proprietary or nonextensible solutions.

Branding and Localization. One of the most important aspects of building a marketplace is creating a unique visual and use experience for participants. Each market maker will want to develop a look and feel that is consistent with the brand identity and the targeted positioning of the marketplace. This is very different from back-office ERP or buy-side e-procurement applications. With these applications, the solution can be implemented almost as it looks when it is installed from the CD. However, a marketplace solution is often rebranded so that it may bear little resemblance to the base application that was loaded from the installation disks. Therefore, it is essential that the marketplace solution can be easily branded to meet different marketplace requirements.

It is almost certain that users from different companies, requiring different languages, will access any given marketplace. Ideally, the solution should not require the customer to completely recode client or server software to support different languages, currencies, or tax structures. The system should, to some degree, be able to dynamically interpret the operating systems of the different users and provide a localized view of the marketplace.

Integrating Best-of-Breed Components. Because every marketplace will operate at a different point in the commerce chain, there is a need to provide different end-user functions and services. For example, a vertical marketplace may want to publish large volumes of industry-specific news and information, while an ebusiness portal may want to provide online news groups or chat capability. A vertical marketplace may require support for more advanced auction functionality, while a procurement marketplace might only utilize basic quote and bid functionality. Regardless of the specific requirements, a viable marketplace solution must provide an open, extensible platform that enables additional best-of-breed modules to be plugged in.

Such plug-and-play capabilities allow a host to easily customize the marketplace solution by adding custom-developed or stand-alone applications. Key areas typically covered by extended commerce modules include the following:

- *Community and collaboration*—An advantage of online marketplaces is their ability to create virtual communities and to facilitate collaboration among their members. Including interactive features, such as discussion forums, email, list servs, and chat capabilities, provides valuable tools for communication among marketplace peers.

- *Information and publishing*—Successful marketplaces will provide additional features to entice its users to return on a regular basis, such as access to relevant information, content, resources, industry publications, and news. In addition to providing external news sources, inclusion of Web site creation and hosting tools would allow a marketplace to assist its users in the creation and maintenance of their own corporate Web sites.

- *Advertising and sponsorship*—An online marketplace offers prime positioning for advertisers and sponsors to generate brand recognition and sales leads for their products and services. To capitalize on this opportunity, market hosts can include internal advertising and sponsorship capabilities. Not only will this give suppliers the ability to advertise, but it can also create a revenue stream for the hosts.

- *Advanced dynamic exchange*—Dynamic exchange technology includes functions and features that allow buyers and suppliers to more easily communicate and collaborate on key sourcing and ordering decisions. Examples of dynamic exchange include Internet-based online negotiations, quote and bid processing, and auctions.

Section Summary

This NetMarketMakers perspective provided a solid foundation of the fundamentals of the e-Marketplace models that are emerging and in practice today. The next section reviews the opportunities and issues associated with connecting a company into multiple e-Marketplaces.

Connecting to Multiple E-Marketplaces

The sheer number of e-Marketplaces that are emerging is daunting. With the promises of improved price efficiencies, improved business process flow, and streamlining of global operations, it has become imperative to have an e-Marketplace strategy. Whether you are building a company "in-house" model or participating in multiple digital markets, both will certainly be a part of everyday business environment. The challenge from a business and technology perspective is deciding which e-Marketplaces to join now and in the future, and deciding how to connect to each of them. To maximize leverage of these new digital marketplaces, you must find a path to connectivity that allows for real-time access to the emarkets from both a buyer perspective as well as a supplier perspective. Also required is a strategy that takes into account all of the various e-Marketplace transaction standards and one that allows the easy accommodation to new e-Marketplaces as the market changes. These new e-Marketplaces will need to be factored into the company's procurement and supply chain strategies, as well as the sales channel strategies. To be successful, integration with these e-Marketplaces should occur at a complete business process level.

Let's review the business issues and then discuss two primary options that are available for developing an e-Marketplace integration plan. First, we will review the option of using an e-services network organization that specializes in providing a single point of connection to multiple e-Marketplaces. Specifically reviewed in this section will be the Ironside Network ASP model as a leading example of this kind of e-service offering, followed by a review of the architectural model from the perspective of building an enterprise Virtual Private Network (VPN). This section will provide an overview of a build versus outsource review of integration to e-Marketplaces.

The B2B E-Marketplace Business Landscape

The following section outlines the B2B e-Marketplace landscape with a quick review of five key types of marketplaces available today. As illustrated in Figure 8-7, there are multiple e-Marketplaces for an enterprise to participate in. On the selling side, there are sites ranging from the pure sell-side commerce site that offers one to many functionality, through to distribution and vertical exchanges that are available for selling products and services. On the buying side of the enterprise are sites offering many suppliers to one buyer, as well as procurement portals offering the ability to aggregate many buyers to many sellers.

The Business Challenge

As enterprises rush into the ebusiness environment and begin the process of either building their ebusiness infrastructure from ground zero or extending their legacy systems into the ebusiness environment through ASPs or packaged solutions, it becomes rapidly apparent how complex the integration of these systems truly is. Compound that with the multiple forms of e-Marketplace technologies, and the complexity becomes even

Figure 8-7. *B2B Landscape*

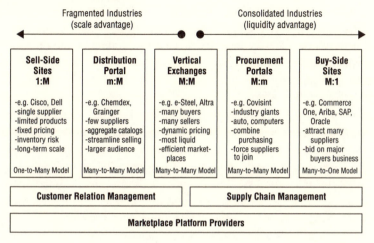

more overwhelming. The horizontal bars in Figure 8-8 show typical enterprise systems that need to be integrated into a sell-side marketplace in order to offer real-time customer satisfaction and long-term business results.

Each of these systems performs a critical function in delivering value to stakeholders throughout the entire value chain, from customer attraction and acquisition to production, distribution, and customer care. The ability to rapidly deploy ebusiness solutions, which map to the company's strategic business objectives and integrate with legacy systems, will be critical to achieving long-term success. There are companies such

Figure 8-8.

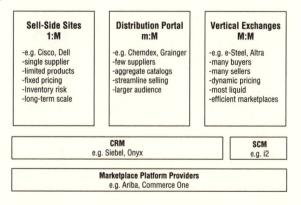

as TIBCO that offer communication and collaboration platforms for integration on a workflow basis.

The challenge for suppliers is to determine which e-Marketplaces to incorporate into a B2B strategy and then seamlessly integrating back-end systems with each of them.

Buyer Perspective Challenge

Let's review some of the emerging channels for buyers to reach suppliers. Figure 8-9 outlines some of the core conecting points that need to be addressed when extending the buying experience through multiple e-Marketplaces and through multiple technologies. The world is increasingly mobile and wireless. This trend needs to be addressed in the e-Marketplace strategy so that access and interaction with the marketplace is possible from not only personal computers but also from other digital devices, such as cellular phones, PDAs (personal digital assistants), and interactive TV.

Figure 8-9. *Buy-Side Connections*

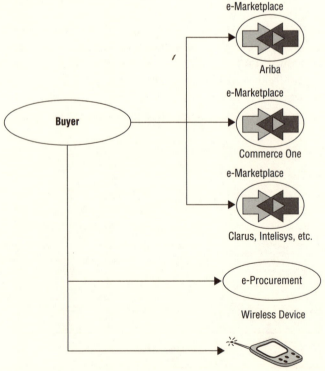

Figure 8-10. *Sell-Side Connections*

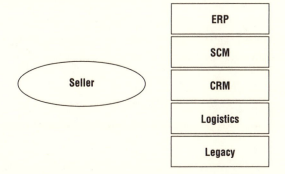

Extending the Enterprise Systems to the Sales Process

When trying to reach buyers through these new online channels, suppliers must integrate both their back-end enterprise systems and their front-end systems with the various e-Marketplace technologies in order to be successful. Figure 8-10 illustrates the multiple systems that need to be addressed in the sales process. This integration needs to bridge the market-facing sides of the business with the employee-facing systems as well as the partner-facing systems to provide a complete holistic integration across the entire value chain.

E-service Networks—Bringing It All Together

There are emerging e-service networks that are in place today to address this critical business issue of connecting suppliers to buyers through these new market channels. Ironside Technologies is one of the companies that offers such a solution. Their solution, called the Ironside Network, shown in Figure 8-11, is an independent ebusiness access service that connects suppliers to multiple e-Marketplaces through one single point of integration. This e-Marketplace hub provides all of the adapters and connectivity needed for real-time integration of supplier systems to the e-Marketplaces, regardless of the transaction standards or protocols employed by each e-Marketplace. This real-time connectivity enables e-Marketplace buyers to access inventory, catalog, and volume discount information directly from enterprise applications and enters e-Marketplace orders directly into enterprise systems.

Figure 8-12 illustrates the e-service ASP model offered by Ironside as a "single-point connection to many marketplaces" solution versus building multiple point-to-point connections to multiple marketplaces. One integration point means lower integration costs, less resources needed for integration, and faster speed to market.

Figure 8-11. *Buy-Side Integration to Sell-Side*

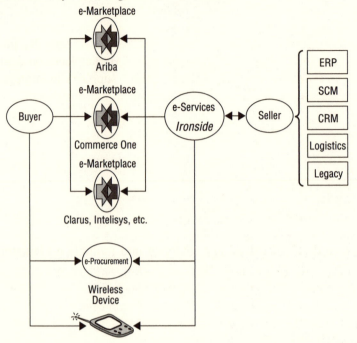

Figure 8-12. *Direct Point-to-Point versus the Ironside Network*

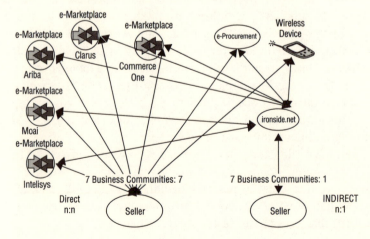

E-service solutions offered by companies like Ironside Technologies solve a growing dilemma for suppliers evaluating the proliferating number of e-Marketplaces—namely, how to reduce the risk when deciding which e-Marketplaces to include in a B2B Web strategy. By providing suppliers the flexibility to enter and exit e-Marketplaces on demand, solutions such as the Ironside Network enable suppliers to strategically manage all emarket channels with minimal risk and investment.

Directly Extending the Enterprise into a Shared Corporate Environment

In this section the dynamics of building an externally focused ebusiness architecture that will extend and integrate into multiple e-Marketplaces are reviewed. Charles V. Richardson, a senior architect at marchFIRST, the world's largest Internet consulting and services firm, explains the shared corporate environment in the remainder of this section.

The concept of a shared corporate environment between business alliance partners is not new. However, how to implement a solution that is secured yet accessible for all the partners may be new to the organization. Obviously, information needs to be provided in Internet time and not pony express. Figure 8-13 offers a single topological network solution that can be easily implemented as a Value Trust Network using readily available and affordable software and hardware technology. Let's break it down and understand the concept behind the architecture.

In the Internet space there exists any given number of n suppliers,

Figure 8-13. *Value Trust Network Topology Model*

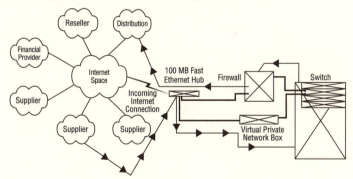

resellers, distributors, and trusted partners that may be spread out from Tahoe to Taiwan. How does an enterprise connect these resources to best utilize what they have to offer? Today's most resounding response would be via VPN, or Virtual Private Network. A VPN allows *n* number of WAN (wide area network) sites to connect using a secure link through a local VPN box at each location.

These sites would all receive access to the shared development environment without restriction, or using a predefined set of rules that define use and administration authorization. When the VPN is connected in conjunction with a firewall at a single administration point, other predefined rule sets on the firewall can allow local corporate LAN (local area network) users to securely access the shared environment as well. Let's look at how the flow of information would occur in our VTN as shown.

Figure 8-13 shows the path that suppliers in, say, Minneapolis may traverse to reach a distributor in another remote location. Upon initiating the connection to the VPN using client software and any available connection to the Internet, the user is locked into the VPN network. His or her data is sent via a secure tunnel through the Internet, into the VPN box, then back out through the firewall to a secure tunnel on the Internet and directly to the VPN box of the distributor.

The only downside of this configuration is that the LAN access that the user may have to his or her local network will be unavailable during the VPN session. One of the overriding advantages is that each site can be protected by a single centralized firewall. This does away with the need to have a costly firewall setup, configured and maintained at each individual site.

Figure 8-14 considers how data may flow when it is necessary to provide information to nontrusted sources. In the figure, data is deployed from any internal source into what is commonly becoming known as the DMZ. The term *DMZ* is a military slang that stands for *demilitarized zone*, a term that denotes a safe area that is fully controlled but exists on enemy territory. A DMZ in computerese simply means a location outside the firewall where nonsensitive data can be deployed for public access.

Note that the data flow is bidirectional on all VPN connections. The only limits to access occur from the DMZ and to the corporate LAN. Also, the reference to "gnatting" refers to the use of internally emulated IP addresses so we don't run out of IPs or space for extensibility inside the firewall. By creating multiple VLANs inside the firewall, we can also provide departmental security and access.

Figure 8-14. *Integrating Internal and External Systems*

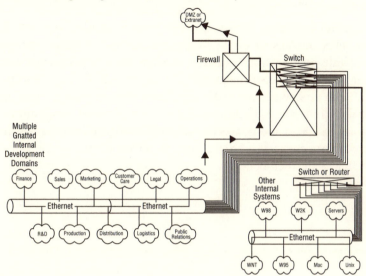

Section Summary

The VPN model by Charles Richardson represents an excellent example of how an enterprise can take a holistic approach to integrating all departments into the ebusiness environment and extending them outside of the enterprise to actively participate in a real-time manner with e-Marketplaces. The alternative or parallel strategy that could be followed is to partner with an Internet solutions provider with integration capabilities, such as marchFIRST, or a technology platform provider, such as Ironsides, Crossworlds, Ariba, or Commerce One. Most likely, a hybrid model would work for most companies.

E-Marketplaces are today, and will be for some time to come, a part of the fabric of the new economy. As such, it is critical that organizations position their strategic business strategies to include connecting to multiple e-Marketplaces and truly leveraging and interoperating with and through these new business models. Properly leveraged, these new digital marketplaces and workspaces can offer tremendous market value as well as significant operating efficiencies. Forward-thinking companies are studying these models.

Chapter Summary

This chapter explored independent and industry-backed current and future business models that are emerging in the e-Marketplace industry, as well as value-added service models for the Net market maker industry. The projected rapid growth of e-Marketplaces will cause a highly competitive environment. The e-Marketplaces that deliver on real lasting value will dominate and ultimately earn for themselves a long-term place in the landscape of the new economy. In the next chapter we will review the customer-centric power shift and the profound impact on e-Marketplaces and their members.

CHAPTER

Value Trust Networks: The Future of Supply Chains

Instant, immediate, personal gratification—that's all customers really want in the Internet generation. So what's so hard about just giving the customer what they want? Well, nothing—except, we have a few things we need to work out first, such as predictable demand forecasting; global distribution on both a physical level and digital level; multilingual, multicurrency, multicultural customer interactions; finished goods inventories; global configuration centers; e-procurement; global supply chain integration, collaborative design, and development within our enterprises and with all 18,000 suppliers and contractors that serve the company— and that's before we break for lunch.

This chapter explores the next generation of supply chains now that Web enablement and networked enterprises are a critical part of our lives. The changing dynamics of supply chains transforming into supply webs, global trading networks, global buying networks, and ultimately into what can be called global Value Trust Networks (VTNs) is discussed.

Global Value Trust Networks

The premise of global VTNs is that supply chains which have been built over years, sometimes decades or centuries, are not going to be replaced overnight with the Internet. The key elements that make a supply chain

Figure 9-1. *Evolution of Value Trust Networks*

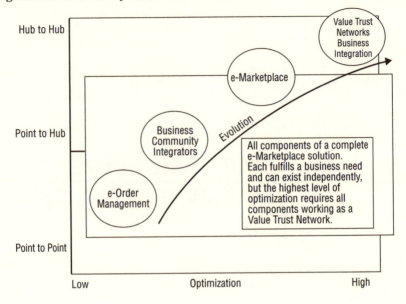

work are not the underlying technologies but more importantly the established relationships and trust that exist between trading partners. For a new global supply web business model to truly work, it must offer real *value* to solve industry pain points. It must offer *trust* to both the suppliers and the buyers. It must leverage the Internet as the ultimate business *network*. (See Figure 9-1.)

Global VTNs cannot just be a Web version of the physical supply chain. Too often in the rush to get business up and running on the Internet, companies have duplicated their old economy systems and process and mirrored it on the Internet. The Internet must be recognized as a new medium for conducting business that has new rules, new advantages, and new risks.

Going global with your company has never been an easy task, and when you factor in the supply chain issues that support the design, production, distribution, and sales of your products and services around the word, the issues multiply. The Internet has provided us with a common platform for global communication and business transactions. The magic is in taking it to the next level towards developing true Value Trust Networks that deliver global customer value both digitally and physically. It is the combination of digital and physical value delivery that will offer the true efficiency and competitive advantages that we are all seeking.

V = Value

New economy supply Web solutions must offer real value to be sustainable and have true impact. VTNs need to solve specific industry pain points and bring new forms of value to market—value that may not have been possible in the old economy business models. Value must be delivered in both a digital and physical blended format.

Digital Value Delivery. Digital value delivery can come in the form of new digital services that leverage the network advantages of the Internet such as:

- Global trading capabilities
- Mass personalization and customization
- Global knowledge exchange
- Global communities
- Collaborative workflow
- Industry-specific (vertical) marketplaces
- Horizontal marketplaces
- Enterprise-to-enterprise connectivity
- E-Marketplace-to-e-Marketplace connectivity

Physical Value Delivery. Long-term success of e-Marketplace business models will depend heavily on leveraging physical value delivery such as global logistics, freight forwarding, warehousing, inspection services, and so on. E-Marketplaces will not need to own these physical service organizations, but they will need to partner with these firms on a global basis to offer complete end-to-end solutions.

T = Trust

Our entire global economic system is based on trust. The paper and metal that we carry around in our pockets that we call money is based on trust. Established relationships and trust are at the core of truly untapping the value of the global network called the Internet. There are numerous e-Marketplace models addressing some of the lower hanging fruit of commodity product and services exchange, where trust is carried with the brands that are being exchanged. As you move further up the value chain, the level of trust needs to be increased proportionally to the importance of the products and services being offered. For example, the purchase of indirect maintenance, repair, and operations (MRO) supplies, such as pens and paper, can be sold based on brand name alone. Trust is even more important in regard to direct materials purchasing. Direct materials are components of finished goods. Therefore, trust must extend beyond brand to include other variables such as quality, delivery terms, collaborative capabilities, and after-sale support.

When we talk about integrated supply chain activities, the trust involves the open sharing of information within and among e-Marketplaces. As a result, e-Marketplaces must support local and international laws, security, confidentiality, and neutrality in order to earn this trust and keep it.

Companies will need to take some leaps of faith when utilizing e-Marketplaces to open up and share information that will create this new value. This means sharing demand and supply forecasting, inventory levels, production and delivery schedules, shortages, and overages in a secure, confidential manner, so as not to lose competitive advantages. This is not an easy step to undertake. Even in the most well-run supply chains, there exists an element of distrust between trading partners, vendors, distributors, and suppliers. Often there is even animosity between trading partners, with each one trying to second-guess the other. This trust issue is at the core of many of the industry's inventory problems.

We have been reviewing the cultural aspects of trust. Another element of trust comes from the technologies that support trust—technologies such as PKI , digital certificates, and SSL (Secure Sockets Layer) compliance. These elements will be reviewed in the infrastructure section under building a *trust infrastructure.*

N = Network

The global Internet is undeniably the mother of all network opportunities. We now have a global standard platform for all forms of content such as data, voice, and video. We also have a global platform for commerce, communication, and real collaboration. The global network effect is so powerful that companies are often taken by surprise by the sheer amount of international business they start generating just by posting a product or service on the Web.

Supply Chains: The Classic VTN

Both traditional and Internet-based supply chain models exemplify VTNs. In a traditional supply chain, each tier must provide tangible value or it will be eliminated from the chain. Many supply chain relationships, particularly those that involve direct goods, are based on trust. Buyers must trust that suppliers will deliver goods on time that comply with certain specifications, such as cost, quality, and customer requirements. Conversely, suppliers must trust buyers to pay for those goods and likewise honor contractual agreements in good faith. Traditionally, the network has depended on human relationships and the physical delivery of goods.

Value Trust Network Model

The Value Trust Network illustrated in Figure 9-2 is an example of how e-Marketplaces will be able to be at the center of the new Internet supply web. The left side of the diagram shows entering the VTN, the classic role of buyer and supplier matchmaker and aggregator services that e-Marketplaces are providing today. E-Marketplaces will begin to add additional value in the form of digital services as well as coordination of physical service offerings. The digital value-added services will represent service offerings from outside partners such as financial institutions, dig-

Figure 9-2. *E-Marketplace Value Trust Networks*

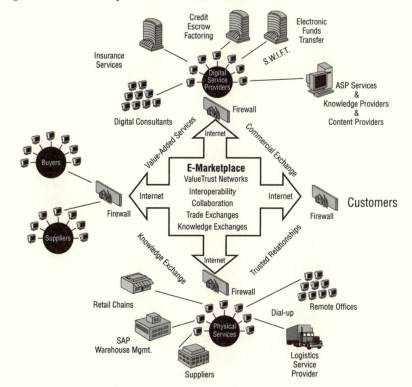

Table 9-1. Solution Offerings

Services	*Description*
Information/Knowledge services	Data mining, customized analysis, and reporting, real-time transaction trends, and consumer behavior tracking
Collaboration services	Web-automated workflow, integrated business process solutions
Supply chain management	Central coordination of global logistics for members including consolidated freight, warehousing and shipping services
Community services	Communities of interest and commerce services
Trading services	Exchange, auction, catalog, aggregation services
Integration services	System/Business integration into e-Marketplaces, trading partners, and service providers

ital consulting companies, and content providers initially designed to complement the decision support and transaction requirements of the members. The physical services will be structured to support the warehousing, freight consolidation, and logistical requirements of the members. Both the digital and physical service offerings outlined above will be provided by outside partners to the e-Marketplaces.

The e-Marketplace will also provide its own unique set of value-added services that will be developed internally as well as through a hybrid set of solution offerings. Shown in Table 9-1, these unique services will differentiate the e-Marketplace and provide real value to the member base. The following outlines key solutions that will be offered through e-Marketplaces.

An Internet-based supply chain represents a slightly different model. In fact, the Internet has caused us to question the value of certain tiers in the supply chain. Take software, for example. Software vendors are moving away from selling boxed products through retail stores. Instead, they are opting to sell software directly to consumers that is downloadable from the corporate Web site. They are also adopting application service provider (ASP) models that enable customers to rent software on a monthly basis as opposed to buying it outright. By selling software directly to consumers, software companies are minimizing (if not completely eliminating) the need for distributors and dealers. Instead, they are increasingly turning to digital production and delivery systems that decrease costs and increase ROI (return on investment).

The Internet will have an effect on B2B supply chains; however, in this case middlemen may not be as easily replaced. Buying all the parts one needs to build an aircraft is a lot different than buying a desktop application software package. Value in business-to-business terms is often knowledge-based. In the supply chain, knowledge-based value is demonstrated by understanding customers' unique needs or helping the customer better understand his or her own needs. Value in the supply chain often boils down to answering questions for customers, as well as helping the customer define the questions in the first place. Either way, the value is problem solving.

In the early stages of Internet supply chain development, we are seeing the benefits described as faster time-to-market and reduced procurement costs, which both solve problems of competitiveness in the short term. Longer-term, Internet-based economics and Internet time will be taken for granted, which will cause a shift in the value proposition. The Internet will increasingly be used as a collaborative tool to solve more complex knowledge-based problems.

Trust in the digital economy must often be accomplished by the use of technology. Global e-Marketplaces enable buyers all over the world to buy from suppliers regardless of their location—theoretically anyway, assuming national and/or international laws allow it. Buyers still care that suppliers are responsive to their needs, and suppliers still care that the checks not only come in but also clear. However, trust is far more complicated than that. Therefore, if we are to conduct real-time business with global trading partners, we must move beyond a trust system that requires a lot of manual labor and other types of human intervention. We must learn to trust each other based on digital trust standards, as well as through our interactions with one another.

In the digital world there exists a number of resources, tools, and solutions available to enable trusted transactions and business negotiations to occur. Table 9-2 compares traditional and Internet-based value trust systems.

Finally, the network is evolving. The Internet has been described as the "mother of all networks." It has flattened organizational structures, penetrated international borders, and changed the way the world communicates. Hierarchies are transforming into matrices where knowledge

Table 9-2. Traditional vs. Internet-Based Value Trust Systems

Traditional	Internet-Based
Paper-based documents	Electronic documents
Photo ID	Authentication
Handwritten signature	Digital signature
Handshake	Email acknowledgment
Physical meetings	Videoconferencing
Qualification	Digital certificate
Authorization	Rule-based access, public key infrastructure
Branding	Branding
Business card	Signature file
Key	Password
Fingerprint	Biometrics

exchange, trust, and collaboration are becoming basic requirements. Supply chains are just now beginning to realize such a transformation.

Why Supply Chains Will Embrace Internet-Based Business Models

One of the leading problems for procurement professionals is inventory. Everyone in the supply chain is worried about getting caught at the wrong time with not enough of the right inventory or too much of the wrong inventory. A lot of this problem can be directly attributed to a problem with reliable information exchange.

Replacing Inventory with Information.   The holy grail of building a new economy supply web is replacing inventory with information. In other words, through open and honest sharing of information starting with customer demand forecasting through inventory levels, production, distribution, and ongoing service, there is a need for information sharing on a perpetual and reliable basis. The emerging consortia e-Marketplace models hope to solve this problem because of their equity-based involvement in the marketplaces that they are trading through. If these consortia can play a neutral intermediary role in opening up the information exchange and setting some standards for methodology and taxonomy, we may see the VTN models emerge with real impact being accomplished.

The Value of Knowledge Exchange.   The first-generation e-Marketplaces are all chasing the trillions of dollars in B2B transactions between companies. This transaction business will be rapidly commoditized to a low- to no-margin business. However, as referenced in other parts of this book, the transaction business is powerful in the sense that it can offer a wealth of information value that can be turned into information services. True value delivery will be demonstrated. For the few digital marketplaces that actually get it and move to a knowledge exchange model, this information and knowledge exchange is really where enterprises will start to see value for their investment in working with global e-Marketplaces.

Perspective: Building Value into the Supply Chain

Mark Hoffman, chairman and CEO, Commerce One

Supply chains in virtually every industry are plagued with inefficiencies. Although most manufacturers, distributors, and dealers have adopted Web sites, business processes have not really improved. Many companies still rely on phones calls, faxed documents, manual data entry, EDI (electronic data interchange) systems, and proprietary systems to get the job done. Simple tasks like order processing often take weeks, even though global business practices are shifting to Internet time. What now takes weeks or months must be accomplished in hours or days if members of the supply chain are to stay competitive. The only way to accomplish this kind of efficiency is to adopt modern business and technology practices that provide tangible economic benefits. (See Figure 9-3.)

Figure 9-3.

e-Marketplace to e-Marketplace
(E2E connectivity)

Complex Business Processes/Direct BOM
(Collaboration, logistics, forecasting, supply
chain management)

Simply buying and selling
(Indirect goods)

Point-to-Point
Phone, Fax, EDI

The quest for competitive advantage will drive the rapid adoption of core supply chain activities. Those companies that enable their supply chains on a global basis will be the clear winners.

Point-to-Point Inefficiencies

Ecommerce has been evolving for more than 20 years. It was first implemented as electronic data interchange (EDI), which required private networks, as well as specialized programmers to set them up and maintain them. These are point-to-point solutions that connect the Fortune 1000 to their key suppliers. Smaller companies are unable to afford these systems, and because of the high cost of connectivity, not all suppliers are connected to the network, which limits the liquidity of the buying community.

The problem with point-to-point solutions is one of scale. It is difficult to scale trading partner relationships one at a time. EDI links must be established on a point-to-point basis, connecting one trading partner to another. It is difficult to process hundreds of thousands of purchase orders when data entry clerks must type the information manually into an ERP (enterprise resource planning) or MRP (materials requirements planning) system. For years, buyers have called suppliers on the phone to verify inventory. If the items are in stock, the customer issues a purchase order, prints it out, and faxes it to the supplier. The supplier then enters the data from the purchase order into his or her inventory control and accounting software and issues an order confirmation. This type of process continues through the entire procurement process resulting in very high labor costs.

Simple Buying and Selling

The Internet provides a means by which people can conduct ecommerce transactions. The first serious Internet solutions for business focused on the buying and selling of indirect goods that are typically maintenance, repair, and operations (MRO) items such as pens and computers. These solutions enable buyers to significantly reduce procurement costs while enabling suppliers to reduce operational costs. Indirect procurement represents only 20 percent of total spend in most industries, however, with the majority portion representing direct goods that are purchased with a bill of materials.

Most Fortune 100 companies have in excess of 40,000 suppliers of indirect goods but purchase less than $10,000 annually from 70 to 80 percent of those suppliers. E-Marketplaces provide an opportunity to consolidate sources and control rogue purchasing that can account for a dramatic savings.

Many indirect procurement solutions are implemented behind the firewall, limiting them to enterprise solutions. Increasingly, businesses are becoming dependent on other businesses to maintain competitiveness. Time-to-market pressures are forcing companies to focus on their core competencies, form strategic relationships, and outsource noncore activities. They need to move beyond tactical procurement solutions to more strategic platforms.

During the last 10 years, ERP has enabled a number of enterprise process improvements, and lately the life cycle of ERP has been likened to the emergence of e-Marketplaces. The technology enabled companies to "right size" and increase overall efficiency by automating processes. ERP successfully reduced cycle times and improved enterprise supply chain efficiency, resulting in higher ROI for the companies that implemented it.

The difference between the ERP era and the e-Marketplace era are significant, however. When ERP was first introduced, the Internet was little more than a text-based search and email system for the scientific community and academia. There was no means of tying together business and business applications together in a way that would enable real-time collaboration. ERP was therefore only an enterprise solution, albeit a very robust one at the time.

Business cycles have also changed radically since the advent of ERP. The business cycle has shifted to Internet time. As a result, efficiencies must be extended out beyond the enterprise to an interenterprise environment.

Supporting Complex Business Processes

Eventually all business processes will have to be streamlined because time-to-market is critical in the digital economy. Workers must be able to able to collaborate on design and planning in real time, which will further reduce the time it takes to manufacture everything from cars to computers.

Indirect buying and selling radically differs from direct bill of material purchasing. Direct goods are components and raw materials that are used in the manufacturing of a finished product, such as sheet metal, semiconductors, and petrochemicals. These direct materials, when combined with direct labor and overhead, make up the cost of goods sold

(COGS). Many of the components used in manufacturing must be customized or custom-built, which obviates the need for collaborative planning and design. The buyer and seller must work closely together to ensure that the finished good meets its original specifications, and if the design changes, then ensure that the new specifications are met.

Currently, the supply chain is linear, which results in several inefficiencies. If a hotel chain wants to purchase 10,000 telephone handsets that have customized features, it would query a wholesaler or distributor for pricing. The wholesaler would in turn query the manufacturer, who must query component suppliers. Some of those suppliers may also have to query yet another tier of suppliers for components or raw materials. Bids, availability, and delivery time flow up and down through the supply chain, and several weeks later the hotel chain receives a quote.

In today's economy a linear supply chain is no longer viable in the long term. Instead, we are moving to a collaborative model where all tiers in the supply chain can exchange information in real time, which has significant advantages. Consumer demand is synthesized and aggregated across channels and stored on the exchange. OEMs (original equipment manufacturers) can mine the demand data and collaborate with the dealers to develop improved forecasts using legacy or hosted planning engines. The OEMs can later elect to post up-to-date forecasts on the exchange, as well as update production plans. The exchange translates demand forecasts and specifies relevant demands for participants at each tier. All participants have access to updated demand forecast information, which enables the entire supply chain to plan based on facts rather than assumptions.

Fact-based planning, as enabled by collaborative supply chain management, reduces the high costs of overestimating or underestimating demand. The economics apply to the entire supply chain.

Other business processes such as payment processing and logistics must also be electronically streamlined to enable the smooth flow of goods and services between trading partners regardless of their geographic location. Conducting business over the Web does not eliminate the need for core and value-added business services. In fact, the value of an e-Marketplace is defined by its ability to provide services that can be applied from design through fulfillment.

Interenterprise Efficiencies

E-Marketplaces are eliminating the inefficiencies of many current business processes. The benefits of streamlined processes are now extending out beyond individual marketplaces. *Intermarketplace* connectivity and resource sharing is enabling new compelling business opportunities.

The need for *inter-e-Marketplace* connectivity becomes immediately apparent in international trading situations and among industries. For example, a London-based manufacturer and a Tokyo-based supplier may collaborate on the design of a good that must be sold to a company in Singapore. Each country has a local language and customs, as well as specific laws regarding tax and trade.

Leveraging services and communities is also beneficial for industries that are dependent on one another, such as the computer and electronic component industries. By connecting e-Marketplaces that have an open platform for interoperable business services, each e-Marketplace can gain access to the expertise of the other, which, if implemented properly, ensures that the needs of all parties are accurately met.

Ultimately, companies want the flexibility to do business on their own terms, which is why openness and interoperability are critical to any e-Marketplace or network of e-Marketplaces. By opening up enterprises and e-Marketplaces, each enterprise may operate around its core competency, outsourcing noncore activities to specialists that provide time-to-market and cost advantages, as well as valuable expertise.

Outsourcing requires the real-time integration of processes so that interenterprise partnering and collaboration can be realized. Capitalizing on these opportunities will require seamless global trading, the rationalization of supply chain processes, and support for locally driven business services.

E-Marketplaces require an absolute level of interoperability where the differences in languages, computer-based applications, business models, and value-added businesses services are openly embraced as part of the whole. For example, an e-Marketplace that already supports auction and procurement services must also be able to support collaborative design and planning, content services, logistics services, and transaction services, and other core supply chain processes to enable a true value chain.

Similarly, locally driven services must be syndicated globally through business partnerships. Services such as IT, import/export, payment, human resources, shipping, and printing are examples of services that are demanded on a local basis. By interconnecting e-Marketplaces, the entire community gains access to regional-specific functionality that can provide a competitive edge.

Section Summary

The dynamic nature of the digital economy necessitates the rationalization of the supply chain. EDI and ERP systems provided the first level of process automation that enabled companies to improve enterprise efficiency. Likewise, the advent of the Internet and ecommerce changed the competitive landscape forever.

E-procurement solutions have provided a means of reducing procurement-related operational costs; however, business process efficiencies must be pushed out beyond the firewall. Enterprises must be linked together at a strategic level to realize the collaborative supply chain model. As we move forward, e-Marketplace-to-e-Marketplace connectivity will enable open enterprises, collaborative groups, and entire industries to realize even greater efficiencies and achieve unprecedented economic returns. We must unshackle the supply chain to realize competitive advantage in the new economy.

E-Marketplace Supporting the "New" Supply Web Through Value-Added Services

The next section reviews several value-added solution areas that e-Marketplaces could offer to secure themselves a long-term annuity business model in the new economy supply web.

E-Procurement Strategies (Direct and Indirect Procurement Solutions)

The Gartner Group predicts that, as a result of ebusiness and e-procurement, more than 70 percent of all buyer and supplier relationships will be nontraditional—that is, long-term, strategic relationships for direct procurement, or short-term, tactical relationships for indirect (0.8 probability).

In some manufacturing industries, 70 to 80 percent of the cost of the product is acquired from external sources, and the end manufacturer adds only 20 to 30 percent of the value delivered to customers. This trend is also surfacing in some service industries as external sources contribute more to the effort involved in delivering a service. In addition, Gartner Group research has shown that large enterprises can spend more than 30 percent of revenue on nonproduction or indirect goods and services. Usually, these goods or services are high-volume and low-value purchases. These two trends in direct and indirect procurement have made supplier relationships more important than ever to CEOs as a means to enhance corporate performance.

According to the Gartner Group, streamlined procurement and vendor management can deliver impressive cost savings and quality improvements. Such savings go straight to the bottom line—often with the same impact as doubling or tripling revenue growth. However, achieving these cost savings requires significant planning and organizational process changes.

E-Marketplaces—Advanced Planning and Scheduling Services

Advanced Planning and Scheduling (APS) has been the hottest segment of the enterprise applications market for the last two years, with a 70 percent compound annual growth rate (CAGR), according to a recent report by AMR Research, Inc. Fueling this growth, manufacturers faced with the challenges of simultaneously reducing costs and improving customer service have been early adopters of APS as part of their supply chain management strategies. While many more manufacturers are interested in APS, the too-good-to-be-true claims and high product costs have caused most companies to proceed cautiously. This section reviews the scope of current APS solutions and provides findings from an in-depth look at existing implementations in a variety of industries.

What Is APS?

APS technology is rooted in the response to the need for fast materials requirements planning and constrained scheduling programs and has become one of the most important advances in business applications. APS leverages the planner's knowledge with responsive decision support tools rather than enslaving him or her with an endless barrage of exception messages. For the first time, manufacturers have planning tools that can absorb vast complexities to produce optimal plans. The key to understanding APS is that it is a new technology, not a rehash of 30-year-old MRP programs. APS leverages the incredible advances in computer technology over the past 10 years. Today's PC and UNIX workstations are capable of storing enormous amounts of data that can support the complex models of contemporary manufacturing operations.

More important than advances in computer technology, APS utilizes new planning and scheduling techniques that consider a wide range of constraints to produce an optimized plan:

- Material availability
- Machine and labor capacity
- Customer service-level requirements (due dates)
- Inventory safety stock levels
- Cost
- Distribution requirements
- Sequencing for setup efficiency

Figure 9-4 references the relationships of major planning systems with typical company data flows. As companies move to map their business process to their systems, it will be critical to have the internal mapping ready to map to external systems and e-Marketplaces as well as those inside the company.

The concept of optimization means that APS weighs the constraints and other business rules to find the optimal use of available material and plant capacity. This enables the business to meet such objectives as minimizing total cost (often from inventory and setup reductions) and maximizing overall plant operations to fill most customer orders on time.

Figure 9-4. *Relationship of Major Planning Functions with Typical Data Flows*

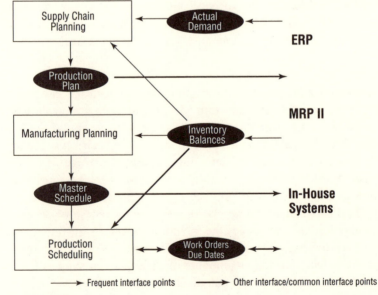

Source: AMR, 1998

During the optimization process, APS engines often look for the best plan by making multiple passes through the planning data. In contrast, MRP programs make a single pass through the data, assuming infinite plant capacity and material availability and simply time-phase production and purchase orders based on customer due dates. Material allocation is done on a first-come/first-serve basis, which often results in suboptimal plans. A good optimization algorithm can be refined to uncover advantageous opportunities.

The Scope of APS

APS is viewed as an umbrella technology embracing the concepts of the following:

- Simultaneous consideration of material and plant resources
- Optimization algorithms that incorporate constraints and business goals
- Real-time decision support
- Real-time available-to-promise

APS Capabilities

- Strategic and long-term planning
- Supply chain network design
- Demand planning and forecasting
- Sales and operations planning
- Inventory planning
- Supply chain planning
- Available-to-promise
- Manufacturing planning
- Distribution planning
- Transportation planning
- Production scheduling
- Shipment scheduling

The scope of APS is not limited to factory planning and scheduling, but has grown rapidly to include the full spectrum of enterprise and interenterprise scheduling functions.

Generally, the planning process is divided into these levels because they are performed by different parts of the organization at different times. From a practical standpoint, even today's most powerful computers cannot simultaneously optimize all of these planning levels. From a process perspective, combining multiple levels of planning in a single application presents organizational challenges, as it often cuts across departmental or divisional boundaries. While APS will support reengineering of the overall planning process, making this a requirement of the initial implementation can cause insurmountable resistance from parts of the organization. Implementing APS at just one of a couple of planning levels lets the manufacturer gain confidence in the technology before making organizational changes.

Improved Productivity Through a Value Trust Network Model

The VTN model of extending the value chain from customer demand straight through the supply web to include all related internal and external levels of the supply and demand response team can now be extended right down to the equipment used for production. The Internet coupled with information and collaboration technologies can now be utilized to solve industry pain points in many areas, including capacity planning, equipment utilization levels, and scheduling, as well as proactive equipment maintenance and repair. (See Figure 9-5.)

Symphony Systems is a leading-edge example of a supply web market maker; it develops and deploys Web-based solutions that maximize the productivity of manufacturing equipment. Its initial market thrust is in the semiconductor industry, whose costly and inaccessible clean-room capital equipment is historically utilized inefficiently.

Productivity of business-critical capital equipment (as measured by such metrics as yield, throughput, and production availability) is essential to maintain and extend competitive advantage. In the semiconductor in-

Figure 9-5.

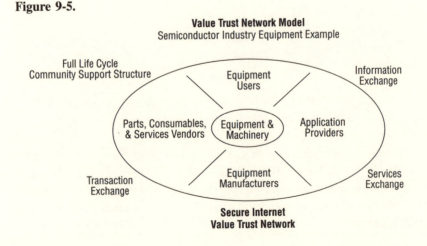

Value Trust Network Model
Semiconductor Industry Equipment Example

dustry, yield has finally surged beyond the 90 percent mark after years of effort, yet the combination of throughput and production availability hovers at less than 50 percent. Change is inevitable. Equipment users are under pressure to increase productivity as they respond to rapidly changing markets. Consequently, they are demanding that equipment manufacturers take responsibility for improving equipment productivity. Both are looking to private, secure networks and the Internet as the vehicle for supply chain partners to collaborate to improve equipment uptime and productivity, and to reduce costs.

The sub-50 percent utilization has repeatedly driven cyclical over-expansions in the industry. More efficient and productive operation and deployment of equipment requires improved information architectures and closer coupling between all tiers of the supply chain. Through the deployment of a Value Trust Network model, a company like Symphony could bridge this gap with a variety of software and Internet technologies, plus hardware enhancements for older equipment to make them Internet-capable.

Timing is critical for any venture, especially one operating on "Internet time." Figure 9-6 illustrates some of the key planning areas that need to be addressed throughout the deployment of the company ebusiness planning process. Certainly, the timing is right in the semiconductor industry. With equipment utilization running in the 50 percent range

Figure 9-6. *Supply Chain Planning Time Horizon*

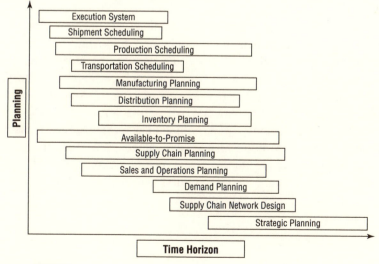

Source: *marchFIRST*

across the highly competitive semiconductor industry, the demand for productivity solutions is intense. Even small increases in productivity have significant financial implications for the semiconductor industry. For example, an increase in equipment productivity from 50 percent to 52 percent would benefit all parties enormously. Under this scenario, chipmakers' annual production revenue of $200 billion would increase by $8 billion—without adding any additional equipment assets.

The opportunity for equipment manufacturers is also impressive. Higher-productivity equipment gives added value to customers, along with increased market share. Diagnostic and customer support capabilities over secure networks mean faster response times with considerable service and support savings. The net result is for equipment manufacturers to continue the trend of receiving a larger fraction of the total semiconductor revenue, and lower total costs the chip makers. Application software providers benefit from a fast, highly efficient sales channel and low-cost system integration. Simply put, information technology is the least expensive method of significantly improving the value of equipment.

Symphony's network-based connectivity infrastructure and suite of software services seamlessly connects people with new and existing equipment within an entire supply chain, creating a Web-based community of equipment, equipment users, equipment suppliers, parts and consumables suppliers, and application software providers.

Chapter Summary

The VTN model provides for both immediate and ongoing productivity improvements of high-demand production equipment. The model is achieved through a collaborative trusted network of independent companies working together in a VTN model. Each participant in the Value Trust Network adds value to the network members, as well as receives significant value from the network. All participants come away with a more streamlined business process, a longer-term integrated customer relationship, improved performance, and valuable information. The powerful information that is gathered through participation in the VTN model can be used to produce better products and services, business model enhancements, and improved bottom- and top-line financials performance for all involved.

CHAPTER

Customer-Centric Power Shift

Consumers in every business sector are becoming increasingly intelligent about products and services as a result of the Internet. The Internet provides easy access to basic product information, price, product reviews, rating systems, and other data points that enable consumers to make more informed choices about products or services. As a result, customers are more empowered than ever before in history.

This chapter reviews the profound power shift from producers to consumers that is causing fundamental changes both from within an organization as well as through the entire value chain. It reviews the sweeping changes in areas such as organizational models, compensation, and distribution networks. At the very forefront of the discussion is a new holistic customer relationship management (CRM) mandate.

The Internet is the primary lever of change in this marketplace and brings with it a whole new set of customer values and opportunities. First and foremost is the dimension of time. Since the number of online business and intermediaries is growing exponentially, the race is on to get more of the customer's time. As businesses become increasingly competitive over customers, those that can expand their services and products to meet additional customer demands will win out over those that can't. Also, because getting more of the customer's time is a gating factor preventing rapid revenue growth, enterprises are shifting their focus from products to customers. In addition, since the Internet is proving disruptive in many markets, fierce competition is producing more customer defection and turnover, requiring companies to be swift and nimble in their response. Not only are businesses fighting each other for customers' time, they are working hard to get more valuable insight into their customers in *less time*. The Internet both enables and fuels these high-velocity markets.

To develop a winning customer-centric strategy, you must think in multidimensional terms, or as they say in the customer relationship management field, multiple "channels." The optimum strategy determines where, how, and when the customer wants to be addressed. In a customer-centric world, companies strive to understand the customer and to come to them or at least be accessible to them on a 24-hour basis through combinations of the Internet, phone, fax, or in person. There are many ways to engage customers and to build lifelong relationships. Savvy companies have a mandate to discover and reach customers through these touch points. (See Figure 10-1.)

The Internet has showered consumer knowledge onto millions of people. It is changing impulse buyers into selective buyers and selective buyers into first-generation relationship customers. The next generation

Figure 10-1. *Multiple Points of Contact in a Multidimensional Business Environment*

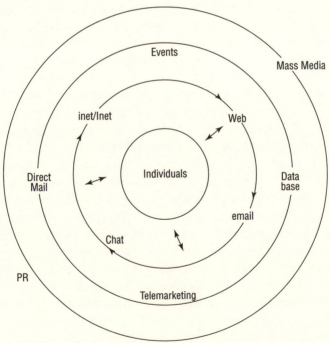

of Internet consumers will demand information concerning products and services. Companies that cannot provide this information and tailor it to the individual or partner will be left behind. While the consumer is becoming more informed, the Internet has also enabled mass customization, creating micro segments of customers. Both these trends are working together to create a very complicated sea of customers and informational needs.

According to Jeff Hammond of Rhea & Kaiser, a digital branding agency in Chicago,

> Interactive communication channels have enabled people to understand the power they have as individuals. Organizations, prices, products, and promotions are transparent to individuals who can share their experiences and knowledge with one another. Consumer research has consistently found that people are looking for solutions to their challenges; they are making purchase decisions differently; and they don't take at face value what faceless organizations say to them. It seems so obvious that people would want to be treated like people, not as targets or segments. But I think it's the widespread use of interactive channels that has galvanized this understanding among "consumers" and, more slowly, within the organizations that serve them. Call it "me commerce," but that's the demand of the online customer.

The combination of smarter consumers, new customer channels, and the effect of customization is forcing companies to make CRM and customer initiatives top priority. Brick-and-mortar along with new electronic business models must clearly understand that this shift is a fundamental business model shift to a customer-centric business model. The customer shift cannot be addressed by yet another one-to-one marketing campaign.

The Three Dimensions of Customization

As the customer shift takes place, the principals that are creating this complexity are also creating the tools and models to enable companies to make the shift along with—if not ahead of—their customers. Just as the consumer is becoming more intelligent, the company in parallel should become more intelligent about the customer. This customer shift is also creating new business channels and even new lines of business altogether. Customization may be the hardest for a corporation to grasp and leverage. Customization in many ways should be the basis for customer relationship management initiatives and will carry a lot of power,

Figure 10-2.

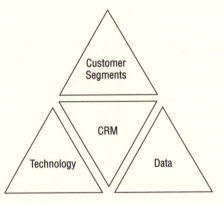

Source: Rhea & Kaiser Marketing Communications

as well as benefits, to the organization. Customization should be addressed as three-dimensional, where the three dimensions are customer
segments, technology, and data. At this time, most organizations only
view customization in the area of broad customer segments. The
customer-centric organization targets segments of one.

Customer interactions occur across a variety of channels: from
phone, fax, and mail, to email, Web sites, and wireless devices (see
Figure 10-2). Ensuring quality customer interaction across multiple channels is a key concern for businesses, especially as these transactions
occur across multiple channels *within one transaction.* Some CRM vendors provide tools to manage and ensure channel parity—that is, to ensure that the brand message and service quality are consistent regardless
of channel.

Customer Customization

The customization of customers segments illustrated in Figure 10-2 is
the result of taking customer segments and breaking them into micro
segments. For example, a company's high-volume or top-tier customers
are now divided into subcategories. The intent is to provide more customized support and interaction with leading customers.

For example, Joe's Luggage Co. may have classified its top-spend-
ing segment as the "elite" customer segment in the past. This customer
contributed x percent of revenue and came through defined channels. The
Internet now adds the additional unknowns about Joe's Luggage Co.
"elite" segment of customers:

- What percentage of the customer base visits the Web site
- The types of information individuals prefer
- Individual buying habits

This is just a very simple example of customization within an Internet segment. In the commodity agricultural chemical industry, many attempts are underway to segment and target the elite customers, which are typically larger growers with more than 250 acres under cultivation. For one company, this has led to a rethinking of the traditional three-step distribution chain relationships, where the three levels are defined as distributors, dealers, and end customers. Because the traditional three-step model hides end-user data behind the administrative layers of retailer and distributor, it can be difficult to communicate with the actual users of the product. To make the distribution channel more transparent, and more efficient, the manufacturer is implementing electronic ordering and commitment management directly with growers, while using the distribution chain only for the value they add, such as shipping, invoicing, and warehousing.

Improving contact through the entire value chain is critical. According to Brad Back of Rhea & Kaiser,

> Having more effective contact with all members of the distribution chain, including the end user, means that awareness-building, mass-media communications can be more narrowly focused to provide "cleanup" coverage for second-tier customers. Payments to the channel can be redirected to more intensive, direct efforts to understand and engage the elite growers. The ability to integrate data from electronic ordering, invoicing, and payments with marketing programs targeted to the end customer (such as rebates, discounts, and regulatory monitoring programs) is providing the company with the ability to squeeze additional margins out of the supply chain. Savings of 1 to 2% out of the supply chain can be achieved by reducing inefficiencies, stabilizing product pricing for retailers, and more accurately managing supply and distribution to growers through improved forecasting and customized solutions to grower challenges.

Technology Customization

The next dimension of customization is technology customization. Technology customization can be achieved by the ability to provide literally all of the relevant corporate data to customers or partners at any give moment. Companies must evaluate what types of information customers and partners want to access from a technology perspective. Second, they must determine which of those customers should have access to such information. Finally, they must analyze how the company can get the information to the customer or partner.

The combination of enterprise resource planning (ERP) and materials resource planning (MRP) systems centralization and several years of customer database data collection has armed enterprises with the beginnings of very customer intelligent systems. The interactive channels that have also been created have blurred the lines of ERP and have allowed the collection and use of logistic, supply chain, manufacturing, and customer data to become customer assets.

Data Customization

The final dimension is the data dimension. The customer-centric shift is breaking the mold of what customer data to capture or leverage. The one-to-one marketing programs are focused on a transactional response of the customer. The data models of the future will need to be more intuitive and layered to capture and return accurate custom relationship data rather than targeted data. Figure 10-3 illustrates that a process and technology–integrated information flow coupled with business rules can

Figure 10-3.

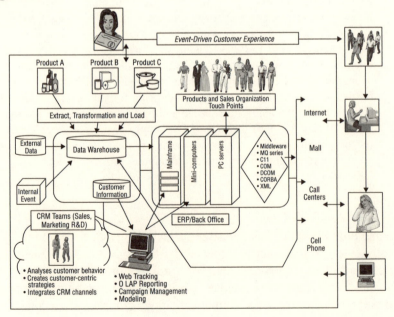

make for an event-driven experience throughout the enterprise. The world is moving toward a requirement for real-time event-driven responsiveness at every step of the value chain. This type of event-triggered activity needs to have a tightly integrated platform available on a 24-hour-a-day basis.

Just as the Internet and the shift in consumer behavior is complicating customer relationships, it is also empowering organizations to be able to accomplish results like never before in history. If the proper planning, models, tools, and approaches are used correctly, organizations will have the customer information to proactively maneuver themselves to optimize profit.

A Shift from Inward Focus to Outward Focus

Companies over the past 30 years have focused internally on their people, process, and technologies, building extensive MRP and ERP systems, optimizing internal business process, right-sizing, downsizing, and so on. The current and future trends are all leading toward an outward focus that is inclusive of the customer and the entire value chain. Companies literally have to turn themselves inside out and expose portions of their operations to various communities that are made up of integrated communities of customers, employees, and partners. This was once the tightly controlled domain of the information systems (IS) department. Now it is a shared by a cross-functional ebusiness effort.

The winners in the next generation of ebusiness will be those that appropriately and securely open up their enterprises to the world.

Business Possibilities

The opportunities for companies to extend their market reach, streamline business workflow, and enter new markets has never been better. The progression to ebusiness is a very personal company path. Some may evaluate their markets, their core competencies, and their company culture and determine to take distinctly different paths. Some may choose to build an ebusiness architecture, culture, and team of people and become an ebusiness. Others may adapt their current operations to capitalize on the Web in a phased approach starting with customer-facing solutions then empowering their internal operations with employee-facing solutions and ultimately integrating with their external partners.

Strength in Numbers

The winners in this game will be those that learn how to set up a marketplace and engage others to join them, and through their aggregated strength of buying power, selling power, streamlined communication, and business integration, they will be stronger together than alone.

The more interactive the e-Marketplace experience is, the more people will become engaged with the e-Marketplace, and this will lead to increased interdependencies. Personalize the experience to all users of the e-Marketplace. The more vested and dependent someone becomes to a certain place, the higher the switching costs are to that person. This is why many e-Marketplaces and portals try to get the members to use free services like calendars, email, and chat rooms.

Building Intimate Customer Relationships

The Internet has provided a medium for companies to have a one-on-one interaction with their customers 24 hours a day, 7 days a week in almost every country in the world. This channel of customer interaction has created an overnight relationship with the customer. The May 1, 2000 issue of *The Industry Standard* references a Boston Consulting Group

Figure 10-4.

Brick-and-Click Firms Lure Buyers Back

Customer Metrics by E-Retailer Type				
	Online Pure-Plays	Multi-Channel (Catalog-Based)	Multi-Channel (Store-Based)	Overall Average
Buyer conversion*	3.5%	4.2%	1.8%	3.2%
Percent of buyers that are repeat buyers	27%	20%	34%	25%
Percent of revenue from repeat buyers	30%	27%	45%	31%
Fulfillment costs per order	$12.50	$10.30	$18.10	$11.80
Customer service costs per order	$3.50	$1.20	$6.20	$2.40

*Percent of Unique Visitors that purchase, all Data Based on financial information for the companies' ecommerce activities only source; Snororg Boston Consulting Group

Source: The Industry Standard

study that reflects the cross-interaction companies are seeing with new interactive channels. (See Figure 10-4.)

The ability to interact with customers at any moment creates the opportunity to gain more wallet share and increase brand loyalty. To take advantage of the intimacy the Internet brings customers, companies must ensure that the quality of online customer service is as effective or better than face-to-face customer service. To begin to understand how to meet customer or partner expectations, a company must start to analyze complete customer life cycles and the multiple customer touch points to the company.

The Importance of Customer Lifetime Value

One way CRM initiatives will be measured is *customer lifetime value*. Customer lifetime value is the total increased value that is generated from a customer by accurately understanding the customer's needs over the entire life cycle. A finance perspective would describe customer lifetime value as the increased profit or loss of profit generated over the entire life of the customer relationship by accurately or inaccurately understanding and predicting customer needs.

The way to get to customer lifetime value is first to determine the *customer life cycle* of a particular segment of customers. The customer life cycle is the groundwork that must be understood to build long-term, intimate customer relationships. To truly understand a customer segment's life cycle, a company must understand the "cradle to grave" concept that begins with the time a company acquires a new customer until that customer is retired and all phases in between.

You should align the company around customer satisfaction, and monitor, measure, and reward for high customer satisfaction ratings. Leading customer-centric companies like Dell Computer have aligned their entire organization around successful customer satisfaction. Making customer satisfaction a top priority takes more that just the words in the annual report. Proactive action-based planning and execution are required to make total customer satisfaction a reality. One of the key areas to focus on is an alignment of top management objectives and compensation plans based on customer satisfaction improvements. (See Figure 10-5.) Customer satisfaction should be an active process of anticipating customer requirements, creating value, and delivering that value by both digital and physical means. A culture of action-oriented people should surround the process. A rapid response should be built in to react to key trigger events throughout the value chain process.

Figure 10-5. *Customer Satisfaction Monitoring*

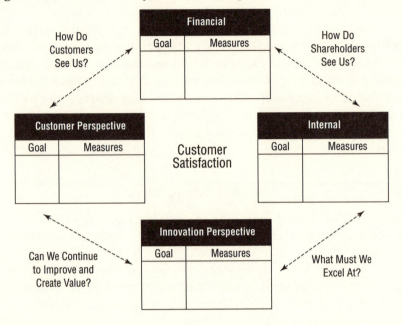

Monitor and Measure Customer Satisfaction

To be a true customer centric company, it is important to align the entire company around customer satisfaction. This includes organizational and business process alignment, as well as compensation and recognition alignment. A critical component to a successful customer-centric model is a workable system of monitoring, measuring, and adjusting to customer satisfaction on a companywide basis every day.

Develop a Balanced Scorecard Approach

A balance scorecard analyzes the following criteria:

- New customers
- Customers lost
- Resubscription rate
- Customer satisfaction
- Customer complaints
- Sales win/loss ratio
- Sales cycle time
- Sales margin

The Devil Is in the Details

To some extent, personalization engines that use real-time techniques, such as collaborative filtering, are already providing real-time knowledge deployment capabilities. Businesses are beginning to develop specific processes and teams around understanding and anticipating customer needs. Increasingly, customer knowledge is being created and classified as an important strategic corporate asset. Just as inventory turnover is a key indicator of supply chain efficiency and demand forecasting accuracy, customer knowledge turnover will be an equally significant measure of how well a business can respond to changing customer needs.

Knowledge Turnover

Technology has a strong role to play in all four of the areas shown in Figure 10-6. The act of creating new insight requires business intelligence and data-mining tools. Dispersing this knowledge to others across the enterprise requires Web application deployment tools. The process of acting on the new knowledge requires internal collaboration and decision-making technology. Finally, the process of measuring and reacting to change requires additional measurement technologies and approaches.

Savvy companies will find ways of integrating technologies with business processes and organizational design to acquire knowledge quickly and make better decisions faster. Over time, we expect to see more organizations infusing technology into work processes. To support this more sophisticated customer-focused knowledge turnover engine, we

Figure 10-6.

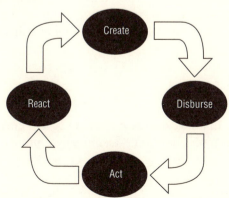

Create
Discover new insights

Disburse
Share insights with others

Act
Get people to move

React
Measure/monitor/adjust and prepare for the next cycle

expect to see vendors add hybrid advanced data-mining algorithms, including techniques such as rules induction, classification and regression trees, logistic regression and other statistical techniques, neural networks, genetic algorithms, and other data-mining approaches within the same product. Sophisticated companies will need to overlay multiple advanced techniques for specific data-mining needs.

Gaining the greatest possible insight into customers will require bringing together multiple streams of data, both online and offline, in a virtual central repository. Over time, we expect to see more legacy system and ERP adapters, specifically designed for CRM. Traditional database marketing has known for quite some time that capturing the correct data is the key to successful campaigns. The intended use for the data being captured traditionally was for transactional-type results that attract and retain customers. The new customer-centric shift is not based on transactional results, however. The key to success within CRM is to take the traditional database marketing techniques to the next level to increase share in the new commodity called customer relationships. The process starts by knowing individual customers and their respective behaviors. Mapping the customer life cycle is a good start to understanding customers and segments.

Organizations should start their CRM approach by diving into the details of their customers and customer segments. The areas that should be completely understood are as follows:

- Customer segmentation
- Segment life cycles
- The most profitable segments

Once an in-depth understanding of customer segments is understood, the organization will then be equipped to create the data structures to address the particular high ROI (return on investment) life cycles and have enough understanding to proactively meet customers wants and needs.

Customer Value-Added Services

In the previous sections, the Internet, database marketing, and customization was reviewed. These topics are very technology-, profit-, and marketing-driven. One major area that organizations cannot overlook is CRM initiatives. Much of the CRM space at this time is driven by technology- or marketing-based solutions. Technology and marketing are large pieces of the customer relationship puzzle, if not the largest. CRM is not something that can be pulled off the shelf and purchased.

Comprehensive CRM strategies are complex initiatives that cover all customer segments and make organizations proactively understand future customer wants and needs. In determining how to approach and develop intimate customer relationships technology, marketing, creative service offerings, employee training, and corporate change management are some of the major components that must be visited.

Once the target segments are identified and the life cycles are mapped within a segment, then all of the CRM levers can be used at any given time to meet the changing needs of that segment. Cross-functional brainstorming should always have a spot on the deliverables list within a CRM strategy process.

One-to-one marketing efforts and life-cycle efforts traditionally have used rewards and point systems to leverage lifetime value. Rewards programs also hold the perception of owning the customer relationship. Studies have been conducted that have shown customer response in these areas.

In the United States the average consumer participates in over three loyalty marketing programs. Over half of the U.S. supermarkets have such programs, yet data show that the biggest shoppers send only half their business to their preferred chain. At least half of all U.S. households now belong to some type of loyalty program. These programs are gathering important information about their customers, as well as driving sales. Yet, very few are building loyalty.

Across the board companies with loyalty programs offer discounts, and a majority of business-to-business marketers do as well, but studies are showing us that's not enough.

In the 1997 Retail Advertising and Marketing Association International Research Project on Loyalty Programs, conducted by Marshall Marketing and Communication, Inc., only 33 percent of consumers said that they are recognized and made to feel special for participating in their loyalty program. Interestingly enough, it was the highest-income consumers ($75,000+) who rated "being recognized and made to feel special" an important element for a loyalty program.

When approaching CRM and customer-centric business models, the data is showing the loyalty programs are just a small piece of owning and managing a customer relationship. Loyalty programs are definitely driving transactional response to drive sales, but they do not engage the customer from a relationship perspective. The reality of the data coming back is showing that truly measurable customer loyalty cannot be bought.

TeleWeb Integration

E-Marketplaces are in a prime position to leverage the multiple touch points that customers have with an organization. The ability to provide a Web interface to all of the customer contact points, such as the marketing, sales, and customer support, is very powerful and cost-efficient. It is now possible to integrate a company Web strategy with a telephone call center support strategy. This integration is known as a *TeleWeb strategy*. A TeleWeb strategy features the ability to provide "live" human interaction on the company Web site with the customers through the integration of live chat capabilities linked to call center personnel or to any other teams or individuals internal or external to a company.

Live Chat or Text-Based Interaction

About 2 percent of all ecommerce players are deploying a chat solution. Live chat is being embraced as e-CRM by top players in different verticals, with financial services organizations taking the lead. With chat up and running, major ecommerce players are able to evaluate its return on investment.

Maximize Sales Opportunities

By extending the length and quality of a customer's visit, live chat technology helps increase conversion rates, average order size, and customer retention. Equipped with live chat, a customer service representative (CSR) can also turn an abandoned shopping cart into a sales opportunity by essentially instant messaging a customer and asking if help is needed.

This is true proactive selling. Up-selling and cross-selling opportunities are also enhanced when a CSR suggests additional products. For example, in a recent test pilot, Intuit, Inc., a leading developer of financial software and services, tested live chat from a leading TeleWeb solution company called LivePerson and reported that 67 percent of its customers who ordered online did so using LivePerson's text-based live chat product. The Intuit technical support department also had similar results. Eighty-one percent of customers obtained help without ever having to interrupt their Web session. At Ditech, the mortgage lending company, and another LivePerson client, they are generating 30 to 50 loans a month worth approximately $3 million per month.

Some organizations are using live interaction proactively. Sales for Hometownstores.com, on online home improvement store, rose 30 percent within a month after a personal greeter service was launched in the fall. The site's chat operators individually greet 14,000 visitors a day.

Reduce Operating Costs

Live chat boosts productivity. The traditional call center works on a support model of one customer service representative (CSR) to one customer call. The TeleWeb model enables a CSR to maintain on average four customer dialogues via the live chat. This dramatic performance improvement enables CSRs to better serve more customer requests in a faster, more interactive manner. Through the use of the Internet, not only does the customer have human contact, the CSR is able to deliver live data to the customer immediately and assist him or her in navigating the existing Web content. This way, companies are able to maximize the quality of the interaction and the time spent with each customer, dramatically reducing the cost per interaction when compared to a typical 800 number call center. In addition, customizable, preformatted responses help the CSR improve productivity and ensure consistency to frequently asked questions.

The lower cost of transmitting information via the Internet or email versus placing a phone call further increases the costs benefits of other customer interaction channels. Gartner Group estimates that when a customer calls in to an organization and actually gets through, the interaction costs an average of $5.01. By contrast, if a company were able to handle a "conversation" with the customer through a Web chat, connecting him or her would cost a center an average of $0.25 to $3.50.

Strengthen Customer Relationships

A lot of lip service is being paid on the concept of one-to-one marketing. Everyone wants to do it. Everyone recognizes it's important. But most make the mistake of thinking technology alone is going to deliver the promise. It takes the impact of a live person to build relationships that last.

With live chat, such as the offerings demonstrated at Live-Person.com, a CSR can interact with customers in real time on a one-to-one basis. They can receive real-time feedback about customer service and technical support efforts, as well as review archived call logs to access a customer's call history and gauge customer satisfaction levels.

360-Degree Customer Satisfaction

Providing 360-degree customer satisfaction refers to the ability of a company to provide a complete circle of information and support to anyone entering and working through the e-Marketplace. The goal is to provide the e-Marketplace customer with complete access to the appropriate people, resources, and information needed to quickly and easily have a productive experience.

To illustrate the importance of 360-degree customer satisfaction, let's walk through an example. The example is a procurement manager named Sam at a high-tech manufacturer. Sam is not currently a customer of the e-Marketplace. He logs into the e-Marketplace and registers himself as a member. While Sam is applying for membership, the site asks Sam to fill out a series of electronic forms that will be used by the e-Marketplace to provide Sam with more personalized service. The e-Marketplace takes the information and, as a result, makes some recommendations that make Sam feel as though the e-Marketplace truly understands his needs. A few moments later, after receiving a welcome and membership confirmation via email, Sam attempts to use the e-Marketplace. When entering the site, Sam is presented the same generic Web pages and begins to go through the buying process as though he hadn't provided any detailed information. The site recommends products inaccurately, and therefore, Sam has to sift through the multiple offerings until he finds what he needs. Sam then continues through the purchase process and is asked to enter much of the same information that he provided when he initially registered with the e-Marketplace.

Unfortunately, this type of experience is far too common. However, when customers find a digital marketplace that accurately customizes the offerings to their needs, they appreciate the personalized value and return to do business again.

To maintain a true customer relationship, a company must provide value back to a customer, particularly when a customer is required to invest his or her time in registering and interacting with an e-Marketplace. It is important to leverage the business intelligence that is gained from the CRM solutions. Not leveraging the intelligence has the effect of diluting the brand and compromising the quality of customer service. The e-Marketplace will lose a valuable opportunity to build a lasting relationship with key customers or segments of customers.

A value-based relationship should be consistent with all channels of communication that are offered at the e-Marketplace. For example, the customer information and preferences should be identified on all portions of the Web site and at the telephone support center, and should also be represented in all external communication between the e-Marketplace and the customer. To make sure that that a constant experience is being provided throughout the entire customer interaction then a *touch-*

point analysis must be part of the overall CRM strategy. This is the process by which a company documents and analyzes all points by which customers interact within the e-Marketplace. This process can be completed in conjunction with the customer life-cycle analysis. Touch points usually change throughout the maturity of a customer's life cycle.

Information Empowerment

Information is the key to creating truly customized experiences. The Internet provides transparency of pricing, availability, and even business models to customers. However, this transparency works both ways. Today more than ever before, companies have transparency to view customer, channel, supplier, and partner behavior and activities. This information is an empowering source of power for companies that learn how to harness it and convert the information into knowledge. The knowledge can then be used to develop products, solve industry pain points, pinpoint customer demands, and create new knowledge services.

Data collection isn't enough, however. It must also be accurately applied. CRM is one of the major initiatives that is pushing this data usage craze forward. The advancement of the Internet and technologies has created endless possibilities for tracking and leveraging user data. These techniques must be reconciled with CRM strategies for maximum benefit, however. The data models and structure must be closely reviewed to ensure they are going to meet the short-term and long-term CRM initiatives.

The current focus on data usage is bringing the powerful notion of *information empowerment* to the forefront. The concept of information empowerment is to model and leverage the data captured and provide knowledge services and value to all customers, employees, and partners. Information empowerment and data usage are also a result of the lines of ERP data being blurred.

An example of information empowerment to customers, employees, and partners illustrates the importance of a multiple touch-point strategy, along with a viewpoint on how the lines of ERP are blurring. As shown in Figure 10-7, in a true real-time organization, business will be conducted with the customers through a frictionless environment in which the ongoing collection, analysis, and use of customer data is applied for the purpose of increasing customer lifetime value. The ERP data is now moving toward integration with CRP, or customer relationship planning. This planning includes all customer systems direct and indirect, marketing, advertising, and corporate culture.

Figure 10-7. *CRM Integration Points*

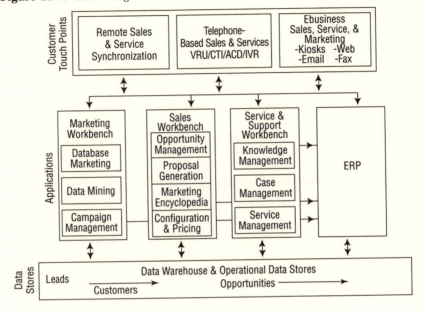

Mass Customization

Mass customization is the ability to communicate in a highly personalized manner with many people at the same time. Customization on the Internet has taken off with sites like MyYahoo and Excite. These sites fueled the portal craze for personalization. The portal push has now evolved into the strategy of mass customization. Along with mass customization strategies maturing, so has the technology that enables mass customization. Mass customization is extremely powerful and will be a major component of delivering a customer-centric business model and value to consumers. On the surface, mass customization seems to have many organizational and technical complexities, and executing it properly does take detailed planning on both the technical and CRM strategy side. A company's mass customization design must meet the CRM objects and the customers' needs, and it must be flexible enough to adapt in the future. Along with the power of customization comes a legal dilemma: How much personal information does a company collect to build a customization foundation? How is that information used or abused? In addition, how much of that information gets leveraged and by what parties? This legal dilemma has the CRM, legal, government, and consumer communities debating. At least part of the solution lies in the area of *permission-based* marketing and support services. Throughout the customer interaction, permission is requested for certain uses of the information. If it is granted, then the customer is satisfied.

CRM and Beyond

Customer-centric CRM efforts within organizations at this time are being viewed as a minimal 24-month investment by organizations. The ROI models are showing that the major returns on customer centric efforts begin demonstrating big payoffs around the 24- to 36-month time frame, depending on the industry. Faster ROIs can be demonstrated on specific initiatives such as adding email responses, promotions, and updates, along with live interactive chat capabilities to e-Marketplaces. A complete, holistic, enterprisewide CRM initiative can be a very complex blend of technology, strategy, people, process, and procedures.

So how does a company begin to approach a customer centric model and begin to launch CRM initiative? Figure 10-8 shows a matrix that can be used when developing a CRM visioning session with corporate executives. The result of this matrix can be the foundation for a CRM maturity model. Figure 10-8 further illustrates some practical areas where a company needs to address the CRM opportunities in a business integration manner.

A maturity approach will identify the current state of the business

Figure 10-8.

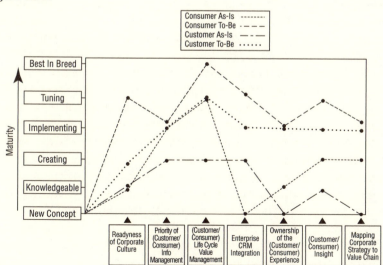

and provide a vision toward the desired state of the business within the main areas of a customer-centric model. The maturity model identifies the gaps and how large the gaps are within the main areas of CRM.

Performing this exercise enables an organization to understand how CRM can be effectively applied in the organization. It allows companies to identify initiatives, capitalize on quick hit opportunities, and lay the groundwork for analyzing which areas will bring the greatest ROI. The maturity process should be a process that organizations look at carefully as a starting point in developing a customer-centric strategy.

As companies improve their sophistication in this new area, more CRM applications will be focused on active experimentation with customers, including surveying and Web-based market tests to better predict what customers will do in response to new product or service offerings. Personalization will evolve from looking at users' behavior from yesterday to predicting what tomorrow's users may do. Expect to see campaign management CRM vendors add better support for online campaign tests and for ecommerce content management vendors to provide better support for real-time test environments, in which different versions of the Web site will be deployed to groups of test users.

Once an ebusiness is established, it quickly becomes a well of highly structured, high-quality customer data. Businesses will need ways to deliver more information about customers to key decision makers quickly. A key measure is what others have called *intelligence density*, which is the amount of information delivered over time. For all businesses, CRM technologies have a strong role to play. The internal decision support and data-mining tools must yield higher intelligence density ratios so businesses can quickly respond to changing market conditions and customer needs.

While the Internet excels as a distribution and transaction medium, perhaps its most promising use is as a highly measured medium. The technology can quickly collect, codify, segment, personalize, and tailor customer interactions for each individual customer. With this fire hose of data at their disposal, businesses will need advanced CRM technologies to process and interpret this data. Those businesses that successfully master these high-velocity approaches will be better at differentiating and retaining their online customers than their competitors. CRM technologies are quickly evolving to provide these capabilities, and the ongoing convergence will produce many effects.

Modern customer information systems must unite field sales, telemarketing, customer service, claims, partners, and customers with an integrated customer information system. A powerful, integrated applications architecture is required across the entire sales and service process.

The Emergence of E-Customer Relationship Management

E-CRM arises from the consolidation of the traditional CRM and the ebusiness applications marketplaces. E-CRM is Web-based and provides a channel in which businesses can continually engage customers, accurately measure and record customer knowledge, and gain flexibility in their product and service offerings and delivery. In a perfect world, e-Marketplaces will be fully transactional environments integrated with ERP supply chain, sales and marketing, logistics, and other legacy systems from which an e-CRM solution can be executed.

The intellectual property of an enterprise is not so much about the products it produces, but the market segment knowledge it possesses. Know thy customer. Do companies really know the value of each customer? Traditional brick-and-mortar companies are fending off the threat of competitors by capturing and using their customer knowledge as a base to wrestle market control from the dot-coms as they reintermediate themselves by building customer-centric products and a set of services to solve customer problems.

As the Internet matures, the customer becomes the focus of attention. To deliver on the customer demands, it becomes critically important to enable direct communication between trading partners.

It is becoming a business necessity to be customer-responsive. Timely response requires rapid communication and integration with all parties involved in the development and delivery of the products and or services. E-CRM solutions leverage the powerful networking and communications capabilities of the Internet. They also allow for both internal process integration, as well as external partner process and communication integration. Figure 10-9 illustrates some of the multiple channels of communication and interaction that are used when working through the value chain.

CRM Channels

Customer interactions occur across a variety of channels. As illustrated in Figure 10-10, these multiple channels can range from phone, fax, and mail to email, Web sites, and wireless devices. Ensuring quality customer interaction across multiple channels is a key concern for businesses, especially as these transactions occur across multiple channels *within one transaction*. Some CRM vendors provide tools to manage and ensure

Figure 10-9.

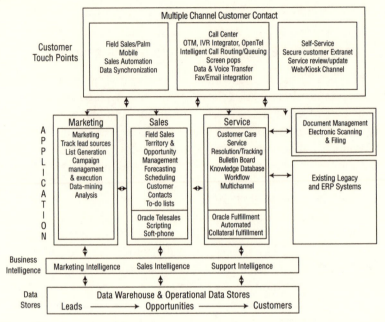

channel parity—that is, to ensure that the brand message and service quality are consistent regardless of channel.

E-CRM Channels

Ecommerce executives are faced with a singular challenge: how to turn browsers into buyers. The key to delivering on the promise of ecommerce

Figure 10-10.

Business	Face to face	**Sales Channel**	Face to face	**End User**
	Video		Video	
	Phone		Phone	
	Voice		Voice	
	Fax		Fax	
	Radio		Radio	
	WWW		WWW	
	Mail		Mail	
	Email		Email	
	TV/Cable		TV/Cable	
	Wireless		Wireless	

is service. And it's clear that customers want to be treated well. They are asking for multiple contact points and options like live interaction. They expect that a company will understand their preferences and respect their privacy.

According to Jupiter Communications, only 37 percent of Web ventures currently combine three or more customer service channels on their Web sites. Clearly, there is room for improvement.

Enter e-CRM, customer relationship management solutions geared to serve ecommerce companies. e-CRM is growing in a customer-centric marketplace. The marketplace is marked by convergence where personalization companies are merging with application providers and traditional call center organizations are merging with each other. Datamonitor estimates that the online customer support market will grow from $150 million in 1998 to $2 billion in 2003. Their studies also show that only 8 percent of the 69,500 call centers in the United States are Web-enabled. They also indicate that businesses lost $1.6 billion online in 1998 by failing to Web-enable their operations. The figure reached upward of $3.2 billion in lost sales during 1999.

An Evaluation of Current Customer Service Solutions

Most current customer service solutions fall into three broad categories: Dynamic FAQs (frequently asked questions), email, and phone. The next generation of solutions is all real time and includes Voice over IP (VoIP) and live chat.

FAQ, email, and phone have important and unique roles to play in an overall customer service delivery solution. By themselves, they fall short because the Internet is a real-time medium demanding real-time interaction. At the same time, live chat and interactive products have a cost disadvantage if not used effectively.

Dynamic FAQ

Dynamic FAQs are a self-service way for customers to get answers to commonly asked questions. FAQs have evolved over the past few years. The most common are in the form of *brochureware*. This tool represents the most basic form of customer service and corporate communication on the Internet. Customers typically scroll down a list to find the answer they need. Brochureware FAQs are limited because there is no way to truly measure their efficiency.

Over time, FAQs have gotten "smarter." Often referred to as natural language query FAQs, these tools deploy "smart" search engine technology to direct the customer to the needed information resources. The customer types in a question like, "What kind of plants should I order for my patio?" and the system interprets the question and provides answers until the customers get exactly what he or she wants. When the activity is complete, the smart FAQ asks if the person making the query got what they wanted and the system updates itself. Office Depot is actively deploying this kind of technology.

A third kind of FAQ is proactive and built into actual applications. These FAQs often pop up on the screen when the customer has trouble. The wizard that comes in many Microsoft programs is a good example of this. Try typing the words "Dear John" in Microsoft Word, and chances are that the wizard will pop up, asking if this is a letter and if help is needed.

Email

Email is an important low-cost, customer service tool. It is ideally deployed in three key ways:

- *By conveying complex information*—Email is ideal for answering complex product questions such as "How do I install my VCR?" or "Why do error messages keep popping up when I install my new computer gaming software?" It's particularly effective when the customer needs detailed information versus immediate information.
- *By updating order status*—Email is also used to let customers know that their order is still packing or that their order has shipped. Nike, LL Bean, and Amazon have set the standard in this area.
- *By generating leads*—Amazon.com, for example, is well known for using email to tell customers that their favorite author has written a book.

Send.com, a site that specializes in helping gift givers choose the perfect item, combines order tracking with lead generation and adds a twist. They provide shipping updates via email and later send a thank-you note from the CEO, along with a box of chocolates. (Send.com sells fantastic gifts, ranging from a day at the spa to Rolls-Royces online.) They follow up throughout the year with personalized gift-giving suggestions.

Managing email is becoming a greater and greater problem. Email is the default channel on the Internet, and ecommerce companies are awash in email. A recent study compared Web site service at ten popular sites in May 2000 to what it was in May 1999. Of the ten companies contacted, four didn't respond after three days. Of those that did respond, the answer had the personality of Hal from *2001: A Space Odyssey*.

Even Amazon.com, which tends be very customer-responsive, has had problems. In 1999, Amazon.com responded in 34 minutes. In 2000, there was no response forthcoming by the third day. Similarly, eBay didn't fare much better, with no reply after three days. In 1999, they replied in an hour and 37 minutes.

Jupiter Communications also recently tracked how fast the top 125 Web sites responded to customer email. They found that 46 percent took five days or more, never responded, or did not post an email address on their site.

Another study examined the Fortune 100 and how they handled email. Twenty-three of the companies couldn't be contacted by email via their Web site, including GTE, Hewlett-Packard, and Intel. Of the 77 Fortune 100 companies that could be contacted by email, a third didn't respond after three months. These organizations included American Express, Motorola, and Walt Disney.

Phone

What does a shopper do if his or her merchandise doesn't arrive? Most would pick up the phone and make a call. It makes sense, right? When it comes to the Web, customers are still very phone-dependent. The phone is an important tool when the interaction is personal (financial services, beauty, health). In fact, call centers have reported a 65 percent call increase as the Internet has grown.

Some companies are so sensitive to this fact that they include a Call Back button on their Web sites. This is an especially effective customer service feature for pure play companies. But it only works if the customer has multiple phone lines in the house.

Ebank.com leverages one channel to another this way. Their site is equipped with a Call Back button. The user just presses the button; a message is then forwarded to an e-bank call center, and the customer then receives a call from a customer service representative.

But not all ecommerce companies are so proactive with their phones. According to a Bizrate.com study, 30 percent of e-merchants aren't offering live phone support, 65 percent aren't offering online order support tracking, and 87 percent don't offer 24-hour support.

What's worse is when a company doesn't even list a phone number on their site. This suggests that a company doesn't care or hasn't really thought through the very basics of dealing with customers. A look at early e-merchant business plans might reveal some of the thinking behind why companies don't support their sales channels with phones.

Many companies never took into account how important phone support would be to their venture. They naively assumed that the Internet was different from other commerce channels. It's not. Goods still have to be packed and shipped. Customers always have questions. Most ecommerce companies overestimated what technology could do, and few realized how much their customers would demand live interaction and real human support. In addition, an inordinate fear of cost also prevails. Ecommerce executives have been known to cringe at the thought of allocating dollars to operators.

And, yes, phone support can also be costly. A perfect example is Amazon. Their traditional call center approach provides great customer service but at a very steep price. Nearly 14 percent of Amazon's 5,000 employees answer phone calls and emails in four call centers around the world. That's a lot of worker hours.

International Data Corp. estimates that at PC companies, support and service calls can cost as much as $25 apiece to fulfill. If the company is a PC manufacturer, for example, selling thousands of units a week, the costs add up. Figure 10-11 illustrates the costs per contract by channel type. It shows that email is one of the most cost-efficient means of communication, at an average of 25 cents, versus a direct technical contact, at an average cost of $11.25 per contract. Customer channels of contact should be viewed as a combined strategy and not reviewed in isolation simply based on cost.

Figure 10-11.

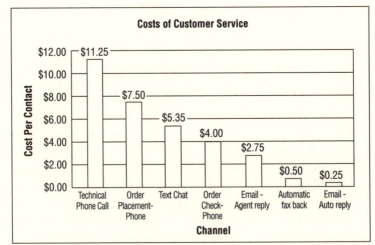

Source: Bain/MainSpring and Forrester

Figure 10-12. *Upstream, Instream, and Downstream Processes*

Upstream, Instream, and Downstream Processes

The business value chain may be divided into three parts for any business: upstream, instream, and downstream. *Upstream* processes involve relationships that a company has with its suppliers. *Instream* processes are those inside a business that allow it to collect and share information among employees. *Downstream* processes are those that manage specific customer and channel transactions and touch points. (See Figure 10-12.)

CRM technologies have historically played a significant role in instream processes, especially in relation to the sharing of customer information. CRM has also played a key role in downstream processes, especially in the area of customer self-service and transaction capabilities. In addition, while normally not considered part of the CRM marketplace, vendors who provide strong upstream and instream software applications (most notably ERP vendors like SAP and PeopleSoft) are aggressively moving to provide strong CRM capabilities. From this technology evolution, the emergence of end-to-end CRM and e-CRM application suites are coming to market. This is achieved by either cobbling together solutions from OEMs, mergers, and acquisitions, or building from the ground up on Web-based technology. (See Figure 10-13.)

CRM Technology Market Overview

Within the last 18 months, there has been significant activity among CRM vendors in product repositioning, mergers and acquisitions, vendor alliances and partnerships, and OEM relationships. While these changes may appear somewhat chaotic, they are a result of the following seven factors:

1. *Full life cycle*—Vendors seek to provide as much support as possible for the full customer life cycle. Niche vendors strive to provide more technical depth in their products and aggressively seek out partnering relationships with other vendors who engage in a broader CRM scope.
2. *Data integration*—Vendors support integration of online and offline data. With the rapid growth of ecommerce, vendors are working to

Figure 10-13.

Customer Knowledge Management					
Campaign Mgmt	SFA/SLA & Contracts	Ecommerce	Call/Support Center	Field Service/ Logistics	Customer Self-Serve
Inbound Email Mgmt		Outbound Message Mgmt (email, fax, pager, voice)		Content Mgmt	
Personalization & Targeting					
OLAP		Data Mining	Web Log Analysis		Reporting
Database Server					
TCP/IP Network					

ensure that legacy and ERP data can be integrated as needed into their CRM offerings.

3. *Web access*—Vendors are deploying solutions via the Web. CRM vendors that historically have provided large (fat) client software are now providing their tools via the Web. In addition, wherever possible, CRM vendors are providing customer-facing interactive tools.

4. *Vertical growth*—Vendors are expanding their product offerings by extending the product either up or down in the hierarchy of needs chart through mergers and acquisitions, partnerships, or internal development.

5. *Real time*—Some vendors will begin to embrace real-time CRM. Personalization and data-mining vendors are already delivering tools that have real-time machine learning capabilities in which customer touch points are enhanced in real time. In addition, with instant messaging, Voice over IP, and interactive Web collaboration capabilities, CRM programs will become increasingly real time.

6. *Downstream reach*—Upstream vendors are converging on downstream vendors. The most notable example of this trend is the acquisition of CRM vendors by ERP vendors.

7. *Instream posturing*—Instream vendors are converging on downstream vendors. Long serving as the backbone for customer information repositories, vendors with tools in data warehousing, knowledge management, decision support, and business intelligence are recasting themselves as CRM vendors.

Generations of CRM Systems and Technologies

Some CRM systems and technologies have evolved from their mainframe roots to client server, and are now Web-based and knowledge-based. Depending on the technical heritage, many vendors are trying to move from first- to fourth-generation technologies. The generations of these technologies are as follows:

> First-generation systems (mainframe-client/server)
>
> Second-generation systems (client/server)
>
> Third-generation systems (Web-based, Web-focused)
>
> Fourth-generation systems (knowledge-based, advanced analytics)

The generations may be considered evolutionary steps, serving increasing degrees of complexity. Generation one was primarily data-driven, generations two and three are mainly information-driven, and generation four is knowledge-driven. Vendors tend to cross multiple generations over time. (See Figure 10-14.)

The various technologies may be viewed as a pyramid in which facts are transformed at each level and ultimately crystallize as a form of succinct yet insightful knowledge (wisdom). (See Figure 10-15.) The key to this pyramid is the concept of intelligence density, which is, simply put, the amount of facts delivered in a unit of time. CRM technologies that can convey the most amount of customer insight *in the least amount of time* can deliver better results. In order to deliver more facts in less time, data must be abstracted using advanced knowledge-based techniques. An example could be increasing value of abstraction or increasing contextual dependencies. As the level requirement for the representation of facts calls for more intervention and interpretation than the complexity of the data, information, and knowledge management requirements increase.

CRM Market Categories

This broad and complex marketplace can be divided into five basic categories, shown in Table 10-1.

Campaign Management/Ad Serving

Unlike the majority of e-CRM tools, which are supported by new entrants into the enterprise marketing automation (EMA) market, sophisticated campaign management tools are produced by both traditional

Figure 10-14. *Vendors Cross Generations*

Vendor	G1	G2	G3	G4
Microstrategy			* * * * * * * * * * * * * *	
Net Perceptions			* * * * * * * * * * *	
Oracle		* * * * * * * * * * * * * * * * * *		
IBM	* *			
Broadvision			* * * * * * * * * * *	
Clarify			* * * * * * * * * * * * * *	
Silknet				* * * * * * * * * * * *

Figure 10-15.

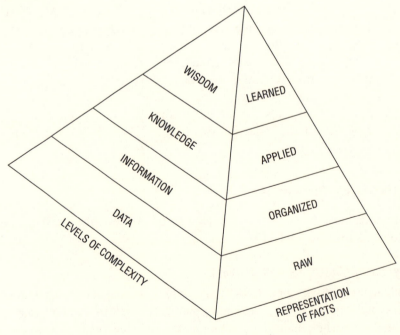

Table 10-1. The Five Basic Categories of the CRM Marketplace

Campaign management, ad serving	These tools help companies manage online and offline marketing and advertising campaigns.
Data warehousing, data processing	This category includes traditional data warehousing, decision support, and business intelligence vendors whose tools are being used to manage and analyze customer information.
Email management	These tools help companies manage primarily inbound email, especially in the support phase of the customer life cycle. They frequently include outbound email management capabilities as well.
Online measurement, personalization, data mining	These tools provide advanced analysis capabilities to develop personalization rules and deliver personalized content on Web sites and segment customers and provide advanced insight into customer information and behavior, both online and offline.
Content management, ecommerce transaction engines	Tools in this category serve up personalized Web content and handle customer purchase transactions in a highly scalable environment.

players and new entrants. Traditional providers, such as Exchange Applications and Prime Response, developed their applications in the early 1990s and developed a strong presence between 1995 and 1996. Their focus was first to bring planning, targeting, querying, and workflow management tools to the marketing manager's desktop and, second, to support enterprisewide, cross-channel marketing campaigns with a single, centralized customer marketing history database and automated reporting tools. They soon integrated with SAS (Statistical Analysis Software) and other mining, modeling, and online application processing (OLAP) reporting tools to further automate traditional database marketing activities. At this time, most companies were utilizing the Web, but the focus was still on brand extension and informational (brochureware) sites. Very few companies were performing customer service online or delving aggressively into ecommerce. Those that did were developing custom applications within their Web site infrastructure to support these processes.

As the market moved from content-based sites to an onslaught of dot-com and "brick-and-click" ecommerce ventures, millions of customers needed to be acquired, serviced, and retained online. The CRM application space, accordingly, welcomed a whole new set of campaign management providers. With outbound email campaign management or online measurement as the crux of their offerings, Rubric, Annuncio, Connectify (purchased by Kana), MarketFirst, and Epiphany came to market with their applications in 1998. Net Perceptions, the leading collaborative filtering and recommendation engine for ecommerce sites, had just introduced its full suite of online marketing automation tools, which included campaign management.

All of these applications provide very similar core campaign management functions for outbound email, online surveys, sweepstakes, and promotions. A single knowledge base (most support both SQL, or structured query language, and Oracle databases) of customer and prospect data is queried by segmentation and targeting functions and by workflow management and campaign definitions (using triggers) to identify qualified targets or respondents.

Workflow management and planning tools are key differentiators in this market, pitting Rubric, Annuncio, and MarketFirst in direct competition with the traditional providers for online-focused activities. Rubric has a more complete integration of call center, sales and direct mail channels. Epiphany and Net Perceptions, with fairly light workflow management tools, are left relying heavily on their deeper analytical functionality to compete with Rubric, Annuncio, and MarketFirst, who are rapidly and aggressively partnering with top data-mining application providers. Rubric was recently purchased by Broadbase, a leading online tracking and data-mining application.

In a new trend, varying degrees of integration with Web personalization and content management are provided by each of these application providers. Epiphany's application, for example, is based on the measurement and data mining of online behavior and includes a fairly robust recommendation engine, which provides real-time offer personalization. This tool is just now being fully integrated into Epiphany's application layer. Net Perceptions' recommendation and personalization engine is tightly integrated with its campaign management functionality and uses existing integration with content libraries to "fetch" content.

Rules-based personalization is supported by both Annuncio and MarketFirst. A field or status code assigned to a customer record can be used to personalize the content of an email with an offer or customer-specific account information such as password, account status, or order status. If a database of content (content library) such as product art is made available to the application through database integration, content can be fetched from this database into an email, yielding an efficient method for creating content and versioning.

For a market that began in 1998 with scale and Web functionality as the two defining characteristics separating the traditional providers from the sexy new online players, the online CRM and campaign management application space is now crowded and competitive across many dimensions.

Data Warehousing/Data Processing

For a couple of decades, businesses have used data warehousing to analyze large volumes of data, typically customer data. It is unsurprising, therefore, to see a traditional data warehouse vendor, MicroStrategy, announce the creation of a "new generation of one-to-one ebusinesses" by using permission marketing and customer information. MicroStrategy's proven multichannel broadcast tools (see www.strategy.com) are a natural for one-to-one marketing via the Web. Clearly, over the past few years, the Web has breathed new life into a somewhat stale market space (data warehousing) by giving vendors the opportunity to rewrite all their analytical tools to be deployed via the Web. That work, however, has been largely complete for some time now, and data warehouse vendors are looking for new feeding grounds.

Microsoft has done much to create this environment. With the release of the very affordable, low-cost SQL Server 7.0 about two years ago (with significant data warehousing features thrown in), data warehousing vendors had to climb up the value-add ladder or face stiff competition on Microsoft's terms. Oracle has resisted the Microsoft charge by continuing to push their ERP-like suite (Oracle Financials) and begin marketing CRM Suite, which is not much more than their existing data warehouse tools recast as a CRM tool set. Hence, data warehouse vendors who relied on the infrastructure part of their suite (database servers, extraction/transformation/loading, and high-performance middleware) are forced to differentiate their applications.

Vendors like Brio, Business Objects, Cognos, MicroStrategy, Oracle, and Seagate have successfully added Web deployment into their decision support tools. Now we're seeing the emerging trend in which data warehouse vendors claim to be ebusiness vendors. One such company, Sagent, clearly a middle-level data warehousing player, has deftly repositioned itself as a Web analysis tool. Sagent has struck up relationships with Siebel and Experián (a supplier of consumer information) and ecommerce player Broadvision. For Siebel and Broadvision, Sagent represents a lower-cost, full-featured data warehousing, extraction/transformation/loading (ETL), and reporting environment. Sagent gets rapid sales growth by riding the Internet wave with these alliances.

While Brio is embedded in PeopleSoft and has relationships with SAP and IBM, Business Objects, the reporting tool embedded in Siebel, is the CRM packaged-application heavyweight. MicroStrategy has a relationship with Exchange Applications, an e-CRM application vendor, to provide decision support capabilities. Cognos seems content to advertise their product as "e-ready," since it allows Web-based business intelligence applications, rather than strike out with another ebusiness partner.

All of this leads to the critical question: With decision support and data warehousing tools finding their way into CRM and e-CRM packages, and with all of the rapid consolidation in the CRM arena, are these CRM tools as well integrated as they claim to be? Savvy organizations will poke under the hood and ask their vendors which parts of the CRM application were manufactured by whom and then drill into the specific technology standards embedded in these components. Examining the family tree of acquisitions can turn up some product integration issues within the CRM vendor's tools.

With the exception of Business Objects, MicroStrategy, and Brio, most of the data warehousing and business intelligence vendors have not boldly entered the ebusiness intelligence arena or provided equivalent functionality found to that within DataSage, Broadbase, Personify, e.Piphany, or NetGenesis Web intelligence products. These products have focused on turning Web and ecommerce data into business intelligence rather than providing general-purpose business intelligence tools. These ebusiness intelligence tools bring advanced data-mining algorithms to bear. Some conventional data warehousing and business intelligence vendors have data-mining add-ons to their product suite, but typically that is not their sweet spot. On the Web, data mining is a natural core product offering.

In addition, none of the data warehouse vendors has added real-time data mining or personalization to their arsenal. Net Perceptions is perhaps the most well-known name in the real-time data-mining space and has partnerships with other well-known ecommerce names such as Art Technology Group (ATG), Broadvision, Engage, IBM Net.Commerce, InterWorld, MicroStrategy, NetGenesis, Oracle, and Vignette.

Another less well-known data-mining company, Information Discovery, which has historically marketed to the conventional data warehouse market, is now focusing their real-time data-mining capabilities on the Web (NovuWeb, Inc.). This tool does not use the collaborative techniques found in Net Perceptions, but instead uses something akin to a rules induction engine that discovers patterns in data that can be expressed as if/then/else rules.

In all, some mildly interesting forays into ecommerce are occurring by the conventional data warehouse vendors, but some much more interesting moves by the new category of Web-intelligence vendors.

Email Management

The inbound email management category as a whole is going through a significant transformation. This transformation is exhibited by the clustering of enhanced chat and collaboration functionality with inbound email management systems. The latest trend is the addition of outbound email functionality to complement the inbound response-handling capabilities already available. The addition of outbound email functionality to existing inbound email platforms will raise the stakes for the category and apply pressure to the Web-based campaign management tools lacking robust response-handling engines. Some vendors appear to be conceding the race for best-of-breed status for inbound email management. Mustang.com, for example, has chosen not to add text chat and Web collaboration to their product set, though most of their competitors offer this functionality.

These are truly the best of times if one is in the market for an inbound email management solution. Baseline functionality and product flexibility are at an all-time high. Customers have the option to purchase off-the-shelf software solutions from vendors like eGain, Brightware, Kana/Silknet, and Island Data or use email management service bureaus like Digital Impact, Talisma, or ClickAction to manage customer interactions. The following features illustrate the depth of the inbound email management platform category:

- Rules-based routing
- Message prioritization
- Message escalation
- Message categorization
- Auto response
- Auto suggest
- Auto acknowledgment
- Spell checker
- Bulk email management
- Web form integration
- HTML email integration

- Sensor technology
- Dynamic content and data-fetching capabilities
- Message and customer history
- Personalized jump pages
- Response monitoring

In addition, several vendors list the following as components of their inbound email management architecture:

- Web self-help
- Dynamic FAQs
- Text chat
- Web collaboration
- Web call-back
- Question and answer and monitoring
- Blended collaboration

The most desirable products were developed by vendors who have managed to look beyond inbound email response handling as the panacea for all Web-based contact management ills. These vendors have examined the user experience and understood the necessity to blend text chat and Web-collaboration into the overall contact strategy. By adding chat and collaboration to the product mix, users will be able to proactively resolve customer issues or questions, instead of reacting to inbound email bombs. Some are taking the category one step further by adding outbound email functionality to their product suites.

Clearly, this is a category that has been transformed over the last calendar year. In fact, inbound email management can no longer be considered a discrete CRM technology category. The incremental functionality within the space like text chat, Web collaboration, and outbound email warrants a new category descriptor. The Kana/Silknet merger has raised the stakes for all would-be contact management suites. Vendors will now be faced with either stepping up or stepping aside.

Online Measurement, Personalization, and Data Mining

The current state of the art of measurement and data mining in the Web-centered area of industry is, in two words, managed chaos. The advance of computing power and data warehousing capabilities, as well as the increased speed and ability of communication brought by the Internet have caused tremendous advances in the availability and quantity of amassed data.

The opportunities brought by this data are clear. The information that can be extracted from this data can, is, and will be of tremendous value to Internet users—in both business and personal capacities. While B2B applications are the "next big thing," data measurement, mining, and the use of extracted information represents another "big thing," albeit a quieter one, in the Internet world.

As with the whole CRM space, there is a degree of convergence in the area of measurement and data analysis. Many software tool and application providers are adding similar measurement capabilities, either through development or acquisition. This is making the distinction between companies a bit more difficult, but in the case of mergers, it is also reducing the number of software providers.

There are predominant categories that can be used to understand the different tools. These measurement and analysis categories are as follows:

- Web traffic reporting
- Analysis of online data
- Traditional analysis tools
- "Incorporating" analysis tools

An explanation of the characteristics of the tools in each of these categories, as well as some discussion about the distinctions and similarities of the tools within each category, is given in the following sections.

Web Traffic Reporting Tools. As the name indicates, Web traffic reporting tools analyze the traffic into a Web site. Until recently, these tools focused solely on technical aspects of site traffic. After installation and some fairly simple configuration, these tools examine the Web site's log files and produce reports containing basic counts of number of visitors, total page requests, number of requests for each page, and so on. These statistics could be viewed either in reports or in graphical format, with titles such as "Hits by day/hour/week/month."

These tools include Accrue's Hit List (formerly Marketwave's Hit List, acquired in September 1999 by Accrue), WebTrends, Macromedia/Andromedia's ARIA, NetGenesis and net.Analysis. Both Accrue Hit List and WebTrends have been implemented and used by marchFIRST successfully on large, robust Web sites. All of these products are now more similar than different. While the tools have focused on the basics, they are now beginning to get slightly more sophisticated in their attempts to add clickstream or path analysis.

At this time, WebTrends allows only user-defined profiling.

WebTrends does not provide automated computer algorithms for profiling and segmenting Web site users. Andromedia has also added capability to intelligently classify users with its LikeMinds product. LikeMinds uses collaborative filtering technology to personalize Web-site content based on user behavior. Like WebTrends, NetGenesis only allows for user-defined profiling. No automated computer algorithms are provided with the software for segmenting Web site users.

Analysis Tools for Online Data.   The development of the World Wide Web has given rise to a number of specialty companies whose domain is mainly analysis of online data. The tools and offerings from these companies go beyond the basic statistical reporting of Web traffic reporting tools.

Personify leads the way in the development of a GUI tool that allows users to mine data that has been extracted from Web log files. Once the user groups have been defined, based on their online behavior, users of the tool can easily "slice and dice" the available data in a number of different ways. This allows the user to discover which site sections users are visiting (defined for each user group) and which items are being sold in conjunction with each other (again for each user group).

Blue Martini's current offering is focused squarely on the ecommerce world. Their main analysis tool enables market basket analysis for cross-selling opportunities and to support customized content efforts. Net Perceptions' offering is focused on real-time personalization. The core of its offering is the Recommendation Engine 4.0. This Recommendation Engine was based on the GroupLens technology developed by the GroupLens Research Project of the University of Minnesota. It is used across offerings for ecommerce, call centers, marketing campaigns, and knowledge management.

Broadbase offers analytical applications that support ecommerce. Its software product, E-business Performance Management (EPM), is tightly integrated with Broadvision. It depends on the Broadvision's Web log file format to analyze the Web site clickstream data. Going further than traffic reporting, Broadbase allows segmentation based on user-defined segments and the data-mining techniques of decision tree and recency, frequency, and monetary value (RFM) analysis. It also has tools to perform sequencing and affinity analysis to learn more about the Web site consumers.

Traditional Analysis Tools.   More computer-intensive and advanced statistical analysis is accomplished using traditional statistical software packages and tools designed specifically for this purpose. While none of the main software providers in this area are focusing products specifically for the Web, the tools they provide have the ability to analyze online data, as well as online data integrated with offline data.

Statistical Analysis Software (SAS) is still the leader in powerful and thorough statistical software. The flexibility, extensibility, and power that it provides comes at a price, however. Typically an SAS programming/analysis expert must develop, execute, and/or deploy the required code and interpret the results. The software's strength lies in its ability to allow users to handle large amounts of data (in the multiple gigabyte range, depending solely on disk space).

In response to the Web, SAS has added at least two relevant capabilities. The reports, tables, and graphs that SAS produces can now be output in simple HTML code. This allows the reports to be posted easily on a Web site. Second, SAS has developed a Web application approach, which allows a Web interface to predevelop SAS algorithms. This allows Web developers to have site users enter data and/or select statistical algorithms to be executed. Additionally, SAS has added an e-intelligence campaign, which is more a marketing campaign than a software product.

Surprisingly, none of the traditional analysis tool companies have developed and packaged a stand-alone online behavior analysis module. All of these companies have the tool sets and skill sets necessary to develop such a useful tool but have not yet done so. This is in contrast to Blue Martini or Personify, who started from scratch and have developed and packaged analysis tools for online data.

IBM is a bit of an exception, although not much of one. Along with their data-mining product, Intelligent Miner, IBM also has a product, WebSphere, which supports online analysis. Intelligent Miner mines relational data such as DB2 and flat files. Intelligent Miner offers algorithms for association, classification, clustering, prediction, sequencing, and time sequence analysis

"Incorporating" Analysis Tools.   While the Web traffic reporting tools, tools for online data, and traditional tools cover all possible existing applications in the area of measurement and analysis, other tool providers are adding functionality that allows them to accomplish some of the same tasks. Some of these tools, which we are labeling "incorporating" tools, are listed here, along with an explanation of their ties into the measurement/analysis area.

Prime Response and Exchange Applications are both incorporating more measurement and analysis tools into their software. Both also have developed hooks into SAS software that allow lists of names in a database to be scored via SAS algorithms and used in their campaign software. Both of these are good examples of companies who have added analytical capabilities to an existing offering.

Engage concentrates its efforts on helping Internet businesses understand their audiences. It profiles Web site visitors and uses these profiles to help companies reach the targeted audience. Along with products for profiling, ad management, and audience identification, Engage has a decision support product, Decision Support Server, that allows the user to conduct detail analysis and provides profile-based reports. Engage also offers I/PRO Research, a service that combines the Web-based data with offline data to deliver analytical solutions and analyses for individual client needs.

Which Tools to Use?   Which tools a company should use depends on the sophistication of the system and analysis that is needed. A beginning dot-com company without an offline component often is satisfied with measuring their Web traffic, thus a WebTrends or Accrue solution is probably all that is needed. A desire for more sophisticated analysis could lead to an advanced implementation of Personify, Blue Martini, or a more robust and complete analytical service offering.

Choosing the appropriate Web site management/analysis tool can also depend on the Web site application environment. If another application environment is used for the Web site, engineers must intercept the installation of the product to ensure proper integration. For example, Broadbase and Andromedia are tightly integrated with the Broadvision product. NetGenesis is tightly integrated with Vignette. On the other hand, WebTrends is currently developing plug-ins for both Broadvision and Vignette. Each time these tools encounter a new Web site environment, plug-ins or other integration solutions must be developed. This can only lengthen the time-to-value of such Web site management tools.

The product a company requires also depends on the amount and types of data it wants to examine. Data can be obtained from many sources. Online data is obtained from online behavior (site use, Web use, navigation patterns, duration, and frequency), online purchase information, and information submitted online (surveys, registration). Offline data may be demographics, life stage/lifestyle, media use, store data (which local outlet of national chain is visited), and product use. A larger analytical service offering is required for companies wanting to take full advantage of the available data.

In the near future, companies will continue to add analytical capabilities as demand for more sophisticated analysis increases. The value of data mining will also become more apparent as companies discover and leverage information to increase sales and customer satisfaction. These, of course, are key objectives of CRM programs.

Regulatory threat is slight. The FTC's investigation of DoubleClick shows both the potential and power of the now-available data, as well as the lack of understanding of what is actually being done by companies with this data. The existence of companies like Axiom and Abacus (consumer and catalog data providers, respectively) are not new. Information about traffic from a Web site clearly belongs to the Web site owner. Use of that data, or its combination with commercial information, is not any more threatening than any previous data uses.

The future will see software providers continuing to add measurement and analytical capabilities to their products. Fully automated analysis, however, will not be achieved, so no software package will be able to provide one "push-button" solution. Companies wanting the most robust analysis will require analytic service offerings, as opposed to solely software-based solutions. More companies will try to leverage the available data, and there will be intriguing case studies and business success stories from such endeavors.

Content Management, Ecommerce Transaction Engines

Ecommerce transaction and content management systems stand at the exact interface between the customer and the computer, so it is natural that these organizations will want to paint themselves in the CRM colors. The dynamics of this market space are fairly simple: Network with partners to add CRM functionality or build the components into the architecture.

Bottom Line. Ecommerce transaction and content management vendors are clearly moving to provide a more comprehensive solution by either partnering, building the functionality, or buying other companies. Since the same analytic and personalization vendors partner with the top ecommerce software vendors, and since personalization and analytic technology can best be leveraged across the full customer life cycle, not just sales and marketing, look for ecommerce and content management software to continue acquiring more analytic and personalization vendors. More importantly, expect that email vendors campaign both management software vendors and customer support vendors to acquire analytic and personalization vendors over time. When selecting an ecommerce and content management package, understanding the direction for personalization and analytics is crucial.

One lingering question remains upon review of this part of the market: Is a purchase of one of these companies by an ERP vendor looming? Since ebusiness is really about value chain optimization in which transactions can flow through the value chain, it makes sense sooner or later to provide tighter integration of the Web store into the back-office applications. In addition, the ERP vendors can leverage such a purchase for fast-track sales growth opportunities.

CRM Makes (Dollars and) Cents

Knowing who the customer is and retaining them is significantly less costly than acquiring new customers. Reducing customer defections by 5 percent can on average increase profits from 60 to 85 percent. Enterprises typically spend five times more on customer acquisition than on retention. (Remember the adage, a happy customer will tell five people about their experiences, while an unhappy customer will tell ten.)

Deployment of e-CRM begins with a vision of how customers and various enterprise stakeholders will benefit. Prioritization of e-CRM functionality enables an organization to provide building blocks for success. IT (Information Technology) organizations should leave the software installation last. Keys to successful deployment of e-CRM include the following steps:

1. Design the customer experience and customer relationship management.
2. Focus on the use of e-CRM: customer segmentation, pricing, personalization, and service.
3. Ensure from the start a plan for multichannel e-CRM integration.
4. Think process, not system: marketing, selling, and service.

Then and only then, think software. Electronic CRM marks a shift of IT from largely focusing its resources and skills on the enterprise's operations to what really matters most—the customer relationship.

Application Service Providers versus Enterprise Solutions

It's a matter of survival: ecommerce organizations have to upgrade their customer service capabilities in order to compete. The question is how to get there and how to do it cost-effectively. Building in-house is attractive because control and customization are seemingly maximized. But building in-house is expensive and perhaps even indulgent—especially for an ecommerce company that wants to be responsive to its shareholders. Building in-house also requires extensive internal project management resources that can coordinate implementation strategies.

ASPs offer an alternative solution, one that is becoming increasingly attractive to ecommerce providers. ASPs essentially "rent" applications via the Internet to companies that need them.

By renting applications from an ASP, up-front development costs are reduced, support is cheaper, and companies are spared the expense of installing server software. In the coming years, an Internet connection and a browser may be the only tools necessary to power a corporation's IT operations.

The ASP model is particularly suited to deliver next-generation customer service solutions to ecommerce companies that don't have the existing infrastructure to handle them. ASPs manage the hardware and software upgrades. They deal with maintenance, setup, and monthly fee ranges around the low thousands versus million-dollar price tags for enterprise packages.

The low costs associated with ASP delivery are compelling. The end result is that line managers are unleashing technology resources into areas of the enterprise that previously might have had to wait or gone through tedious approval cycles.

The ASP model also enables companies to test newer technologies at lower costs. Let's face it. Technologies like live chat, Voice over IP, and even natural language query aren't mature. By working with an ASP, a company can try new technologies, and if they meet expectations, that company can move on with minimal disruption.

The market for rented solutions is already taking off. By the year 2003, when the software market is expected to grow to $20.6 billion, Forrester Research estimates that 25 percent of these revenues will go to ASPs. IDC (International Data Corporation) predicts that this space will grow to $7.8 billion by 2004 up from $300 million last year. Also emerging are ASP aggregators. These are companies that pull together various ASP applications (customer service, human resources) for a complete solution.

Chapter Summary

The highly personal and immediate nature of the Internet is forcing enterprises to reexamine continually and adjust their business models and their internal organizational structures. Sound disruptive? It is.

Enterprises that manage disruption and work with disruption to open up new opportunities will set themselves apart. Much of this disruption centers on the customers. A customer service imperative is currently at play. It's huge and everyone is feeling it. Companies can no longer rely on the rigid demographic information used in years gone by. The Internet is empowering individuals of all ages with access to information, resources, and more selection and options then were ever available easily before. Less important are mass demographic groups of people that span two generations; more important are the specific requirements of individuals as we move forward, if indeed companies want to increase customer lifetime value. Companies that accurately address the needs of individuals will be the ones who reap the benefits of customer loyalty, repeat purchases, and referrals.

The customer has more power than ever before and is in effect shaping the twenty-first-century enterprise's product and services directions. To survive, let alone conquer, companies must embrace CRM strategies that accurately address the needs of customers. Then they must put this knowledge to work internally within their organization and externally across their entire value chain. The following chapter reviews business models that are in place or under development to capitalize on this new customer-centric business environment.

CHAPTER

Developing Your E-Marketplace Organization, Culture, and Strategy

Success in the twenty-first century requires a new way of thinking, organizing, and doing business. The Internet has in fact touched almost every part of business in one way or another. This chapter provides an outline of some of the new organizational models that are optimized to leverage these new business dynamics. Also reviewed are the business cultural implications to take into consideration, as well as an eleven-step outline to developing an e-Marketplace strategy business plan.

Innovation Organizations

In the new economy, organizations are struggling with how to move at Internet speed, how to create corporate agility, and how to attract and retain talent in an increasingly competitive job market. Companies like Cisco on the hardware side of the business and marchFIRST on the professional services side of the Internet industry are good examples of forward-thinking innovative companies. This section reviews a few models that may provide some insight as to how to build the twenty-first century organization model.

When entering the e-Marketplace space, your company can approach the opportunity from a number of ways depending on your strategy. The first step is to understand the opportunities and the competitive landscape of your industry with regard to the impact of e-Marketplaces.

Three Key E-Marketplace Models

There are three primary e-Marketplace models. A company can choose to participate in one or all of these models. Each has its benefits and limitations. As the company sets its ebusiness and e-Marketplace strategies, it is important to know up front which models will be pursued. This decisions will directly impact the company strategy from a financial, technical, cultural, and personnel basis.

The three models are as follows:

- *Direct B2B e-Marketplaces*—These are one-to-many models that reflect a company developing their own e-Marketplace to support their own customers and suppliers. Cisco Systems and Dell Computer are examples of this type of direct e-Marketplace model.
- *Coalitions or consortium e-Marketplaces*—These models reflect a many-to-many model in which major industry players come together to aggregate their buy-side and supplier-side leverage to increase operational efficiencies and leverage buying power around an industry supply chain. Almost every major industry has announced the formation of one or several consortia. For example, Boeing, Lockheed Martin, BAE Systems, Raytheon, and Commerce One announced plans to create the Global Aerospace and Defense Trading Exchange. The exchange will allow aerospace and defense companies to have a secure electronic marketplace where buyers and sellers around the world can conduct business.
- *Independent e-Marketplaces*—This model is typically a neutral intermediary historically providing either a buy-side focus or a supplier-side focus, or in the more forward-thinking independent e-Marketplaces, a balanced win/win model for both suppliers and buyers. Examples of independent e-Markplaces include Chemdex for the chemical industry and e-Exchange for the high-technology industry.

A company can participate in a single model or any combination of the above models. If the model is a start-up, it may not have as many issues with legacy systems, culture, and speed. However, if it is an existing company that is extending into the new ebusiness environment with an e-Marketplace strategy, then it would be prudent to pause and choose the right model to match the opportunity. The organizational model options are many but may include one of the following:

- Build an e-Marketplace to capitalize on your leverageable assets, such as company brand, reputation, operations, global assets, management team, and industry experience, and support it with the existing organization and resources.
- Create an autonomous separate business unit of the company to leverage the e-Marketplace opportunities. Have the unit report to executive management directly and operate with support of the organization without being encumbered by the organization.
- Spin off a separate company to capitalize on the opportunity. Develop an Internet culture, organization, compensation plan, and location that will attract and retain the right talent.

The New Innovation Fundamentals

Whatever model is put in place when building an ebusiness organization, several fundamental elements must be addressed. When comparing the old economy business models and management teams to the new economy success models, certain key differences become apparent. The differences show up predominantly in the areas of management, sense of speed, action, willingness to take risks, and the corporate culture. This section outlines a few of these key fundamentals.

Create an Externally Oriented Culture

For many years companies focused on their systems, process, and people to optimize their own internal business models. In today's global networked economy, it is critical that companies focus not only on their own internal operations but on being an active participant in the global Internet revolution that is changing the dynamics of business. To achieve this goal, companies must take an external viewpoint of their operations and look outside of their enterprise to the entire value chain, from customer demand to production to product and service delivery. This requires integrating and interoperating with multiple external organizations including customer organizations, channel partners, e-Marketplaces, supplier organizations, and outsourced partners.

Spheres of Innovation

Figure 11-1 illustrates the foundation from which CEO- and executive-sponsored innovation and change emerge from within an organization following a four-step innovation process:

Develop innovation teams—All great innovations start with an individual or small team that has an inspiration about how to innovate

Figure 11-1. *Value-Delivery Spheres*

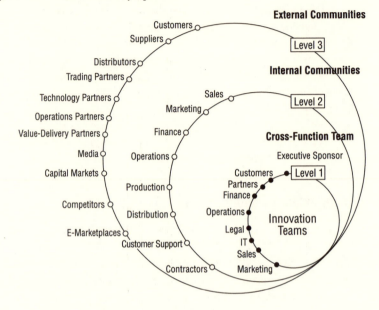

within a department, organization, or even within an industry. From the seeds of this new innovation team comes the initial plan that is formulated. Once formulated into a proposal that is accepted by management, a cross-functional team is formed to execute the strategy.

Develop cross-functional project teams—Develop cross-functional teams from across the enterprise and also include customers, trading partners, and suppliers to round out the team. The objective is to provide a holistic innovation movement throughout the organization.

Integrate with internal communities—From the foundation of the innovation leaders and the cross-functional teams, build linkages into each of the internal communities that exist in the organization.

Integrate with external communities—Identify key external communities that are critical in the value chain of the business. Include customers, suppliers, trading partners, and external contract organizations.

Develop a Customer-Centric Organization

One consistent lesson that has been time-tested and learned thoroughly by the leaders in the Internet age is that building a customer-centric organization is critical, as illustrated in Figure 11-2. The customer should be *the* central focus when developing an e-Marketplace strategy.

As Jeff Hammond, director of interactive media for Rhea & Kaiser,

Figure 11-2. *Internal and External Factors*

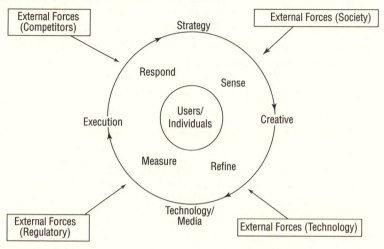

notes, "We've worked with both old economy companies and new economy companies who've found out the hard way that a successful strategy—online or off—must deliver against customer-defined needs while, at the same time, accounting for the forces that impact or influence how those needs are defined at any moment. Just because it's on the Web doesn't mean people are more willing to accept poor fulfillment, billing, and service."

Doing business in the networked economy means that careful consideration to all points of customer contact and influence, both internal as well as external, must be taken into consideration. The Internet can offer new ways to deliver value to customers, and it offers multiple ways to support your clients, from the early attraction and informing stages through to conducting commercial transactions and providing ongoing customer support to your clients. The e-Marketplace strategy should be designed to support clients through the entire customer life cycle. Careful consideration should be given to both the digital connecting points as well as the physical points of customer contact.

Develop a Culture of Innovation

The work environment is a critical component to building an innovative workplace. To create an innovative attitude, the employees and employers must regard the company as a collective adventure. This type of attitude generates excitement, enthusiasm, and a sense of being a part of something great. Aspiring to greatness is one of the keys to creating innovation. Develop a culture of individual empowerment. People can do amazing things when they are driven to achieving greatness and have a sense of speed and urgency. To truly empower individuals within a company, you must provide them with access to information and knowledge tools and the authority to take action.

Develop a Culture that Supports "Real" Partnering

Partnering is one of the key success factors for the twenty-first-century organization. Through the use of advanced thinking coupled with advanced technologies and the Internet, it has never been more possible to develop real operational partnerships between companies. This new business era requires focus on core competencies. Partnering allows companies to do what they do best and outsource or partner for the rest. True partnering means developing win/win models that provide a profitable, sustainable relationship for all parties concerned. It also means sharing information, knowledge, facilities, resources, people, and even customers.

Keep Your Structures Small

In the twenty-first century, successful companies have small organizational structures and divide their operations into small, accountable teams that drive rapid success. Avoid rigid hierarchy; the organizational models that are put in place today are relatively flat, with clean lines of communications and authority.

Foster Direct Informal Relations

Develop a sense of informal access to decision makers in the company. This will allow ideas to flow freely and foster an environment where innovation is encouraged and rewarded.

Develop an Ability to Mobilize People and Resources for Projects Quickly

Know what resources are available both from within the company and externally from partners. Build a competency database and keep it updated.

Develop a Productive Work Style

The work style should be fast paced, hard working, but still reflect productive energy through use of appropriate colors and workspace design. Every company has a set of values and a culture. This should be reflected in the work environment. If the company is promoting openness and interactivity and high technology as key cultural elements, these can be communicated through the environment.

Establish a Dress Code that Supports Your Company

How people dress in a workplace affects the spirit and culture of a company. The dress also reflects on the business principles and can be used as a motivational tool. A dress code can be used to attract and retain key employees, partners, and customers.

Employ Stock Option Remuneration

The new model for compensation at high-growth pre- and post-IPO companies is driven significantly by the inclusion of stock options as part of the compensation plan for employees. Employees share a common sense of ownership in the company's success.

Create a Start-Up Spirit in Large Enterprises

There are several models that can be put into effect within a large organization to develop an entrepreneurial spirit within the company. Several are reviewed briefly in the following list:

- *Use focused innovation models.* Develop small business units that have autonomy from the mother ship but are still tethered to the company resources as needed. These small entrepreneurial teams should have the freedom to innovate.
- *Establish a direct reporting structure to senior management.* The success of these small business units is important, so empower the business unit with a direct reporting relationship to senior management.
- *Motivate the business unit to move at Internet speed.* The rationale for developing a small team is so that it is unencumbered by the larger organization from which it was spawned.
- *Change from functional organizational models to process organizational models.* As companies move toward Web automation of both internal as well as external business processes, it may make sense for businesses to realign their organizations around the full customer support process, from customer attraction through to fulfillment and ongoing support.
- *Incubate innovative start-ups.* Develop an internal incubator within your organization that allows your employees to put their best ideas forward, utilizing organizational resources, internal as well as external funding, and partnerships. Maintain equity in the ventures.

Customer-Centric Organizations. A customer-centric organization is one that is structured so that all employees are measured and

compensated by customer satisfaction. All employees are in close touch
with the customers that they serve. Dell Computer is an example of a
company that has structured their organization to support customer focus.
Dell established a "Customer Experience Council" that reports directly
to a corporate vice chairman. The council is made up of a cross-functional team of senior executives from each of the company's lines of
business. Dell has made it a top corporate objective to track and measure
customer satisfaction. In a recent *Harvard Business Review*, Dell Senior
Vice President Paul Bell explained that Dell looks to apply the same
rigor to tracking customers as most companies do tracking financial results.

> Every public company tells shareholders how it's doing every quarter, but
> few companies have a metrics that measure the customer experience from
> month to month, quarter to quarter [as we do]. Dell tracked the customer
> retention, satisfaction, and behavior and found three key drivers of cus-
> tomer loyalty: order fulfillment, product performance, and post-sale ser-
> vice. The council determined the best way to measure performance in each
> of these areas and set up a system to track performance and they com-
> municate the results every day to the entire company. Aggressive improve-
> ment targets are set, and management bonuses are tied to achieving these
> targets. This type of clear focus and accountability on customer satisfac-
> tion and loyalty represents a customer-centric organization.

People-Centric Organizations.   A company that fosters an environment of individual empowerment and support can prosper in this new
era of entrepreneurial enterprises. This model has worked well for the
service-oriented industries—for example, consulting/professional services firms such as marchFIRST, legal firms, accounting firms, and real
estate firms such as Century 21, which provides company support such
as advertising, offices, administration services to their real estate agents.
Each individual can have a sense of driving his or her own destiny and
success, as well as being part of the overall company success.

If people are truly a business's greatest asset, then the companies
should organize to support that fact. Development of people-centric organizations will remain a competitive advantage for companies developing their twenty-first-century enterprises.

Project-Centric Organizations.   As speed becomes a corporate
imperative, it becomes critical to be able to rapidly pull together cross-
functional teams around projects that will keep the company moving at
Internet speed. A project-centric organizational model encourages and

rewards people for being part of business acceleration teams. By dividing critical success factors into a series of projects, a business can accomplish the rapid, accelerated results.

The key to success through a project-centric approach is to develop a spirit of teamwork among the various groups in the company. Then divide up the many tasks needed to accelerate the growth of the company into smaller, more manageable project deliverables that can quickly be assembled and deployed into action. Create an environment that allows for a highly focused set of objectives and deliverables to be set and measured. Provide a sense of identity and purpose to all employees participating in a project. Develop a sense of urgency for the project with frequent management reviews and deliverables. Communicate a clear accountability for the team. If possible, structure projects in a way that allows for employees to choose projects that interest them and keeps them motivated and inspired by their work environment. While the projects are underway, make an effort to provide a venue for cross-training and sharing of diverse experiences and points of views.

When launching and executing projects, brand the projects with an identity and a visionary, high-impact message about the project and its importance to the company. This will provide a sense of pride of participation in something exciting. The short-term nature of the project provides a sense of accomplishment and completion to the project team members, as well as to the company overall. In many corporate functional jobs, there is no real sense of completion—just a sense of ongoing routine workflow. Having highly visible projects that are launched, executed, and delivered is a great morale-building exercise.

When setting the stage for the project, provide a big picture point of view. Being part of companywide projects allows participants to be able to bring their experiences to the table and see in real time how their part of the company is a critical component to the success of the entire organization. This creates a sense of importance and value to employees. Operating in an accelerated project cycle mode creates a culture that supports the rapid mobilization of resources around critical company objectives. Traditional silos and barriers within company structures tend to be lowered if not removed over time.

Create a Sense of Destiny

A project-centric organization can be a stimulating, dynamic organizational model. It may not be the model for every business, but it has worked well across multiple industries. The automotive industry uses this model to focus resources on building new lines of cars, trucks, SUVs, and so on. The high-tech industry uses this model when developing new lines of computers or consumer electronics.

In the early 1980s Steve Jobs had a now infamous internal battle within Apple Computer about the future direction of the product line. At the time, the Apple II line was doing well and had achieved great success in the marketplace. There were some that advocated sticking with the status quo and continuing with an evolutionary development of the product line. Steve Jobs was adamant that the company had to grow beyond the current product line and continue the personal computer revolution. His now infamous tactics of pulling together his project team and taking over a building in Cupertino, California, locking the doors, and raising a pirate's flag outside the building is one of the most extreme examples of a project-oriented organization. His efforts, and those of his project team, developed what was to become the Macintosh Computer line.

The Macintosh redefined what personal computers should be and did in fact create a revolution in software development and industrial design that has forever left its mark on the way people and computers interact. The lessons learned from this were outstanding. This project team had its own sense of direction and even a sense of destiny. They felt that they were changing the company. To many, the Apple vision of changing the world that was deeply rooted into the corporate culture became a reality through this project involvement. The sense of teamwork and project identity ran through the veins of the company. In fact, on the inside cover of all of the early Macintosh systems produced, you can find the project team members' names etched for prosperity and pride. It is easy to see similar practices with software companies who list the key programmers by name as their customers load up their new software packages.

Create a Sense of Purpose

Creating a sense of purpose, focus, and clear goals and objectives is critical for the success of any organization. Sometimes this can be an elusive task for managers of twenty-first-century companies. Often a sense of urgency is instilled, but not of purpose. There is often a sense of reactive activities that keeps the pace of the organization moving quickly, but by the end of the day, the troops feel physically and emotionally drained. In most companies, there is no shortage of work to be done. But far too often, there is a severe shortage of vision and sense of purpose in today's workplace.

The new dot-com phenomenon, fueled by supportive capital markets, has sparked a new sense of optimism in the workforces around the world. The challenge to the current management teams is how to create an environment that fosters innovation and a sense of entrepreneurial spirit throughout the organization. It is becoming a major factor in the ability of companies to attract and retain top talent.

The Twenty-First-Century Organization

The mark of a twenty-first-century organization will include certain characteristics that will set it apart from its old economy counterparts. These characteristics include key guiding principles such as having a highly focused customer-centric culture that is aligned from the top down to provide exceptional customer value throughout the entire company. The new-economy companies will be purpose-built to operate in both the digital and physical worlds through a multidimensional business model that capitalizes on the best of both. These companies will use the most advanced technologies to empower their people with communication and collaboration tools, as well as access to information resources. Their management structures will be relatively flat. This will encourage an environment that fosters rapid decision making. These organizations will optimize their internal process and systems as in the old-economy companies but will do so with an external focus knowing that they must build their business process and technology platforms in a way that integrates with external organizations, including customer enterprises, trading partners, exchanges, and suppliers. The twenty-first-century enterprise will think and act in a global manner.

In today's knowledge society, knowledge workers are the key assets of a company. In fact, in today's networked economy, physical assets can be a severe liability over smaller, digitally oriented competitors that are taking major mind share and market share away from traditional brick-and-mortar companies. A balance must be struck in order to succeed in the knowledge society. Companies need to take a long, hard look at their culture, people, resources, and assets, as well as their external relationships, and take a surgical focus on what they do best to provide highly differentiated customer value. Then they must eliminate or outsource the functional elements of the company that they do not do best.

Communication and *collaboration* are critical success factors when building a successful knowledge enterprise. Fostering an open communication between employees, customers, and partners is critical. Both internally within a company's four walls and externally when working with customers and partners, providing knowledge tools to the knowledge workers is of utmost importance. These tools will take different forms when supporting customers, employees, and partners, but each group will have its own set of knowledge tools that they require to navigate and succeed in the digital economy.

Developing an E-Marketplace Strategy

Following are the steps necessary to develop a successful e-Marketplace strategy.

Step One: Define the Vision

Determine what the key objectives are for the B2B strategy: Define the questions listed on the following page as a starting point to setting the strategic vision. Then prioritize the answers into the most critical to the least critical objectives. This will help you define quickly what the top objectives are for implementing a successful e-strategy.

Once these questions are answered and prioritized by the level of importance to the business, you are ready to take the next step in defining your vision.

Step Two: Define Your Core Competencies

Take an honest assessment of the company. If the company produces a product, where are the best company strengths? Is it through leading-edge design of great products? Is quality a key strength? Are the strengths found in the convenient distribution of products? This exercise should be done with brutal honesty. Once completed, ask customers why they work with the company. Equally important, you should also find out why others do not choose to work with the company.

Next, define a list of what is considered to be core competencies, then review this list. For each item on the list, determine whether this function adds customer value. Once completed, this exercise helps to define the business focus on a set of core competencies.

Step Three: Focus on What Your Business Does Best and Stop Doing the Rest

Decide what is critical to the success of the business going forward, and define who is the absolute best to perform these functions. In some cases, it is a core competency of the company. In many cases, external outsourcers, financial service providers, the sales channel, or logistics and distribution partners are better at their particular specialty. If the company is doing some functions today that are not core business functions and

E-Marketplace Strategy Questions

1. Is a primary goal to maximize leverage over your suppliers?
2. Is a primary goal to broaden your supplier base?
3. Is a primary goal to reduce operating costs through efficiencies offered through the use of B2B marketplaces?
4. Is revenue generation a key objective?
5. Is a primary goal to create a B2B strategy that provides competitive advantage in your market?
6. Is a primary goal to leverage existing e-Marketplaces?
7. Is a primary goal to create and own an e-Marketplace?
8. Is a primary goal to take a vertical approach or a horizontal approach to developing the e-Marketplace strategy?
9. Who are the target customers? Are they end-user clients? Are they vertical market buyers and/or suppliers?
10. What is the market that is being addressed?
11. Does the company have extensive experience in the market that is being addressed?
12. Can this experience be turned into a definitive competitive advantage over competition?
13. If developing an e-Marketplace, does the company have industry influence in this space?
14. Is it realistic to believe that the company can reach critical mass within the chosen industry?
15. Can the company realistically achieve liquidity in a reasonable amount of time? (Liquidity is defined as reaching sufficient critical mass of buyers and suppliers to ensure a permanent, profitable place in the market being addressed.)
16. Is the market being addressed highly fragmented, with many buyers and suppliers? Or is it more centralized around a few major buyers and many suppliers (for example, the Big Three auto manufacturers in the United States)?
17. Who holds the most influence in the industry over the buying and supplying of products and services?
18. Can a commitment be locked up from several of these key industry influencers to the e-Marketplace business model?
19. From the current starting point, can a business model be built that guarantees neutrality?
20. Who would provide the funding for the venture? Is the funding internal, external, or private placement or venture capital funding? (Each has its own advantages and disadvantages.)
21. Are there other successful models that can be seen in practice within the industry or in a complementary industry?
22. Is the primary motivation driven by protection or defense of the current market position or toward aggressive market advancement?

not adding value to customers, then it should stop doing them. If the company is doing functions today that it is not particularly good at, then it should stop doing them as well. Take this time to redefine the company value proposition to customers, and take a surgical focus on doing only what adds value to the customers, the long-term business viability, and shareholder value.

Step Four: Know Your Competition

When developing an e-Marketplace business model, begin by going online and experiencing what the marketplace, clients, competitors, and other industries are doing on the Web. Study their business models. Identify the various models that exist in the digital world today, project what will be coming tomorrow, and start to build your model by leaping ahead of where the competition is today. Following a simple "me too" strategy will not launch you into a leadership position in your market.

Entering a market with existing participants means that there will not be a first-mover advantage. Thus, there will be a need to innovate and to include everything that the others offer and more, or to take a difference approach than the competitors are taking and attack the market from this new perspective.

Step Five: Develop Your Ebusiness Landscape Matrix

Define where you want to play in your industry. Do you want to offer a wide range of products or services? Or do you want to address a vertical market and go deep into servicing the customers in that vertical market opportunity? Create an ebusiness matrix for your industry that shows the current and future landscape. For example, you can start by looking at Figure 11-3. This figure provides a tool or a planning exercise for reviewing the functionality and competitive landscape of e-Marketplaces in a particular industry. The first quadrant provides a space to list digital markets that offer only a single branded product; for example, Dell or Cisco selling their products in a direct marketplace. The next quadrant provides a space to list the e-markets that offer multiple brands of products, usually owned and operated by an independent company. The next quadrant provides a section to review digital markets that offer integrated products and services; for example, a site that offers computers with software and extended services bundled with the sale. The next quadrant to the right features sites that allow customers to customize their purchasing. The final quadrant provides a section to list e-Marketplaces that not only offer products and services but also offer an ongoing set of services that provide a complete customer life-cycle experience. An ex-

Figure 11-3.

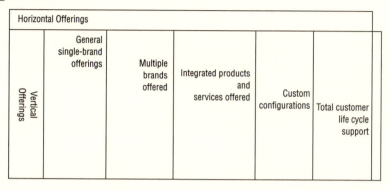

Horizontal Offerings					
Vertical Offerings	General single-brand offerings	Multiple brands offered	Integrated products and services offered	Custom configurations	Total customer life cycle support

ample of this type of digital marketplace would be a site that provides financial products, services, and support.

While developing an e-Marketplace strategy, it helps to develop a model similar to the matrix in Figure 11-3. Once populated with specific lists of competitors, it demonstrates where the opportunities may be to capture market share.

Develop Your Ebusiness Landscape Matrix. Define where you want to play in your industry. Do you want to offer a wide range of products or services, or do you want to address a vertical market and go deep into servicing the customers in that vertical market opportunity? Create an ebusiness matrix for your industry that shows the current and future landscape. For example, you can start by looking at Figure 11-3.

Map where your business is today in this matrix and where the competitors are. This will help you define your market space clearly and also provide you a view of how much competition you are up against. Next, map to this where most of the spending is occurring in your industry and where it is projected to be. Then highlight the areas of the business that are most profitable and least profitable for you to provide.

This exercise will help you define your market, the areas of profitability, and where you wish to participate.

Step Six: Build the E-Value Chain

Define the "e-value chain." Start with the customer. For a moment, ignore your current organizational structure or how your industry has up to this point created and delivered value. Build the customer value chain from the customer outward. Think through the new e-value creation and delivery options that best address your targeted market of customers and customer segments. Gather intelligence; find out who your customers are and create an optimum customer profile. Uncover which of these customers is likely to be online. Understand how customers perceive value-added and strive to understand what other kinds of value they would be willing to pay for. These may include time savings, convenience, cost saving, ease of use, efficiency gains, important information, or access to a community.

Step Seven: Define Your Value Proposition to These Customers

Starting with the most complex customer, develop a list of products and services that will be offered to customers. Define which of these products and services can be offered online and which need to be provided offline. Provide justifications in either case. Why are some products better suited to online sales? For example, in the case of software, traditional packaging and distribution costs can be completely eliminated, which translates to a higher return on investment. Compare your strategy to the online and offline strategies of your competitors. How do they differ? What have they thought of that you haven't? How can the strategy approach be transformed into a long-term competitive advantage?

Next, define your content strategy. Consider what types of information buyers will use as tools to make purchasing decisions, and look for areas where your e-Marketplace can provide added value. Consider the community aspects of your e-Marketplace, and define how your site can create "stickiness," as well as facilitate relationships between community members. Finally, define your commerce strategy, taking into consideration the various revenue types that may be possible to leverage.

Starting with your most complex customer, develop your list of products and services that you will offer to your customers:

- Define which of these products and services can be offered online and which must be provided offline.
- Define which products/services competitors are currently offering online.
- Define benefits/negatives of using the Internet as the vehicle for servicing these customers.
- Define content strategy.
- Define community-building strategy.
- Define commerce strategy.
- Define partner strategy. Draw out the e-value chain from the customer through delivery and define which values you will provide and which will be provided through partners.

Step Eight: Define Your Timing

In the digital economy, timing is everything. Time-to-market is essential; however, it may make more sense to publicly launch your e-Marketplace at a particular point in time based on new industry events, the ratification of a standard, or other variable. E-Marketplaces do not launch themselves. As with offline businesses, the launch of an e-Marketplace must be carefully planned and executed to ensure maximum and positive impact.

The timing of content rollout is also important. Underpromise and overdeliver, always keeping the business needs of trading partners in mind. Communities take time to build and may not be ready for prime time at the time of your launch. That said, you can create a forum to seed your community or, better yet, initiate a community among your initial customers or the founding members of your e-Marketplace to get the ball rolling.

Define Key Impacts (Internal and External—Economic/Organizational/Industrywide). What effect will e-Marketplace have on customers? Not all e-Marketplaces are alike. Some will focus on price, while others focus on quality. Accept the fact that the e-Marketplace may evolve slightly or radically over time. To anticipate these changes, pay attention to changing customer habits, the competition, and industry trends that relate to the e-Marketplace business model.

The company e-Marketplace initiative will affect the company whether it is completely online or not. If it is, the entire organization will be focused on some aspect of succeeding in the digital economy. If the company is a traditional "brick and mortar," realize that the Internet initiative will take on a life of its own and impact the existing business. The e-Marketplace may prove a vehicle to streamline selling costs, but it might also create channel conflict issues within the traditional core organization. Further, the culture of the Internet team may prove to be radically different from the core corporate culture—and it probably should be! If the organization is inherently bureaucratic, there are two choices: Give the Internet team autonomy and allow them to execute in Internet time, or change the corporate culture. Although companies are adopting both strategies, the former is a better short-term strategy. In the meantime, plan to Internet-orient the entire company sooner rather than later. Figure 11-4 is a representative example of a creative team.

An organized approach for executing the customer experience online ensures that skills and competencies can be brought to bear at the right time and for the right reasons.

Figure 11-4. *An Example of a Team Deployed to Develop and Maintain a Customer-Centric e-Marketplace*

Strategy—Producer/Product Manager*
Manage—Project Manager*

Analysis	**Design**	**Build**	**Rollout**
Content Developer*	Creative Director*	Tech Designer*	Interactive Specialist*
Interactive Specialist*	Interactive Designer*	Tech Developer*	System Admin
	Interaction Designer		Customer Svc
	Video/Audio Producer		

Develop Your Ebusiness Marketing Plan. Include the following considerations in your ebusiness marketing plan:

- Determine ebusiness product/services offerings (content, catalogs, chat rooms, bulletin boards, search and directory services, ecommerce, value-added services, and so on).
- Define primary target customers, vendors, advertisers, and sponsors.
- Create an advertising/PR plan (traditional media, online, comarketing strategies, imbedded marketing strategies, and so on).
- Target initial strategic customers/members (target communities that you can engage, and win an entire community at a time instead of just a customer at a time).
- Define revenue sources from your ebusiness (transaction fees, advertising, sponsorships, commissions, referral fees, subscription fees, shared revenue models, and so on).

Step Nine: Develop the Business Case

Developing a solid business case that drives quickly to value and profitability is critical to the long-term sustainability of your e-Marketplace strategy. The business case should incorporate an evaluation of your internal capabilities, resources, strengths, and weaknesses. Then it should be positioned with a competitive analysis of your industry and the key trends of online ebusiness models. The industry should be viewed from the perspective of competition from traditional competitors, as well as competition from new online competitors.

The business case should include defined impacts of the successful execution of the e-Marketplace's strategy on customer relationships and market share, company perception, market valuation, and so forth. Define the content, communities, and commerce models to be organized around key business process issues including:

- Types of customer needs to be met
- Market size of the communities being addressed
- Range of products and services offered to these customer communities
- Revenue models generated from each strategy

Step Ten: Define Technical Architecture

Technical architecture at a minimum should be open standards–based, robust, and scalable. More important, it must be interoperable with the systems of your trading partner community and overall Value Trust Networks. Technology decisions should be based on the business requirements of the e-Marketplace and its user base. Setting up and managing an e-Marketplace may require more time and expense than it's worth, depending on its scope. If you plan to manage all the technical aspects yourself, align yourself with some savvy technology partners who can ensure your e-Marketplace enables business transactions seamlessly and reliably. If you don't want to manage all the technical aspects, consider a hosted solution or an application service provider (ASP). But remember that you are ultimately the only one that will be responsible for the stability and growth of your technology platform.

Specifically:

- Define e-value chain business/customer needs, then map to technical functional requirements.
- Define which functions should be in-house and which can be outsourced or partner provided. Regarding information architecture, remember that information and the knowledge that it creates is the secret weapon that your e-Marketplace has to provide outstanding customer, partner, and stakeholder value.

Step Eleven: Develop a Partnership Plan

Partnering for success will be one of the key success factors of modern e-Marketplaces and for twenty-first-century enterprises in general. It is critical to define the following areas at a minimum when setting your e-Marketplace strategy:

- Define the e-value chain. Assess skills/asset/resource gaps relative to goals.
- Define partnership candidates.

- Determine the degree of ownership you are willing to give up to partners. What is negotiable, what is not?
- Define a preemptive strike strategy. Identify where your aggregation of partners, customers, content, and communities will leapfrog your ebusiness, and create barriers to entry for competition.

The three key areas in which partnering will immediately be valuable to the e-Marketplace business model are as follows:

- *Technology partnerships*—Given the rapid acceleration of technology solutions, it may prove advantageous to partner for certain technologies that drive the e-Marketplace business model.
- *Marketing partnerships*—Given the wide global reach of the Internet, it is likely that a global alliance and partnership strategy would be a powerful addition to your strategy so that the e-Marketplace strategy is able to address offering value in multiple markets, multiple languages, and multiple currencies.
- *Value-added services partnerships*—Offering value-added services to customers will be a key differentiator for e-Marketplaces. Many of these value-added services will best be provided through partners. For example, global financial services, logistics, insurance services, and warehousing all would make excellent partnering opportunities.

Focus on Core Competencies

Companies should focus on what they do best. Focus business models on an area of the market that complements the company's industry experience and that of its management team. If a company plans to develop its own e-Marketplace, the company should enter the market in a focused area of the industry where it is confident that it can achieve the critical mass required to ensure long-term sustainable success. Critical mass in terms of an industry vertical e-Marketplace would be the capture of a significant enough percentage of the buyers and suppliers to achieve liquidity.

E-Marketplace's Success Factors

There are certain foundations from which all e-Marketplaces must start in order to achieve long-term viability. One of the primary foundations is that the e-Marketplace should be a neutral player in its markets. Or in the case of consortia owned by major industry players, there should be a neutral management team in place.

E-Marketplaces should choose either to be horizontally focused across multiple industries, products, or services or focused on a vertical market opportunity and have deep domain expertise in their chosen market. In the case of a vertical market focus, they should target highly specific areas of value offered to solve industry pain points for the business model.

One such industry pain point usually centers on the lack of a unified business language and terminology used by multiple players in the market to describe their products and services in catalogs. A winning e-Marketplace model would address the ability to bring unification of an industry schema or common business language for all e-Marketplace participants.

The e-Marketplace should be able to achieve critical mass in their selected markets (that is, it should have a sufficient number of the buyers or suppliers in their chosen market to support ongoing liquidity/profitability). The e-Marketplace model should support the aggregation of buyers' and sellers' demand and supply. The business model should support long-term value and motivation for both suppliers and buyers. In addition, negotiation is a key growth area within the e-Marketplace industry and should be included as a critical functional component of the business model.

Secure transactions, administered by a trusted management team and organization, are also a must-have in the e-Marketplace sector.

Top Ten E-Marketplace Success Factors

The following factors will determine whether an e-Marketplace is successful:

1. *Openness*—Enable the maximum number of participants.
2. *Neutrality*—Don't pick sides. An e-Marketplace that favors either suppliers or buyers will lose the other.
3. *Domain expertise*—Leverage it from within or acquire it. The most successful e-Marketplaces are built on a specific expert knowledge base.
4. *Perceived and real value*—Enabling basic transactions is only the beginning. Move to value-added services as quickly as you can.
5. *Common processes*—Focus on industry standards and standard practices.
6. *Critical mass*—Strive to aggregate 30 percent of all trading in your industry or region.
7. *Liquidity*—Focus on long-term sustainable profitability rather than short-term gains.
8. *Ease of use*—Make it easy to conduct business. Give more than lip service to ecommerce efficiencies.

9. *Flexibility*—Plan for change. Your industry, competitors, customers, and e-Marketplace will evolve with time.
10. *Interoperability*—Build an e-Marketplace that transparently supports leading, buying, and selling applications.

Chapter Summary

Developing and executing winning strategies in this new era requires a new innovative mind-set. Capturing the opportunities presented by building or participating in e-Marketplaces requires a mind-set that embraces change, thinks and executes on multiple dimensions, and is above all a customer-centric mind-set. A focus on value, true win/win partnering, and customer satisfaction may sound like old economy principles, but they apply today as strongly as they ever have. Build a strategy on a solid foundation of proven business principles while leveraging the power of the global Internet opportunities. Work to build a culture that empowers all members of your Value Trust Network. Reward and encourage innovation, and never let success blind you to the needs of your customers.

Glossary

authentication—The use of a password, biometrics, or other methodology that verifies the identity of a user.

B2B—Business to business. Used in reference to ecommerce transactions.

B2C—Business to consumer. Used in reference to ecommerce transactions.

brick and mortar—A retail storefront.

buyer—Any person or business entity that purchases or attempts to purchase a good or service.

click and mortar—A retail storefront that has also established a formidable Internet presence.

content management—An electronically organized means of storing, gathering, filtering, organizing, modifying, and distributing information.

customer lifetime value—The direct and indirect dollar value that any customer contributes (positively or negatively) during the lifetime of the relationship with a company.

dot-com—A business that solely operates on the Internet.

ebusiness—A company that conducts business on the Internet. This includes businesses that are wholly or partially Internet-based.

ecommerce—Short for electronic commerce; however, typically refers to Internet-based commerce as opposed to EDI (see below).

EDI—Electronic data interchange. A legacy industry standard that defines business document exchange.

e-Marketplace—A digital marketplace for the buying and selling of products and services.

e-tailer—An Internet-based retailer.

first-mover advantage—The first person or business entity to establish the definitive e-Marketplace, ebusiness, or commerce site in an industry or geographic region. This is currently considered a competitive advantage.

HTML—Hypertext Markup Language. HTML graphically displays data on a computer screen, enabling Web pages that combine text, graphics, audio, and video.

HTTP—Hypertext Transport Protocol. Enables the transport of HTML data. It is a subset of the Standardized General Markup Language (SGML).

IP—Internet Protocol. This is an abbreviation of TCP/IP, which stands for Transport Control Protocol/Internet Protocol.

IT—Information Technology. Generally referred to as the business of managing computers and computer networks.

Java—An object-oriented programming language developed by Sun Microsystems that operates independently of the underlying operating systems.

legacy system—Any computer system, network hardware, or software that has been superseded by a newer technology. In the past, this term referred to mainframe computers; however, it now is applied to products or services that are not the latest commercial version.

PKI—Public Key Infrastructure. This is an Internet-based security technology and practice that utilizes key pairs to establish temporary secure channels between the sender and receiver. The keys (each pair is mathematically related but not identical) are managed by a public key authority.

seller—Any person or business entity that sells or attempts to sell a good or service.

SGML—Standardized General Markup Language. A language developed by the U.S. government that separates data from format.

SSL—Secure Sockets Layer. An Internet security standard that is commonly used for the secure exchange of sensitive information.

supply chain—A classic tiered distribution model that includes some combination of manufacturers, suppliers, distributors, wholesalers, and dealers, among others.

time-to-market—The time it takes to launch a product, service, or business. Quick time-to-market is currently considered a competitive advantage.

trading partner—A buyer or seller.

value chain—A knowledge-enhanced supply chain in which all parties contribute qualitative or quantitative value.

VAN—Value-added network. A private network that is physically established between companies over leased (dedicated) lines. Historically, large companies have used these because they are inherently secure.

VAS—Value-added services. Premium services that are offered at premium prices.

VoIP—Voice over IP. Voice services that are offered over IP networks as opposed to the Public Switched Telephone Network.

VPN—Virtual Private Network. A secure private network that utilizes the Internet for data transport. This is an economical replacement for leased line networks such as VANs.

VTN—Value Trust Network. A knowledge-based network enabled by a value chain (value), trust systems (trust), and technological and human elements (network).

XML—eXtensible Markup Language. An industry standard developed by the World Wide Web Consortium (W3C) that enables the development of "intelligent" documents and machine-to-machine connectivity. It is an enhanced subset of SGML.

Bibliography

Books

Hagel, John III, and Arthur G. Armstrong, *Net.Gain: Expanding Markets Through Virtual Communities*, Boston: Harvard Business School Press, 1997.

Korper, Steffano, and Juanita Ellis, *The E-Commerce Book, Building the E-Empire*, San Diego, CA: Academic Press, 2000.

White Paper

"Epicentric: Building B2B and B2C Portals, The Fusion of Commerce, Content and Community," Q1 2000 from Epicentric, Inc., 333 Bryant Street, Suite 300, San Francisco, CA 94107.

Unpublished Manuscript

"Fast-Track Innovation: ASAP" by Desander Mas and William G. Raisch, © 2000.

Magazine and Web Articles

Machlis, Sharon, "Build Community, Build a Market," *Computerworld*, January 19, 1998.

Essex, David, "Get Into Web Portals," *Computerworld*, March 15, 1999.

Watson, S. J., "E-commerce Companies: Creating Sticky Communities," *Computerworld*, November 15, 1999.

Schwartz, Mathew, "How Big Can a Community Get?" *Computerworld*, April 10, 2000.

Schweitzer, Carole, "Your Portal or Theirs?" *Association Management*, May 2000.

Schweitzer Carole, "Portal Partnerships," *Association Management*, May 2000.

McIntyre, Carrie, "Co-Branded or Private Label: Choosing the Most Effective Approach to Portal Partnering," *Association Management*, May 2000.

Burns, Susan, "Co-Ordinating Behind the Scenes: The Importance of Integrating Web Applications and Business Processing Systems," *Association Management*, May 2000.

Knowledge Management and Education Resources

"Blackboard Overview White Paper," May 2000, Blackboard, Inc., Washington, D.C.

"Start Talking and Get to Work," by Michael Zisman (Vice President of Strategy, IBM Software Group, Executive Vice President, Lotus Development Corp.), Remarks at KMWorld '99 in Dallas, TX, September 23, 1999.

White Paper: The Lotus and IBM Knowledge Management Product Road Map, December 1999, Lotus Development Corporation, 55 Cambridge Parkway, Cambridge, MA 02142.

Caterinicchia, Dan, "Making Knowledge Accidents Happen," *Federal Computer Week*, June 22, 2000.

Roberts-Witt, Sarah L., "Knowledge Management: Know What You Know," *PC Magazine*, June 26, 2000.

"Knowledge Management: The Next Big Thing?" Lotus Development Corporation, 55 Cambridge Parkway, Cambridge, MA 02142.

"The Knowledge Paradox: How to Manage Your Most Strategic Asset," Cambridge Information Network, 539 Bryant Street, San Francisco, CA 94107.

"Innovation, Leadership and Knowledge Management," *Dataquest*, The Complete Computing Magazine, January 15, 2000.

"Corporate Learning—On the Threshold of Dramatic Change: An interview with Elliot Masie," May 16, 2000, Lotus Development Corporation, 55 Cambridge Parkway, Cambridge, MA 02142.

Recommended Knowledge Management Reading on the "Knowledgemanagement.com" Web site maintained by Knowledge Transfer International (KTI)

Myers, Paul S., "Knowledge Management and Organizational Design Resources for the Knowledge-Based Economy"

Davenport, Thomas H., and Laurence Prusak, "Working Knowledge—How Organizations Manage What They Know"

Stewart, Thomas A., "Intellectual Capital—The New Wealth of Organizations"

Nonaka, Ikujiro, and Hirotaka Takeuchi, "The Knowledge-Creating Company How Japanese Companies Create the Dynamics of Innovation"

Koulopoulos, Thomas M., Richard Spinello, and Wayne Toms, "Corporate Instinct—Building a Knowing Enterprise for the 21st Century"

Womack, James P., and Daniel T. Jones, "Lean Thinking—Banish Waste and Create Wealth in Your Corporation"

Bancroft, Nancy H., Henning Seip, and Andrea Sprengel, "Implementing SAP R/3, How to Introduce a Large System into a Large Organization," Second Edition.

Holtshouse, Dan (ed.), and Christopher Meyer, "The Knowledge Advantage: 14 Visionaries Define Marketplace Success in the New Economy"

"The Knowledge Management Yearbook 1999–2000," John A. Woods and James W. Cortada (preface)

"Harvard Business Review on Knowledge Management," Harvard Business Review Series

Recommended Knowledge Management Reading by Lotus Development Corporation

Peppers, Don, and Martha Rogers, *Enterprise One to One.* This book provides a compelling argument for the need to create customer knowledge using technology. The authors discuss how to be responsive to customers and to develop a mass customization model.

Nonaka, Ikjiro, and Hirotaka Takeuchi, *The Knowledge Creating Company.* This book got the whole knowledge management movement going in the 1990s. A good place to start to cover the basics.

Hamel, Gary, and C. K. Prahalad, *Competing for the Future.* Discusses in business terms the core concepts found in the Lotus Knowledge Management Framework: innovation, responsiveness, productivity, and competency.

Kao, John, *Jamming: The Art and Discipline of Business Creativity.* Kao argues that competitive advantage can be found in the unleashing of the creative power of workers. He suggests that innovation activity requires a special form of semi-structured collaboration—like improvisational jazz.

Edvinson Leif, and Michael Malone, *Intellectual Capital: Realizing Your Company's True Value by Finding Its Hidden Roots*. The authors outline the process for developing, nurturing, and measuring intellectual assets. The book covers Skandia's first attempt in 1995 to provide to its shareholders an intellectual capital annual report.

Stewart, Thomas, *Intellectual Capital: The New Wealth of Organizations*. Like Edvinson and Malone's book, it makes a compelling argument that an organization's success will be determined by its ability to develop, measure, and sustain its knowledge resources.

Prusak, Laurence, and Thomas Davenport, *Working Knowledge*. This book provides vivid examples of how companies are beginning to manage what they know through the creation of new processes, organizational roles, and uses of technology. As long-time consultants in this area, the authors have a firsthand look at what works and what doesn't. Prusak has also compiled an anthology of articles,

Knowledge in Organizations. Discusses knowledge management from a variety of perspectives, including sociology, economics, and management science.

Savage, Charles, *5th Generation Management*. It posits that the new enterprise requires processes for cocreation through virtual enterprising, dynamic teaming, and knowledge networking.

Barabba, Vince, *Meeting of the Minds*. Barabba, General Manager of Corporate Strategy at General Motors, argues that market leadership is attained by transforming information into shared knowledge, which then becomes embedded in core decision processes in the enterprise.

Harvard Business Review has several articles that condense many of the knowledge management themes in the above titles. "A Note on Knowledge Management," by David Garvin and Artemis March, traces the history of the knowledge management practices of Andersen Consulting and of Ernst & Young. Both cases describe in detail the use of "Notes" as a technology foundation.

Sloan Management Review published a series of articles in the summer of 1996 that fall under the heading of knowledge management, including "Improving Work Processes," by Thomas Davenport, Sirkka Jarvenpaa, and Michael Beers. The authors observe that "The most promising technologies for knowledge management are tools such as Lotus Notes or the World Wide Web." In the same issue, "Three Cultures of Management: The Key to Organizational Learning," by Edgar Schein, examines the clash of differing philosophies of management and its impact on knowledge management.

The American Productivity and Quality Council (www.apqc.org), a nonprofit trade association, has published its own white paper, *If We Only Knew What We*

Know, which describes some of the knowledge management activities of four companies, including the use of Lotus Notes.

The Ernst & Young Web site (www.ey.com/knowledge) has an impressive set of documents on knowledge management, including a number of case studies in which the use of Lotus Notes is mentioned.

There are also a number of Web sites that serve as knowledge management clearing houses, including the Business Researcher's Interest (Brint) Web site (www.brint.com/OrgLrng.htm), the University of Texas at Austin (www.bus .utexas.edu/kman), Massachusetts Institute of Technology (learning.mit.edu), and the Stanford Learning Organization Web (www.leland.stanford.edu/group/ SLOW).

Contributors List

Keith Krach, Chairman of the Board and CEO, Ariba
As chairman, CEO, and cofounder of Ariba, Keith Krach is responsible for the management and strategic direction of the company. A pioneer in the field of ecommerce, Krach was recently honored at the World Economic Forum in Davos, Switzerland, where Ariba was presented with the Technology Pioneer Award. Krach was also recently named a Year 2000 Ernst and Young Entrepreneur of the Year. Under Krach's leadership, Ariba was named among the Hot 100 Companies of 1999 by both *Upside* and *Red Herring* magazines. Krach was named a 1998 Top Ten entrepreneur by *Red Herring*.

Mark B. Hoffman, Chairman of the Board and CEO, Commerce One
Mark Hoffman has more than 20 years of proven senior management experience. As chairman and CEO of Commerce One, Hoffman drives the overall direction of the company. Prior to joining Commerce One, Hoffman cofounded Sybase, Inc., in 1984. As president, CEO, and chairman of Sybase, Hoffman managed the company's dramatic growth from a software start-up to the number two relational database management system vendor and sixth largest independent software company in the world with annual revenues of nearly $1 billion in 1996. Hoffman is currently chairman of the board of Intraware, Inc., and is a director on several other companies' boards. Hoffman earned a B.S. in Engineering from the U. S. Military Academy at West Point and an M.B.A. from the University of Arizona.

Gideon Gartner
Gideon Gartner is an entrepreneur, having built from scratch three successful firms in the computer field. He founded Gartner Group, Inc., Soundview Tech-

nology Group, and Giga Information Group. Gartner is currently working on another information model, which is being called gideon.com. He studied at M.I.T. (Massachusetts Institute of Technology), earning his B.S. in Mechanical Engineering and his M.S. in Management from M.I.T.'s Sloan School. He is on the Board of Advisors of four Internet companies and is a past member of the Board of the Society for Information Management where he was Special Appointee to the President.

Anne Perlman, CEO, Moai

Anne Perlman brings over 20 years of experience in Silicon Valley to her leadership role at Moai's helm. Just prior to joining Moai, Perlman had been a strategic management consultant assisting Internet start-ups and other high-tech companies. Before that, she was employed at Tandem Computers as VP and General Manager of Multimedia, VP of Marketing, and President of Tandem Source Company. At Tandem Source Company, Perlman experienced firsthand the challenge of managing personal computer–related inventories when new models became available every few months. Before joining Tandem, she spent four years at Computer Curriculum Corporation, where she was Director of Marketing. Anne holds an M.B.A., a B.A. in mathematics, and a B.A. in economics from the University of California.

William P. Kane, Eastern Regional Managing Executive, marchFIRST, Inc.

William Kane is a visionary leader within the Internet professional services global leader marchFIRST. Kane and his organization focus on strategy, brand building, and technology. He has managed a number of Internet enablements in the B2B and C2B sectors for a variety of clients including manufacturers, retailers, and services organizations.

Rich Sheldrick, Group Technology Partner, marchFIRST, Inc.

Rich Sheldrick has over 21 years of experience in information technology, serving diverse industries in distribution, retail, and manufacturing. His responsibilities include providing strategic consulting, thought leadership, and business development for ebusiness at multiple offices throughout the organization. A primary focus is helping client organizations envision their business-to-business opportunities for realizing increased market share and cost reductions. His primary areas of expertise are in business-to-business supply chain and customer-facing technologies. Sheldrick has provided direction to Corporate Solutions Engineering in defining product offerings. He has managed partner relationships with key ebusiness alliances throughout his region. He has been a speaker for client executive education seminars, and for several seminars and Web casts regarding customer-facing technologies. Sheldrick has contributed to best practices, white papers, and project methodologies.

Eric A. Crump, Associate Partner CRM Solutions, marchFIRST, Inc.

Eric Crump is an associate partner in the Northwest CRM Solutions Group for marchFIRST based in San Francisco. Crump is responsible for the creation and execution of comprehensive cross-functional CRM solutions. He joined marchFIRST in early 1998 as the practice lead for the Information Technology Engineering organization, concentrating on enterprise infrastructure design and integration. Along with managing the Information Technology Engineering Practice, Crump has been the managing associate partner for the NetStructure and the e-Solutions business units, which included the following practices: e-strategy and branding, ecommerce, collaborative technologies, and information technology engineering. He has been creating and assisting in the completion of business strategy and information technology initiatives for manufacturing, media, financial services, and high-tech sectors for over 8 years. The market capitalization of these organizations has ranged from fast-growing start-ups to International 1000.

Lisa L. Morgan

Lisa Morgan has 16 years of business management, marketing, consulting, and professional editorial experience. She is an executive adviser to high-technology organizations on business development and marketing-related issues, and often develops strategic documentation such as business plans and positioning pieces. Morgan works with notable pre-venture, pre-IPO, privately held and public clients, which recently include Commerce One, Digital Island, Stream Theory, Spirent Communications, Fresher, Redback Networks, The Horn Group, Pretty Good Privacy (PGP), Technology Transfer Institute, Pilot Network Systems, and Com21, among others. In addition to working with client companies, Morgan is a regular contributor to *E-Commerce Business, The Washington Post, InternetWeek, Planet IT, Wireless Developer,* and *Software Development Times.* She is the author of *How to Expedite Your Career Through Publishing* (IntelliPress Publishing, 1999) and coauthor of *Implementing Internet Security* (New Riders, 1995) and *The Internet Security Handbook* (IDG/Mecklermedia, 1995).

Carole Palmer

For the past 15 years, Carole Palmer has uniquely combined her M.A. degree (emphasis on motivation and learning theories) with her M.B.A. degree (in finance and marketing) to assist her clients in determining an approach to investing and estate planning that is suitable for their individual needs. Palmer says her most challenging task has been to help her clients clarify their personal goals. How to allocate their assets is easy in comparison. Without identifying intrinsic personal goals, investment and estate plans fall apart. The last 2 years, Palmer has adapted her technique to create a new field of mentoring executives in the IT world, dealing with entrepreneurs in start-up phases. Her goal is to

reduce and smooth out the inevitable friction evident in start-up and rapidly
building enterprises; plus, facilitation to improve effectiveness in arranging business functions—legal, personnel, and organizational values and culture.

Todd M. Stafne

Todd Stafne started The Co-Venture Group (CVG) in January 2000, which specializes in forming strategic business alliances in Latin America. CVG provides
marketing assistance to new and fast-growing companies to sell their products
and services in Latin America. Stafne lived and worked in Latin America for
19 years. His company represented various U.S. companies selling products to
heavy industry in Chile, Panama, and Costa Rica. His client list includes Flour
and Daniels, Becthel, The Corp of Engineers, Occidental Chemical, Codelco,
the National Copper Company in Chile, Coca-Cola, and the like. Start-up efforts
included setting up corporations, registration of brands, advertising, marketing,
sales, importation, and fabrication of special industrial materials under license.

Tony Ward

Tony Ward, Vice President-Supply Chain, is the founder of marchFIRST's
Global Supply Chain practice. At present, the Supply Chain practice is a major
force in the marketplace with over 300 consultants worldwide. Companies such
as Grainger, ConAgra, Emerson Electric, United Stationers, Bosch, Toys R Us,
and Du Pont have entrusted marchFIRST as their trusted adviser to assist with
their supply chain needs. Ward has spoken at CLM, WERC, and many other
supply chain forums. He has been featured in more than 40 articles, and he is
a contributing author to several books. Ward is a member of the Council of
Logistics Management and the Supply Chain Council.

William G. Raisch

Bill Raisch is a principal of the American Group of Companies, Inc., an enterprise focusing on new-venture development, especially in the areas of knowledge
and education. He is also cofounder of the American Innovation Network, an
initiative focused on the systematic enabling of innovation in organizations.
Raisch has participated in start-ups, strategic acquisitions, and partnerships in a
variety of markets. He has served as director of strategic planning for Smith
Barney, International, and as president of Cornerstone Resources Inc., a venture
capital organization. Bill received his B.A. and M.B.A. from Cornell University,
where he currently serves on the Advisory Council of Cornell's Entrepreneurship
and Personal Enterprise Program.

Neal Goldman, Director, Internet Computing Strategies (ICS), The Yankee Group

Neal Goldman is the Director of Internet Computing Strategies at The Yankee
Group. ICS counsels clients on the core infrastructure of the Internet revolution,
providing strategic insight on enabling technologies for ebusiness. The planning

service examines how enterprises design, build, and integrate Internet technologies into a scalable, secure, and personalized ebusiness infrastructure. Goldman brings 20 years of industry experience to The Yankee Group. He has been VP of Business Development for both Smarterkids.com and Dr. Solomon's Software, where he managed worldwide strategic alliances, technology licensing, and mergers and acquisitions. Previously, Goldman held a variety of senior marketing and product management positions at such companies as FTP Software, Liant Software, and Symantec. He is also the author *of The Complete Idiot's Pocket Reference to the Internet* (Alpha Books, 1994) and is a frequent speaker at industry trade shows.

Julie Perkins

Julie Perkins became employee number forty with LivePerson, Inc., in August 1999. From start-up through the current LPSN company status, Perkins sells the LivePerson ASP solution of live customer support to key accounts. Julie has enjoyed the sales communication process for over 20 years, building relationships with many types of buyers in the real estate, legal, telecom, and art markets. Two bachelor of arts degrees with honors in Comparative Religion and Sociology from Trinity University have been the springboard for a continuing interest in viewing the Internet and telecom industries as an emerging global web with enormous potential for positive change in mass society.

Scott Jordan

Scott Jordan has 18 years of experience in high-tech business development and turnarounds, including a broad range of product development, marketing, research, and general management roles in areas as diverse as software, process automation, semiconductor process equipment, photonics, and mass-storage fields. He has led several high-tech endeavors to rapid growth through technical and market innovation and close partnership with customers and suppliers. A veteran evangelist, he is widely published—and a familiar speaker—on topics ranging from photonic packaging automation technologies to submicron processes to the use of small computers for manufacturing resource planning. Jordan's current business focus includes novel photonic devices and advanced robotics optimized for production process automation in sensitive photonics packaging operations.

Mercedes Kronfeld Jordan

Mercedes Jordan is a Silicon Valley educator, writer, and consultant with almost two decades' immersion in fields ranging from primary education to software start-up ventures. Ms. Jordan has built on her early interest in international relations and a lifelong commitment to education. She has served as Vice President, Marketing of a software start-up, was a private school teacher and administrator, was president of her local public school's PTA, and spearheaded her district's successful all-volunteer wiring of an elementary school for high-speed Internet access during NetDay '96. Ms. Jordan holds a bachelor's degree in German Literature with a History minor from the University of Pennsylvania, and a master's degree in German Literature from the University of California, Irvine. Active in civic and cultural affairs, Ms. Jordan makes her home in San Jose, where she consults on education and ecommerce projects.

Index

About the Author

Warren D. Raisch is the executive director of ebusiness for marchFIRST, the largest global ebusiness solutions company. As the founder and CEO of WorldCast Networks, Inc., he developed the first online business-to-business (B2B) trading exchange floor for the Information Technology (IT) market. Mr. Raisch has spent more than 20 years working with lending companies, including Apple Computer, 3Com Corporation, Gateway Computer, and others, providing innovative leadership and applying advanced technologies to real-world business models.